Social Work Evaluation

Principles and Methods

Leon H. Ginsberg

University of South Carolina

Allyn and Bacon

Boston • London • Toronto • Sydney • Tokyo • Singapore

Editor-in-Chief, Social Sciences: *Karen Hanson*
Series Editorial Assistant: *Alyssa Pratt*
Marketing Manager: *Jackie Aaron*
Production Editor: *Christopher H. Rawlings*
Editorial-Production Service: *Omegatype Typography, Inc.*
Composition and Prepress Buyer: *Linda Cox*
Manufacturing Manager: *Julie McNeill*
Cover Administrator: *Brian Gogolin*
Electronic Composition: *Omegatype Typography, Inc.*

Copyright © 2001 by Allyn & Bacon
A Pearson Education Company
160 Gould Street
Needham Heights, MA 02494

Internet: www.abacon.com

Between the time Website information is gathered and then published, it is not unusual for some sites to have closed. Also, the transcription of URLs can result in unintended typographical errors. The publisher would appreciate notification where these occur so that they may be corrected in subsequent editions. Thank you.

Library of Congress Cataloging-in-Publication Data

Ginsberg, Leon H.
    Social work evaluation : principles and methods / Leon Ginsberg.
        p.   cm.
    Includes bibliographical references and index.
    ISBN 0-205-30495-8 (alk. paper)
    1. Social service—Evaluation.   2. Evaluation research (Social action programs)   I. Title.

    HV40 .G558 2001
    361'.0068'4—dc21

                                                                    00-056559

Printed in the United States of America

10   9   8   7   6   5   4   3   2   05   04

Contents

Preface

Since my earliest years as a social work practitioner, program evaluation has stood as one of the most complicated and controversial areas of practice and responsibility. On my second job, in Tulsa, Oklahoma, in the early 1960s, I was assigned to work with the local United Way on a priorities study, an effort to determine where the limited funds available for private agencies might best be directed. Results of similar studies in other cities, I learned, were often controversial because they pitted such traditional and popular programs as scouting against services for those with serious personal problems, such as physical and mental disabilities.

In those years I attended my first meeting of the now-defunct National Conference on Social Welfare. It was an impressive experience that included seeing leading political figures and some media personalities. One of the sessions I attended dealt with the future of social group work, which was my area of social work practice. A representative of a traditional group-work agency was placed in a position of debating a major social work educator. The educator thought the limited numbers of group workers should serve those who needed help most, rather than relatively prosperous young people whose needs were for leadership training and quality leisure-time programs. I heard a similar debate at the first Council on Social Work Education annual program meeting I attended in 1963. Emotions were high, and the debate continued for years, although those who thought social workers principally belonged in services for those with disadvantages more or less won the argument.

I learned early that program evaluation is not for the meek. It's a tough process, no matter which methods or procedures are used. In some cases, people lose their jobs because of program evaluations. In other cases, people win promotions and salary increases. Agencies may lose or gain substantial amounts of money, or they may merge with other programs or even go out of existence because of evaluations. Therefore, for me, evaluation is not a dull subject, although many of my students initially believe it is. Evaluation is exciting—sometimes a bit more exciting than one would want.

A word of warning, however. This book is about evaluating programs and one's professional practice with individuals, not employees. Evaluating employees in human services agencies and other organizations is a completely different enterprise. Varieties of management and supervisory systems are used. Evaluation results can determine one's employment status (permanent or temporary), one's salary, and even one's continued employment. No doubt these are of great importance in social work and other human services. However, these processes are part of the personnel or human resources function and are not a focus of this text.

Although a program evaluation might look at personnel or human resources processes, it does not typically delve into individual cases of evaluations. One example, however, is included that shows a crossover from a program evaluation effort that became a highly charged personnel issue—for the program being evaluated as well as for the staff who commissioned and conducted it. There are many books and other guides for those seeking to develop better approaches to personnel processes, just as there are guides for other elements of an organization's production or activities. This book, however, is not about the specific improvement of any part of that production or those activities. It is not about effective service delivery, fund development, or public relations. It is about the methods that may be used to conduct evaluations of any or all of those processes.

It is also true that this book is not an introduction to basic social science research methods or to social statistics. It is assumed that readers already have backgrounds in those subjects. Some chapters review fundamentals to show how they are applied to program evaluations; however, clarifying the basics of research and statistics requires revisiting texts, class notes, and experiences in those fields. To the extent possible, leading texts in research are cited so the reader can follow up on new or enhanced interests that this book might foster.

This book is intended to fill a gap in a subject I am often assigned to teach at the College of Social Work, University of South Carolina. Although there are several high-quality texts on social work's use of evaluation in print, none of them quite fits the approach I take to teaching. Perhaps because I have been involved—both as an evaluator and as a subject of evaluation—in social work evaluation efforts for about 40 years, I have found that the professional literature rarely covers evaluation as I experienced it in private and public social agency practice.

For example, audits and accreditations were often the evaluation methods that preoccupied the agencies where I worked. As a public official in West Virginia for 10 years, I was heavily involved in licensing and in other forms of evaluation that determined whether programs could operate. Clearly, licensing is a major issue for child day care and group-care facilities, nursing homes, and other facilities that require state sanctions to operate.

As commissioner of Human Services, I was involved in granting programs the authority to operate. We were also subject to evaluations. When our state implemented the first "work experience," or workfare, program under President Ronald Reagan's 1981 Omnibus Budget Reconciliation Act, we were chosen to be evaluated by the Manpower Demonstration Research Corporation (MDRC). (MDRC's work is discussed later in this book.) The evaluation was carried out with financing from some major foundations that wanted to learn more about the impact of work programs on assistance clients and their families.

As a professor at three different state universities (University of Oklahoma, West Virginia University, and University of South Carolina), I often directed or participated in evaluations of programs under contract with governments or organizations that wanted to be evaluated. I have served on or chaired social work accreditation teams for many years. I helped train workers in Oklahoma child care facilities in which training was based on evaluations. I also worked as an evaluation team chair or member in the evaluation of Head Start programs in some of the areas where I lived. Those evaluations were conducted under contracts between the federal government and private corporations, such as the company whose main business was the manufacture of private airplanes, including the Lear Jet. I learned that many major corporations operate research and evaluation programs in addition to their primary tasks. In earlier times, I worked with other corporations and business groups. Today, one of the leading social-welfare planning and evaluation organizations is Lockheed Martin Corporation, which manufactures airplanes and is involved in many other non–social-welfare businesses.

Later, as chancellor of the West Virginia Board of Regents for Higher Education, the organization I served was legally authorized to determine who could operate higher education programs in the state, clearly a matter of significance for educational institutions.

As dean of the West Virginia University School of Social Work in the 1960s and 1970s, I was also involved in several evaluations that were not associated with accreditation. One was a study of the costs and benefits of social work education, commissioned by the U.S. Department of Health and Human Services (then the Department of Health, Education, and Welfare), which chose my school as part of the study sample.

This book is a consequence of my thoughts and efforts in program evaluation. Evaluation is a major part of social work practice everywhere, and it has the potential for improving services to clients and providing accountability to the public in systematic, reliably scientific ways. Of course, this book goes well beyond my own ideas and experiences and draws heavily on the diverse and rich literature of evaluation.

Acknowledgments

This book is not simply this author's project; I want to thank the many people who have been great supporters of the ideas and work that have gone into this effort: Michael R. Stone, of the State University of New York at Brockport, who intended to coauthor this book, helped define the book's contents. Although personal circumstances required his withdrawal, I'm grateful for his work in planning this book. Dr. Stone helped obtain some of the materials on outcomes indicators that appear in Appendix 1, for which I am grateful to the United Way of Rochester, New York. Judith Fifer, former social work editor for Allyn and Bacon, had faith in this project and its different approach to social work evaluation. Alyssa Pratt of Allyn and Bacon was a great help in completing the book. Larry Shaw, formerly president of Family Service of the Midlands in Columbia, South Carolina, helped with materials on the Council on Accreditation of Family and Children's Services, Inc. Cathy McRae of the Georgia Regional Board in Savannah provided many of the evaluation devices used in mental health. George R. Wise, CPA, of Camp, Moring, Wise, and Cannon, Certified Public Accountants, helped with the chapter on auditing, accounting, and budgets. Joyce Shaw, administrative assistant in the College of Social Work, provided dedicated help on manuscript preparation and research. Graduate assistants Ji-in Yeo and Julie Spinks helped with manuscript preparation. Karla Walsh of Omegatype Typography has been enormously helpful with many elements of this project. Thanks go to Ann Koonce for copyediting. Thanks also go to Dean Frank B. Raymond III, and the University of South Carolina for recommending that I be granted a sabbatical for the spring semester 2000 and to the university administration for granting it. The sabbatical provided time to conduct the intensive research and writing this book required.

In addition, I want to thank Michelle Mohr Carney, University of South Carolina, College of Social Work; Abraham Wandersman, University of South Carolina, Department of Psychology; and Larry Nackerud, University of Georgia, School of Social Work, for contributing chapters to this text. I am grateful to James H. Dalton, Jr., of Bloomsburg University of Pennsylvania for editing the content that appears in Chapter 11, and to Wadsworth Publishing Company for its permission to adapt the content in Chapter 11 for this book. Thanks also to Edward Potts of the United Way of the Midlands and Meg Plantz of the United Way of America for their assistance with the materials on the United Way outcomes measurement approach. Finally, I want to thank my wife, Connie, for her support and understanding and for helping me stay connected with human services practice through her work as executive director of Family Connection of South Carolina, Inc.

The Context of Evaluation in Social Work

The first three chapters introduce current issues in social work evaluation and factors that led to them. Chapter 1 outlines the history of evaluation efforts and the increasing demand for social workers and social welfare programs to measure and document their effectiveness. Some of the profession's critics—both internal and external—and their influences in pursuing evaluations are discussed. The chapter also outlines some of the alternative approaches to conducting evaluations.

Chapter 2 explores some of the alternative procedures that are used in carrying out evaluations. Some evaluations are conducted internally by organizational staff. Others use external organizations and firms. Still other evaluations are conducted by funding organizations as means for monitoring the uses of the support they provide to social welfare programs. The ethical issues associated with evaluations also are covered, especially those contained in the Code of Ethics of the National Association of Social Workers.

Chapter 3 introduces the various approaches to evaluation, many of which are covered in detail in later chapters. Some approaches not always associated with social work evaluation—fraud and abuse detection and journalistic exposes, for examples—are briefly discussed.

Part I lays a background for the more specific, technical, and detailed chapters that follow.

1

Introduction—Accountability and Evaluation in Social Work

What some call a revolution in accountability is among the most important current influences on social work and the other human services professions. For most of the history of the human services and charitable efforts, public attitudes accepted as valid and valuable the efforts made by social workers and others to help people overcome their personal and social problems. The public and those who supported social welfare activities were appreciative, more than anything else, of what the helping professions did. That was true in all fields of human service.

For example, the medical healer who did all that was possible was the accepted and often revered image for much of the history of medicine. Knowing how to cure all illnesses or having the means to save all lives was beyond the expectations of most people; therefore, physicians and other health care personnel were not held to high and specific standards for their efforts. Gratitude that a physician had done his or her best was the reaction to medical care, even when the results were unsatisfactory or ended in death. Similarly, teachers have historically been loved by their communities. In many cultures, there is no higher honor than that accorded teachers, who are often treated with reverence. Even if students sometimes became rambunctious or failed to be attentive, their parents, the board of education, and the community at large viewed teachers as dedicated, wholesome, underpaid people who were doing their best to achieve complex and critical social goals. Nursing, with its image of Florence Nightingale and other angels of healing and saviours of the sick, received similar respect.

Of course, this also is true for social work and the human services agencies and settings in which social workers are employed. For much of its history, human services and charity were indistinguishable for the larger public, which cared about charitable causes and only wished that it could help more. Those who carried out the work of the human services organizations were likely to be idealized as conveyers of mercy and good will. Social workers were viewed as low-paid, sometimes unpaid, heroes who cared for the sick, dependent children, people with disabilities, and older adults.

However, beginning with the end of World War II, all these public attitudes began to change. The changes were largely the result of the successes of the professions as much as they were products of changes in public acceptance of those professions' services. For example, in health care, new knowledge of human physiology, new medicine—especially antibiotics—new technically sophisticated equipment, and new surgical procedures, meant that many people who would have died in an earlier era now survived. If one thinks of the major medical discoveries and procedures that have changed health care and public expectations about medical care in the past half-century, it is overwhelming. The antibiotic drugs, for example, meant that many illnesses that would have been fatal before the invention of drugs such as penicillin were now treatable and curable, often within a few days. New knowledge of exercise and diet kept many heart patients alive who earlier would not have survived a first heart attack. Diagnostic tests to determine the exact type of coronary problems were developed. New and powerful medicines and surgical procedures, such as the heart bypass for those with coronary blockages, were developed and applied to what earlier would have been terminal cases.

The transplantation of kidneys, hearts, lungs, livers, and other organs—the subject of horror films only a few years before—was perfected and used to save and prolong lives. With all these developments, medicine and health care personnel were no longer viewed only as heroes but also as skilled scientists and technicians who could apply various means for saving lives. The expectations for health care became greater because health care could do more. Doctors, nurses, and hospitals could do things for people that could not have been done in the past. Health care personnel and health care organizations were held to high standards because patients and their families expected recovery. When recovery was not the result, actions were often taken against physicians—malpractice law suits, for example. Similarly, Morbidity and Mortality Committees (Gawande, 2000) in hospitals now evaluate unsuccessful surgical outcomes and place responsibility on physicians and other health care providers who do not perform their duties satisfactorily and who lose patients. Professional Service Review Organizations (PSROs) set up formal systems for physicians to evaluate the work of other physicians on a regular basis. Insurance companies set limits on the amounts they will pay for surgical procedures, based on current and prevailing charges. They also specify maximum hospital stays for patients, based on what they statistically determine will be sufficient for each condition or procedure. The Diagnostic Related Group (DRG) approach to reimbursement means that every procedure has its price and that less costly care will be rewarded by insurance and other providers. Although they continue to be highly respected, physicians no longer have the unanimous and perpetual praise of those they serve and those in their communities. They are expected to produce and to produce efficiently—because they now are viewed as being able to do so.

The formerly saintly profession of teaching is no longer assumed to be wonderful or its practitioners to be revered. In today's education world, there are tight and strict evaluation procedures, including student evaluations of the teaching abilities of instructors. Many public officials have pressed for the implementation of tests to determine whether teachers are competent. Schools, school systems, states, and politicians pore over detailed comparisons of student scores on Scholastic Assessment Tests and American College Testing Program tests for evaluating high school students for college admission. Debates over teacher competence are common in state legislatures and in community forums throughout the United States. The importance of standardized test scores is so great in evaluating schools and teachers, that it became something of a scandal. *Newsweek* magazine devoted a detailed article to the issue in 2000 (Clemetson & Brant, 2000).

Of course, social work is also subject to similar criticisms and measures. It is no longer assumed that social work service is, on the face of it, always a useful service. Financing organizations such as foundations, governments, and United Ways want to know whether the social welfare programs have made a difference in the lives of clients. They want to know if services have been delivered by the most effective means. Funding agencies want to evaluate the extent and quality of services provided through government funds in order to determine the per person costs and to learn if services were effective for clients. Did it work or didn't it? Could it have been done better? Could the same goals have been achieved at lower cost or with a different set of activities? What do we know about this kind of client or client system and the ways in which they may be helped?

Government Performance and Results Act of 1993

The emphasis on results and the demand for accountability were codified into federal law in the Government Performance and Results Act of 1993. Congress said that waste and inefficiency in the programs of the federal government undermined public confidence. It also said government managers had difficulty performing effectively because there had not been enough articulation of goals and objectives and there was insufficient information on performance. Congress members also said they had difficulty making spending decisions and evaluating programs because too little attention had been given to results and performance.

The law requires strategic planning by government agencies that focuses on results—also called outcomes—and the ways in which they will be achieved. This act includes a requirement for performance goals and indicators of how well those goals have been met.

Clearly, this law requires the kinds of evaluation efforts discussed in this text.

Meeting the Demands of Funding Organizations

Those who provide funds for social work programs also demand results and performance indicators. This is true of government as well as private funding sources such as foundations. For example, virtually all grant application packets require an evaluation plan along with the operational plan or proposal for an activity. This set of instructions and requirements, from a funding program sponsored by the United States Information Agency, is typical of what one encounters in any grant application process:

> Project Evaluation: Proposals should include an effective evaluation plan which defines and articulates a list of anticipated outcomes related to the project goals and activities and procedures for final evaluation as well as for ongoing monitoring and midterm corrective action. Proposals should describe specific intermediate objectives to be achieved.
>
> Cost effectiveness: The overhead and administrative components of the proposal, including salaries, should be kept as low as possible. All other items should be necessary and appropriate.
>
> Value to U.S.–Partner Country Relations: Proposed projects should receive positive assessments by USIA's geographic desk and overseas officer of program need, potential impact, and significance in the partner country. (United States Information Agency, 1998, p. 14)

Effective social work is expected to demonstrate its effectiveness systematically and concretely. It is not enough to do good work—or what the social worker believes is good work. It must be systematically shown to be good and effective by measures that are sometimes prescribed by the funding organization or, in other cases, developed by the organization receiving the funds and ultimately approved by the funding agency.

Purpose and Scope of This Book

That is essentially what this book is about: how social workers and others in the human services demonstrate the quality and outcomes of their efforts. A demand for social workers to evaluate their practices, whatever the level of intervention with which they work, is now widespread. Virtually all government agencies and other funding sources insist upon evaluations before they will continue funding and, in some cases, before they will even initiate funding. An evaluation of services cannot be a simple addition to a grant proposal or any other plan. It must be a carefully structured, systematic arrangement, built into the overall design of the work that is being done. Whether an agency provides social services, mental health, public health, or a voluntary services, the demand for good, clear, systematic evaluation is virtually universal.

It is not unusual for men and women to complete their bachelor's or master of social work degree armed with extensive information and ideas about serving clients but with minimal information about evaluation. Social work education heavily focuses on preparing people to directly counsel individuals, couples, families, and small groups. It also pays attention to preparing people for roles in larger system work, such as community organizing and social planning.

However, many new social workers often find that the preoccupation of their employers is something other than professional practice with clients or client systems. Although they are usually expected to carry out professional practice appropriate to the agency, workers are often expected to readily understand and be able to evaluate the effectiveness of their work—to demonstrate the value of what they do.

A focus on evaluation should not be surprising or even unfamiliar to newly graduated social workers. If there is any institution that focuses on evaluation it is education. From the beginnings of life in the public schools, pupils work for, speculate about, and become upset over grades. What did you get? That's a common question from age 6 through doctoral education. It should be no surprise that social agencies are equally subject to evaluation for successful results.

If an agency is preparing for accreditation (a subject discussed in Chapter 6), that may be the organization's preoccupation. A purchase of services agreement may require documentation of effectiveness as a condition of continued funding. That documentation may become a top agency priority. An audit, which is discussed in Chapter 4, also may cause great change within an organization and focus its attention on that kind of evaluation. This book is a call for social workers to know more about more kinds of evaluation because evaluation may sooner or later constitute an important focus of their responsibilities.

Effective social workers need to know how to evaluate their own efforts and the programs in which they are involved. There are few jobs in social work that do not require some knowledge of evaluation, some ability to conduct evaluation procedures, and some ability to understand and interpret evaluation results to boards, staff members, and the larger community. Clients want to know if an agency and its workers' efforts are effective. Workers, themselves, want to know if their work is effective. Therefore, the pressure for social work, in some ways more than other professions, to be able to evaluate itself is great.

Another theme of this book is that evaluation should not be viewed as an aversive or negative process in the human services. It is a reality of practice in the environment of the 2000s, and it should be viewed as something other than a necessary, but unpleasant activity. Instead, those whose efforts are evaluated ought to view the process, no matter what the form of the evaluation, as an opportunity to learn from skillful observers. Similarly, this book is written to encourage evaluators to understand their work as that of helping a program better understand itself and improve its work. Evaluators should not view their efforts as searching for deficits. Although it is important for deficits to be identified and addressed by a program, the evaluation process need not be a club with which a program is hurt. Instead, the program being evaluated should be candid and forthcoming about everything and should understand itself as benefiting from the evaluation. This ideal notion of the way things should work is not always the way in which evaluations are conducted, but it should be the usual nature of evaluations as well as the ideal model.

Historical Origins of Evaluation

There are some specific sources of demands for social work evaluation that have come from different directions.

Beginning with the Kennedy administration in the 1960s and continuing since then, social work has experienced extensive demands that it evaluate and justify its efforts. Simply knowing that something is good and asserting that it is is no longer enough.

This does not mean that social work, as a profession, has diminished. In fact, it grew remarkably during the second half of the twentieth century. The U.S. Bureau of Labor Statistics now identifies about 600,000 people it considers as social workers. Although many of these have not had professional social work education, even the National Association of Social Workers, which is composed of people who have had such education, now has about 160,000 members. Traditionally, only about half the professionally educated social workers join NASW, so there are probably more than 300,000 professionally educated social workers working in the United States at the beginning of the new century. There are also more than 40,000 undergraduate and graduate students enrolled in social work in any given year in more than 400 accredited undergraduate, about 120 master's, and about 50 doctoral programs in colleges and universities throughout the nation. In other words, social work is a major profession with large numbers of practitioners. Obviously, governmental bodies, foundations, and charity groups that finance social work services want evidence that their services justify the billions of dollars spent on them. These demands for evaluation and documentation of effectiveness often come from the profession's friends and supporters.

However, social work also has critics. Some emerged during the presidencies of John F. Kennedy and Lyndon B. Johnson, eras during which social work and social services enjoyed great numerical growth, as well as broad public acceptance of the belief that social workers delivering social services could solve human problems.

Among the most important reasons for the growth of evaluation for social workers was the advent of the War on Poverty through the Economic Opportunity Act of 1964. It added a number of new programs to the U.S. social services system, such as Head Start and Community Action. Although social workers were not the designers of the act, ultimately many social workers became staff of national, state, and local, antipoverty programs. Because many of the new programs were designed quickly and aroused skepticism among many public officials, the media, and citizens, evaluations became important.

Another 1960s development that led to greater evaluation of social work programs was the passage, under President John F. Kennedy, of the 1962 Social Security amendments.

The 1962 Social Security Amendments

The 1962 amendments to the Social Security Act provided larger roles for social workers and more intensive opportunities for financial-assistance clients who participated in the Aid to Families with Dependent Children (AFDC) program to receive social work services. Wilbur J. Cohen (who later became the secretary of Health, Education and Welfare under President Johnson and was an architect of the original Social Security Act) along with Robert J. Ball, a Social Security official, wrote about the 1962 amendments in *Public Welfare* (1962). Cohen and Ball say President Kennedy claimed he had approved a bill that made possible the most far-reaching revision of public welfare since it was enacted in 1935.

Perhaps this was the first language hinting at the nation's steps toward what has come to be called welfare reform. Kennedy added that the new law stressed "services in addition to support; rehabilitation instead of relief; and training for useful work instead of prolonged dependency" (Cohen & Ball, 1962, p. 233).

It is important to note that at the time of these amendments and statements, social workers in public welfare combined both social services assistance and eligibility determination in their work. That is, all those who applied for assistance such as AFDC—the program described by Cohen and Ball and lauded by President Kennedy—saw social workers who took their applications for assistance, evaluated them, and recommended whether they could receive assistance and the level of the assistance to be provided, based upon agency policies. It was assumed that financial need was only one of the needs. Clients also required, the wisdom of the era suggested, "casework" or counseling services to help them better budget their resources, maintain their families, and become self-sufficient through work, marriage, and education.

There were several reforms that Cohen and Ball (1962), as well as the President, were describing. For example, the 1962 changes made it possible for families that had fathers to receive assistance, even if the reason for the need was that father's unemployment. Until that time, if there was a man in a household, it was assumed he either was or should be working and providing support to the family. The AFDC–Unemployed program, which could serve two-parent families, became a state option under the federal-state AFDC program, although only about half the states ever adopted it.

Another reform was the disregard of earned income. Families with earnings could keep a portion of those earnings, rather than see their assistance checks reduced by exactly the amount of their incomes. Essentially, the program began to serve the working poor. The policy was famously called the "30 and a third disregard" because it allowed assistance families to retain, without penalty, the first $30 and one third of the rest of their earned income.[1]

Funds were also set aside for education and training to help families become self-sufficient. The federal matching formula for social services increased with the 1962 amendments from 50 percent to 75 percent, which made additional services possible.

Perhaps most important, as far as social workers were concerned, was the requirement that families receive augmented social services from social workers

---

[1]Excellent and detailed discussions of the evolution of modern assistance programs can be found in McBroom (1977) and Carrera (1987).

employed by state welfare departments. Some experiments had suggested that families that received social services from professionally educated social workers could become independent of the assistance system (Brown, 1968). The social services were geared to helping family members become rehabilitated and independent through work or other arrangements, such as establishing or reuniting a self-supporting family. However, the experiments used fairly intense social services, which meant that social workers were available to families regularly and that the social workers initiated regular contacts with those families. That, in turn, meant that the number of families served by each social worker had to be relatively small. In the regular AFDC programs of the states, however, each social worker was likely to serve a large number of families—too many in most cases to be available to help or to make regular contacts. It had been the contention of professional social workers that if they had had enough time for intense contact with families, they could have solved some of the severe problems faced by those disadvantaged families who were served by the public welfare system.

The 1962 amendments put specific restrictions on the numbers of families per social worker, with the intent of making it possible for the workers to help rehabilitate the families. Of course, the numbers were not such that the services could be as intense as in the experiments. Generally, states were required to limit caseloads to 40 families per worker and to expect each family to have contact with a worker every three months. Therefore, the operational definition of intense social services actually applied in state AFDC programs was much different than the efforts made in the experiments.

During the years after the 1962 amendments were implemented, the desired results did not appear to follow. In fact, the results were the opposite of those desired. According to the U.S. Bureau of the Census (Lerner, 1975), there was steady growth in the numbers of people served by AFDC as well as a steady growth in the dollars expended on that open-ended entitlement. The more people entitled to benefits, the more dollars were allocated by the federal government to match state dollars—without limit.

In 1962, when the amendments were added to the Social Security Act, there were 932,000 families constituting 3.5 million people receiving AFDC. By 1965, there were 1 million families with 4.4 million people on the rolls. By 1970, there were 2.5 million families and 9.6 million individuals receiving assistance. In terms of dollars, the program cost $1.2 billion in 1961. In 1970, the cost was $4.8 billion.

Although it is not totally clear what happened, there was speculation. Those most suspicious of social workers and their methods thought that the more intense services led social workers to encourage their clients to seek more and more benefits—and to tell their friends and neighbors. Other analysts thought that low assistance payments, inflation, unemployment, and normal population growth led to the changes. Another hypothesis was that many people who were eligible for financial help did not seek it before the more encouraging climate for services of the 1960s.

Social work was criticized for asserting its value in ending poverty without documenting supporting results. As McBroom wrote, "Spokesmen for the social work profession have advanced services . . . as the best way to interrupt the cycle of generation-to-generation poverty. It has become increasingly clear, however, that no form of social work will serve this purpose in the absence of grants adequate to meet minimum need" (1977, p. 1159).

The net result of the 1962 amendments and social work's perhaps overly enthusiastic suggestion that its efforts could address and overcome dependency and poverty was a requirement for stringent evaluation, reliable data, and other efforts to prove theoretical perspectives, rather than simply assert them.

The 1967 Social Security Amendments

By the late 1960s and especially with the 1967 amendments to the Social Security Act (McBroom, 1977; Carrera, 1987), social work was less credible than it had been in the early years of the decade. Several initiatives were undertaken by federal government officials and welfare directors in several states. One of the primary changes was the separation of the eligibility and social services functions. Although social workers and others with professional degrees would be required for social services work (in many states that had formerly required a master's of social work degree for its services workers, persons with master's in other social science and professional fields were authorized to fill social services jobs), those who determined eligibility for financial assistance would simply be technicians or clerks with a minimum of high school preparation. Simply because a family needed financial assistance did not also mean that that family required social services, federal and state administrators decided. Clients could just be living through unemployment or personal troubles that caused them to be in need of financial aid. Determining their eligibility required only some technical analyses and computations—not social services. Meanwhile, social services workers would be free to provide guidance, child protective services, and similar help to families who required it.

The 1967 amendments' focus was on simplification of the assistance process. Along with the separation of income maintenance and services would come support for a "declaration system" (Carrera, 1987). As Carrera, who was an official in the federal portion of the AFDC program, described it, "The declaration system was based on the premise that poor people were just as honest as other people and that AFDC should be based on applicants and recipients attesting to the fact that they were eligible" (p. 129). The complicated and often long processes of investigating eligibility would be replaced by clients completing simplified applications. Compliance would be checked with audits, much like those used by the income tax system.

Optimism for Changing the System

The literature of the early 1960s as well as the policies enunciated by the Kennedy and Johnson administrations suggested that some genuinely major changes were in the offing. Primary among them would be a guaranteed annual income (McBroom, 1977). There was hope that such a guarantee would end welfare as it was understood and operated at the time.

Indeed, President Richard M. Nixon proposed such a plan in his Family Assistance Plan in 1972, but it was defeated by Congress. President Carter proposed a similar plan in 1977 that also failed to gain congressional approval. However, the "welfare reform" plan that finally gained congressional approval, the Personal Responsibility and Work Opportunity Reconciliation Act of 1996, changed the system in ways that were quite different than a guaranteed annual income. With support from President Bill Clinton and the Republican leadership of Congress, the bill imposed strict work requirements. More significantly, it imposed a lifetime limit of five years of assistance on any family, with provisions that states could reduce that limit to as few as two years.

Thus the modern evolution of public assistance in the United States went from the optimistic 1962 amendments to the 1996 law, which is comparatively punitive.

Built into all the initiatives as well as into the research that helped determine which policy options would be chosen were a variety of evaluation initiatives and requirements such as some of those explained in this book.

The phenomenon of requirements for evaluation is not limited to the United States; it is worldwide, and examples may be found in many other nations. Fiona Gardner, a social worker in Australia, writes, "Currently, evaluation is very much on the agenda in health and social work. There are greater expectations of agencies and individual workers to justify funding, methodologies, and effectiveness" (2000, p. 176). She also identifies the serious problem social workers encounter in evaluations—finding ways to evaluate their work in ways that fit with the way they go about that work.

Evaluation efforts of social welfare programs started much earlier than the 1960s. Rossi, Freeman, and Lipsey (1999) suggest that the emphasis on evaluation rose from the transfer of human services efforts to the governments in the 1930s. Before that era, programs were local or voluntary. With the growth of programs such as Social Security at the federal level, however, major expenditures by government began and human services became public human services, to a large extent. The pressure to use "scientific management" in operating and understanding these programs evolved into program evaluation. Thus the kinds of efforts described in this book were in effect long before the 1962 amendments.

Error Rates and Quality Control

In the 1970s, the federal government began requiring the states to use a form of evaluation that earlier had been confined to industry instead of public efforts and human services. Because of its concern that funds were being given to ineligible people, the government instituted a program of quality control and enunciated error rates that might be tolerated before sanctions were taken against states for committing errors (Carrera, 1987). At one time, the federal government wanted zero tolerance, or no errors at all. However, it generally accepted rates of 3 percent to 5 percent. The quality control process of evaluation is discussed in another chapter. Essentially, the federal government would review a quality control evaluation developed by and implemented by a state through the careful examination of a small number of cases. The percentage of errors over the tolerance level would be applied to the whole state caseload, which could make the state liable for millions of dollars in repayments.

External and Academic Critics of Social Work

The criticisms of human services and social welfare have also come from sources other than disappointed government officials. For example, one of the most influential social welfare policy books of the late twentieth century is Charles Murray's *Losing Ground* (1984). Murray, a sociologist who identifies himself as a political libertarian, is not concerned about the effectiveness of social workers' efforts. His belief is that social welfare programs such as food stamps, Temporary Assistance for Needy Families, unemployment compensation, and most others cause the problems they are designed to cure. He believes that problems of poverty, disadvantage, family breakup, and the like are much more severe because of the programs designed to prevent and treat them than they would be if those programs did not exist. The economist George Gilder (1981) shares a similar negative reaction to social services programs, as do dozens of other conservative political figures, scholars, and journalists (Ginsberg, 1998). Therefore, social welfare workers and especially social workers are called upon to show that what they do is effective rather than harmful, as some of their critics suggest.

For years, there have also been unrelenting attacks on social work, its efforts, and its practitioners by conservative radio talk show hosts and other notable figures. Social work is on the defensive regularly against many who believe the profession is causing harm rather than solving problems. The need to document social work's effectiveness, whenever possible, is obvious in such an environment.

Internal Critics of Social Work

Social workers, themselves, have recognized the need to be more specific about what they do, how they do it, and how effective they are. Some of the strongest challenges have come from social work educators and scholars such as Joel Fischer (1973), Betty J. Blythe and the late Scott Briar (1987), and others who challenged the idea that social work services were, invariably, worthwhile and effective. In a landmark article, Fischer examined eleven studies of the effectiveness of social work and found few that showed social work services were effective.

In Fischer's (1973) article, "Is Casework Effective?: A Review," he looked at evaluations of "social casework," or what is now more commonly called "direct practice" or "micro social work practice," meaning practice with individuals, families, and small groups instead of community change efforts or work with larger institutions.

Fischer (1973) rejected about 70 studies of effectiveness because they did not meet his basic criterion, which was that there would be a control group. He believed a control group was essential as a means of comparing subjects who did not receive treatment or experimental services with the results of those being served (or, as one might define them, the treatment or experimental group members). He concluded that it would be impossible to determine whether a group of people were actually changed by services unless a control group was used for comparison purposes. That, of course, is the criterion for defining a true experiment—an experiment from which one might be able to draw inferences about the treatment or intervention being evaluated.

Ultimately, Fischer (1973) found 11 studies that met his criterion of having a control. He found that the actual results of those studies demonstrated that, in comparison with control groups, none of the subjects improved as a result of the social work treatment that was used with them. He also asserted that half the subjects actually deteriorated—were worse off after the casework intervention than they were before it was provided to them.

Fischer noted that many of the subjects were involuntary and were children or youth. Many were juvenile delinquents. However, whatever the circumstances and research designs, Fischer's findings led to major changes in the ways that social work approached its services. They also led to what the journal in which he had published his article, *Social Work,* called a "Furor over Fischer" (May 1973).

Some students of social work evaluation noted that it is difficult to document the effectiveness of a service such as social casework. They suggested that the methodologies used by social scientists do not always lend themselves to accurate assessment of services. Others insisted that Fischer's conclusions had also been reached in psychology and other service fields and that he was essentially correct. Whatever the comments, it became clear that social work would have to change its approaches to helping and to evaluating the effectiveness of its work.

Blythe and Briar (1987) found that social work's questioning of its own practice effectiveness began much earlier than Fischer's work. One example was Richard C. Cabot, president of the National Conference on Social Work, who in his 1931 presidential review urged social workers to study practice effectiveness. Mullen and Dumpson (1972) cite Cabot's challenge.

Blythe and Briar (1987) state that Fischer's critique was one of the best known, but many other were conducted. All used different criteria for examining or choosing not to examine practice successes.

They also point out that statistically significant results, alone, do not prove practice effectiveness or significance. Changes in client behavior or symptoms might appear to be significant in statistical terms but those by themselves may only mean a small improvement in the client's functioning. They also note that clinical significance is not well defined, and better efforts are needed to determine more concretely what practitioners mean. Blythe and Briar (1987) support single-subject design as a means for better determining client change, a subject that will be explored later in this and another chapter.

Implications for the Study of Evaluation

Because of these trends and developments, human services has focused more and more heavily on evaluation of its work. Most government and foundation grants require an evaluation component as part of the operational funds provided to each agency. Increasingly, social workers in agency jobs need to know how to conduct evaluations, especially in organizations that receive external funds.

Learning to evaluate one's own practice has also become a crucial part of social work. It is never quite enough to assume that one has done an adequate job with a client, family, or group. Funding sources, such as insurance companies, managed-care programs, and government-funded programs such as Medicaid, increasingly require concrete information on how a client was helped and how much a client was able to change in relation to the client objectives because of the service that was provided by the social worker. Specifying and justifying the outcomes of service are critical elements in social work practice today. Being able to quantify the services that are provided as well as the results is a skill that all social workers need in the climate of professional accountability and systematic evaluation that has emerged in recent years.

In addition, agencies find that they must document their effectiveness and their compliance with the highest professional standards to more effectively serve the public, reassure their clients, and satisfy those who provide financing for them. Therefore, accreditation has become a critical issue in the human services, from social work education to agency practice. A variety of accrediting bodies, which are described in Chapter 6, set standards and evaluate agencies for compliance with those standards as a part of their work. Accreditation sometimes has significant effects on the ability of graduates of schools to receive licenses and the ability of agencies to receive public funds for the services they provide.

In addition, individual human service workers now find that they must comply with a variety of professional standards and document their knowledge and their continued professional development through legal and voluntary regulation.

Every state has some form of licensing or certification for social workers and many other human services professionals, such as marriage and family therapists, just as they have had for lawyers, nurses, and physicians for many years. Each state licensing or certification law is different, and not all the state regulatory bodies are reciprocal. That is, being licensed in one state does not necessarily mean that one will be automatically licensed in others. There are also rules about whether one needs a license to simply use the title of social worker or to practice social work, no matter what title one uses. In addition, social workers are required to renew their licenses or certifications periodically and, in most states, to document their participation in professional development and continuing education to demonstrate that their knowledge and skills are current. All these factors of legal regulation are discussed in Chapter 5.

A variety of voluntary organizations provide credentials to social workers who apply for their certifications and who meet their standards. There are special certifications for school social workers, social work managers, clinical social workers, marriage and family therapists, and sex therapists. These are in addition to the Academy of Certified Social Workers credential, which is available to members of the NASW who have specified periods of professional practice and supervision.

All these credentials are examples of the evaluation and quality control of professional social work practice.

Not all evaluation, however, is designed to require agencies or social workers to comply with specific standards. In many cases, evaluation methods are used for agency improvement. Discussions of outcome-oriented agency work and quality control are provided in subsequent chapters. Again, these are less focused on evaluating the quality of programs and more focused on identifying problems and resolving them within the structure of the organization.

Types and Methods of Evaluations

This book is organized around and focuses heavily on the variety of ways in which evaluations are conducted. There are, obviously, many different ways to look at programs objectively. These include needs assessments, accreditation, accounting and auditing, program monitoring, and quality control, as well as a number of approaches that are adapted from those already mentioned.

However, the two basic categories of evaluations into which all the approaches may fall are called *summative* and *formative* by most of the scholars who write about evaluation. Weiss (1998) points out that formative evaluations are those that provide information on a program's activities. They tell the evaluator— and ultimately the consumer of the evaluation—how the program is progressing. That information is useful for a number of reasons. Ideally, it is provided to help an organization develop and improve a program. In some cases, it is used as an ongoing assessment of how well a program complies with a set of standards and similar requirements. Much of accreditation activity is formative in that sense.

Summative evaluations, on the other hand, examine how well a program has achieved its goals. Such information is useful to funding agencies in determining whether to renew or continue a program. It is also valuable information for others who want to know about the effectiveness of a specific program.

Weiss (1998) is one author who does not accept the formative–summative rubric for all evaluations. She says two other concepts are important: process and outcome evaluations. She writes that the formative–summative concept deals with the intentions of the evaluator—what the evaluator sets out to do. Process and outcome, however, deal with the phase of the program being studied. Process evaluations occur while a program is in operation, whereas outcome evaluations deal with the results of a program for the client and community. She points out that evaluators' intentions may change during their work. What started out to be a summative effort may shift to formative objectives, designed to help a program improve rather than to summarize its achievements or lack of them. She also notes that formative and process evaluation activities occur during the same phase of a program's operations as summative and outcome evaluations. However, the spirit and nature of the two kinds of evaluations are quite different.

Much of the evaluation literature suggests that formative evaluations are conducted during the operation of a program and do not necessarily indicate whether the program has succeeded. On the other hand, summative evaluations are designed to assess the achievements of programs in terms of their objectives—helping children develop, removing mental patients from institutions and placing them in communities, and all the other myriad goals that programs support.

Conclusion

This chapter is a backdrop to the balance of the book. It traces the evolution of evaluation in social work in many forms and specifies the ways in which it has developed from a variety of concerns about social work practice and theory.

Some of the historical developments that led government agencies to question the ability of social work services to solve human problems are detailed, as well as some of the solutions used to more effectively evaluate social work contributions. The origins of such efforts as quality control in the public social services are also discussed.

The chapter shows that evaluation in social work applies to individual programs, to agencies, and to individual practitioners. Clearly, a thorough, detailed knowledge of evaluation concepts and methods is essential to modern social work practice and must be part of every professional social worker's array of skills. This chapter puts the practice of evaluation into context so readers will better understand its origins and some of the principles under which it operates.

Any historical and current-practice assessment of social work makes it clear that evaluation is now central to all elements of social work practice. For social workers, that makes evaluation content as important to effective practice as understandings of social policy, practice interventions, and human behavior. It is simply not possible to discharge one's professional social work responsibilities without a working knowledge of the broad range of evaluation methods and concepts.

The style and content of this text is different than most in the social work literature. It includes information on a broad range of the evaluation activities included in the profession and in the field of human services. Most texts that deal with evaluation focus either on carrying out experimental research designs in social agencies or single-system designs for evaluating one's own or others' professional practice with clients. This text includes both those subjects. However, it also discusses subjects such as accreditation, quality control, auditing, and accounting, which are not covered extensively in most of the literature. Other often-overlooked topics such as monitoring are explored, and detailed examples of some significant social program evaluations are given to help readers put a concrete face on the sometimes-difficult concepts of program evaluation.

The author's initial interest in writing this book came from his own experience as a social welfare administrator, so some of the text includes personal examples and personal observations about evaluation work. There are few better possibilities for learning about a subject than being directly involved in it, either as an evaluator or as a subject of evaluation. The author is heavily involved in social work education evaluations. He has served on or chaired several dozen bachelor's and master's accreditation site visits throughout the United States and Canada for more than 30 years. He also has taught courses on evaluation at the University of South Carolina, where he has been a professor since 1986. He has served on evaluation committees within the university as well. When the book's explanations and conclusions are based on the author's personal experience with evaluation programs, that fact is clearly stated. The author hopes that these personal examples will give concrete information to help the reader understand some of the complexities and pitfalls, as well as the basic principles, of social work evaluation activities.

Questions for Further Study

1. Discuss the reasons that social work evaluation has become a major function and issue in recent years.

2. In your opinion, what are the likely positive as well as negative consequences of the greater emphasis on evaluation of programs and professional social work practice?

3. How might the formative–summative and process–outcome approaches to program evaluations be distinguished from one another?

4. Assume you are a government official who has authorized a grant of $1 million for an early childhood development program. What kinds of evaluation information would you seek? How would you define the questions you would ask a program evaluator to answer about the program?

References

Blythe, B. J., & Briar, S. (1987). Direct practice effectiveness. In A. Minahan, R. M. Becerra, S. Briar, C. J. Coulton, L. H. Ginsberg, J. G. Hopps, J. F. Longres, R. J. Patti, W. J. Reid, T. Tripodi, & S. K. Khinduka (eds.), *Encyclopedia of social work* (18th ed., pp. 399–407). Silver Spring, MD: NASW Press.

Brown, G. E. (1968). *The multi-problem dilemma: A social research demonstration with multi-problem families.* Metuchen, NJ: Scarecrow Press.

Carrera, J. (1987). Aid to Families with Dependent Children. In A. Minahan, R. M. Becerra, S. Briar, C. J. Coulton, L. H. Ginsberg, J. G. Hopps, J. F. Longres, R. J. Patti, W. J. Reid, T. Tripodi, & S. K. Khinduka (eds.), *Encyclopedia of social work* (18th ed., pp. 126–132). Silver Spring, MD: NASW Press.

Clemetson, L., & Brant, M. (2000, June 19). When teachers are cheaters. *Newsweek,* 48–52.

Cohen, W. J., & Ball, R. M. (1962, October). The public welfare amendments of 1962. *Public Welfare,* 191–198, 227–233.

Deming, W. E. (1986). *Out of the crisis.* Cambridge, MA: MIT Press.

Fischer, J. (1973, January). Is casework effective? A review. *Social Work, 18,*(1), 5–20.

Gardner, F. (2000, March). Design evaluation: Illuminating social work practice for better outcomes. *Social Work,* 176–182.

Gawande, A. (August 7, 2000). Annals of medicine: When good doctors go bad. *The New Yorker,* pp. 60–69.

Gilder, G. (1981). *Wealth and poverty.* New York: Basic Books.

Ginsberg, L. (1998). *Conservative approaches to social welfare policy.* Chicago, IL: Nelson-Hall.

Lerner, W. (1975). *Historical statistics of the United States: Colonial times to 1970.* Washington, DC: Bureau of the Census.

McBroom, E. (1977). Public assistance and Supplemental Security Income. In *Encyclopedia of social work.* (17th ed., pp. 1156–1161). Washington, DC: National Association of Social Workers.

Mullen, E. J., & Dumpson, J. R. (Eds.). (1972). *Evaluation of social intervention.* San Francisco: Jossey-Bass.

Murray, C. (1984). *Losing ground: American social policy, 1950–1980,* (10th anniversary ed.). New York: Basic Books.

Points and Viewpoints: Furor over Fischer. (1973, May). *Social Work, 18,*(3), 104–109.

Rossi, P. H., Freeman, H. E., & Lipsey, M. W. (1999). *Evaluation: A systematic approach* (6th ed.). Thousand Oaks, CA: Sage.

United States Information Agency. (1998). *NIS college and university partnerships program: Project objectives, goals, and implementation* (p. 14). Washington, DC: Author.

Weiss, C. H. (1998). *Evaluation* (2nd ed.). Upper Saddle River, NJ: Prentice-Hall.

2

The Administration and Ethics
of Program Evaluation

Program evaluations vary widely, depending on the program involved and the organization that commissioned the evaluation. There also are many purposes for evaluations, each of which carries its own suggestions for the kind of evaluation organization or evaluator that should be selected. This chapter deals with the selection and deployment of evaluations as well as the ethical precepts under which evaluations should be conducted.

Evaluations are sensitive for many reasons. They can determine whether large numbers of people continue to receive services that they may need. They can also determine whether key staff members maintain their employment. Millions of dollars may change hands because of an evaluation because funding organizations often base their decisions about continued support for a program on the evaluation results. Similarly, many personnel decisions are based, at least in part, on the results of evaluations. Therefore, the accuracy, honesty, and independence of evaluations are critical and must be foremost in the minds of those who carry out evaluations.

The Business of Program Evaluation

It is critical that students in social work and other human services programs understand that program evaluation, like other kinds of research and consultation, is a business of significant proportions. Millions of dollars are spent in the United States each year to evaluate all sorts of programs. Much of the money comes from state and federal government sources. In fact, for the federal government, research and evaluation are significant activities, especially in an era in which the national government provides fewer and fewer services. Research and evaluation are the remaining functions, and they are central functions in several agencies, including the departments of Agriculture, Defense, Labor, Health and Human Services,

Housing and Urban Development, and Education, as well as others such as Energy and State. However, human services researchers normally focus on the departmental efforts listed here. There are many special institutes in the federal government established to fund research on various subjects. Also, of course, the federal government's efforts have been highly significant in controlling and reducing many health, mental health, and environmental problems.

Evaluation research has grown to be such a large business that it has attracted major corporations. Lockheed Martin, which has expanded well beyond its aerospace business, conducts evaluations. It also has demonstrated its ability as a private corporation to establish and operate human services programs that were once under the total control of governments.

Because of their high profile and the many dollars expended on them, evaluations have become major professional employment opportunities for social workers and others in the human services fields. Those with skills and interest in research and evaluation have great possibilities for eventual employment—usually highly paid employment.

This text describes some types of evaluations and their purposes. How an evaluation is conducted and who conducts it depends on the auspices under which it is organized and, more important, the purpose or purposes for which the evaluation is conducted. Some of the purposes and the possible choices of evaluators or evaluator organizations are explained next.

Evaluation Ethics

Social work's major professional organization, the NASW, promulgates a Code of Ethics (1999) to which its members are supposed to adhere. In addition, state licensing boards may adopt the NASW code or develop their own ethical codes. The basic principles of social work ethics are pervasive for social work practice, as well as research and evaluation activities. The sections dealing with research and evaluation are most applicable to evaluation work.

In some forms of evaluation, many of the central ethical issues are enforced by the rules of the organization that provides the evaluation. For example, in accreditation programs, such as those conducted by the Council on Social Work Education, specific rules apply to the structure of visiting evaluation teams and the conduct of everyone else associated with the accreditation. For example, evaluators can have no other relationship with the school being examined, such as serving as a consultant or even as a recent member of the faculty. Generally, alumni do not evaluate the schools from which they graduated. The rules prohibit persons from the same state as the school being studied from serving on accreditation teams. Members of accrediting decision-making commissions or committees are expected to excuse themselves from deliberations if they have any conflicts of interest of any kind with a program under consideration. If rules are violated, schools under evaluation can appeal or even file legal actions to require the accreditation to be disregarded and repeated.

Of course, not all evaluations of social or social work programs are conducted by social workers. In some cases, those who commission evaluations believe that professionals with different backgrounds should be the evaluators. For example, accountants, auditors, physicians, educators, or any number of other categories of evaluators may be chosen to conduct evaluations. In some cases, evaluation teams include practitioners and consumers of services.

Rossi, Freeman, and Lipsey (1999) cite a survey conducted by the American Evaluation Association of its own members in 1993. Twenty-eight percent of the members were professional evaluators, 19 percent were researchers, 18 percent were involved in administration, 13 percent were teachers, and 8 percent were consultants. Forty percent were employed by colleges or universities, 12 percent by private businesses, and 11 percent by nonprofit organizations. The federal government employed 10 percent of the members, and state governments employed another 10 percent. Four percent were employed by school systems. In terms of their primary disciplines, 22 percent came from education, 18 percent from psychology, 16 percent from the evaluation discipline, 10 percent from statistics, 6 percent from sociology, another 6 percent from economics and political science, and 3 percent from the field of organizational development. Twenty-one percent were from other fields, including social workers, although this writer noticed at a meeting of the American Evaluation Association that few were social workers. Even so, many social workers are heavily involved in evaluation work although most of them may not affiliate with national professional organizations in the evaluation field.

Under the NASW Code of Ethics (1999), social workers are encouraged to participate in and support program evaluations as a means of improving social work practice and to help build knowledge about the profession.

Social workers are also encouraged to critically evaluate, stay current with, and use research and evaluation in their practice. However, those who engage in social work evaluation are also admonished by the code to live up to a variety of professional ethical mandates in their evaluation work.

Most of those mandates replicate the human-subjects protections required for research in most institutions, especially those that receive federal funds of any kind and for any purpose. These protections were created after revelations about research projects that posed potential harm to the subjects or participants either because of medical interventions or, in one celebrated case, the lack of medical intervention, or through the possibility of information about the subjects becoming known to others.

Universities and other organizations that engage in research establish procedures and guidelines for protecting subjects. They also establish procedures and review boards to screen proposals for research projects and evaluations. All those in an organization who intend to carry out such programs must submit their plans, evaluation or research designs, and instruments such as surveys and questionnaires, as well as clinical procedures they intend to use. The human-subjects review board must give its approval before work can begin. If the board members have questions, they may make suggestions about how the project can be modified to conform to their standards.

Perhaps the best known ethical case was a Tuskegee, Alabama, study of syphilis in the 1930s (Jones, 1993). In the study, public health officials from the U.S. Public Health Service identified a panel of 399 African American men in the rural Tuskegee community who had syphilis, for which, at the time, there were no cures. The purpose of the study was to better understand syphilis and its course. Some painful medical procedures such as spinal taps were used in evaluating the patients and their disease. Although the subjects were told they had "bad blood," they were not told they had syphilis. They were to be compensated with medical checkups, some meals, travel to clinics, and funds for their burials when they died (not necessarily from syphilis). The ethical issue arose when penicillin was developed in the 1940s. Penicillin was and remains a relatively fast cure for syphilis. However, the patients were not given penicillin after it was discovered and the study continued. Proper protection of the subjects would have cured their illness as soon as that was possible.

A number of other studies of a more social or psychological nature also led to requirements for the protection of human subjects. The Lawd Humphreys studies (Humphreys, 1970) in the 1970s provided observation of anonymous, male homosexual acts and, through license plate tracing, identified the participants, who were later interviewed by the researcher. Many of the participants were married and many could have suffered in their employment if they were identified publicly. Another set of studies by Stanley Milgram (1965) tested the willingness of subjects to inflict pain and, they thought, injury on another person through electric shocks. Actors who were paid a fee for their participation, were separated by a screen from the subjects. They behaved as if they were in great pain and even physical danger from the shocks. In fact, there were no real electric shocks and no one was injured. However, in neither the Humphreys nor the Milgram studies were the participants notified in advance of the nature of the studies, nor did they consent to participating in the studies in which they became subjects. Both researchers reported the nature of the studies to the participants after the projects were completed—but not before. In fact, these two projects (although not the Tuskegee example) could not have been conducted as they were if the subjects had been informed about what was going to happen.

Although evaluations are not always comparable to research projects, some of the same needs for human-subjects protections still apply. For example, employees in an agency or program could reveal information about their employer that could lead to negative recommendations. If the agency managers learned who revealed the damaging information, that person's work situation or even continued employment could be threatened. Using recipients of foundation or government agency funding as informants in evaluating the foundation or agency could lead to a reduction or elimination of funding, or revealing information could cause unpleasant interpersonal relations on the job. An evaluation or accreditation of an education program that interviews students could lead to problems of all sorts for students who write or say negative things.

The NASW Code of Ethics cautions social workers who conduct evaluations to obtain voluntary and written informed consent from participants when that is appropriate and to assure them there is no penalty for not participating. The code also suggests that evaluators take human-subjects protections principles into consideration in planning their work. When it is possible, the code also suggests using review boards to screen evaluation as well as research plans as a means of avoiding the mistreatment of the subjects.

Part of the ethical mandates apply to the relationships social work evaluators may have with the subjects of evaluations. One of the provisions of the Code of Ethics says that social workers engaged in evaluation or research should avoid conflicts of interest and dual relationships: "Social workers engaged in evaluation or research should be alert to and avoid conflicts of interest and dual relationships with participants, should inform participants when a real or potential conflict of interest arises, and should take steps to resolve the issue in a manner that makes participants' interests primary" (NASW, 1999, p. 26).

One of the classic ethical conflicts is the evaluator who is told with some degree of clarity what the contracting organization wants the evaluation to conclude. That is, an organization may hire an evaluator or an evaluation organization as a means of confirming some of its prejudices. The organization wants to eliminate or drastically overhaul a division, or it wants to document the poor performance of one or more key staff members. An ethical evaluator certainly wants to consider the concerns of top officials of the organization. However, it is not ethical to draw conclusions before conducting the evaluation or even to agree with the authority figures if there is little basis for doing so. Of course, there may be organizations and evaluators who develop reputations for concluding whatever their employers want them to conclude. However, such actions are ethical violations, and though they may be profitable, they conflict directly with the ethics of most professions and scientific work in general.

The ethics of evaluation would also apply to relationships between an evaluator and the organization that is the subject of the evaluation. For example, a social worker or other professional who has worked for an organization as a consultant would obviously not be a sound choice to conduct an evaluation of the program. It is possible that the evaluator would want to justify his or her recommendations as a consultant by, consciously or unconsciously, reporting that the program had done well. In some cases, potential evaluators may have independent relationships with the agency board or staff. The evaluator may have the potential for future employment with the evaluated organization either as a staff member or consultant. Generally, if one expects to be involved in a postevaluation relationship with an organization, it is usually best to not serve as an evaluator of the organization and especially of the area in which one might be employed. On the other hand, for work with a larger organization, someone may appropriately be employed to evaluate a segment of the organization with which there is no possibility of later employment. Evaluators may demonstrate their abilities to understand and describe the program and at the same time show their desirability for later employment—perhaps to conduct evaluations for the larger agency. However, of course, evaluators should avoid situations in which they might be invited to apply for positions of employees who have been terminated, in part, because of a negative evaluation of the organization that was conducted by job candidates. Thus the evaluators have improved their employment, intentionally or not, through an organizational evaluation. It happens in human services—but, ethically, it should not. A social work ethics audit is a means for ensuring ethical compliance (Reamer, 2000).

Minority Issues and Evaluation

A recurring issue in the social sciences and social programs is the relationships between research and evaluation activities and minority groups, especially minority groups of color. This is a critical ethical issue for evaluations. Those who organize and direct evaluations must always work to ensure that their designs and implementation are fair and respectful of those they study. As early as the 1960s, minority group members who were social scientists objected to majority group social scientists writing about and, in effect, criticizing minority groups of color.

John H. Stanfield II, a sociology professor at Morehouse College in Atlanta, Georgia, in a complex article (1999) suggests that the conventional wisdom and the behavior of the academic world is "racialized." Stanfield says that racist ideas and behaviors permeate the academic world, even though—as the title of his article suggests—the twentieth century was the "people of color" century. Although there are efforts to diversify university faculties and student bodies, minority group members and women have not been integrated into the higher levels of decision-making. Studies of minority communities, he says, refer to those who are studied as informants and human subjects. Those who are studied are rarely participants in the design and operation of the research or evaluation. Stanfield adds that much of the power over the design and implementation of studies rests with white men, who are usually those who make the major decisions for private as well as governmental funding organizations. Researchers enhance their careers on the basis of their studies of people who are often of low income and minority status. Often, the experts have no firsthand contact with the communities they study. "The ability to claim expertise without firsthand contact has also encouraged the persistent tendency for social scientists to view those they study as commodities, as objects, while those studied view the university professor (or evaluator) as an exploiter only interested in extracting data and then disappearing" (p. 419).

Stanfield (1999) suggests that the social sciences and evaluation research are products of deeply racialized roots. Race, he says, is no more than a myth with no real basis in fact. People create the idea of race and then act as if it is significant and relevant. In other words, skin color does not, inherently, have anything to do with behavior, ideas, or abilities. However, because society believes in race and assumes that all people of a particular skin color have similar personal characteristics, it ascribes social differences to racial differences. The myth ultimately has real consequences for the larger society.

The author points out that black culture as well as other so-called racial groups are diverse. Not all black people are alike, by any means, Stanfield (1999) says, nor are all Native American or Indian groups or all people with Asian backgrounds. All the socially defined racial groups are actually diverse, complex, and multicultural. The fundamental differences in society are between individuals, not between groups. Stanfield's solution is for the social sciences, especially in their evaluation and research activities, to be more inclusive of people of different cultures. He advocates the empowerment of minority communities so that they are involved in defining and carrying out research.

Several evaluation specialists responded to the professor's critique and generally agreed with what he said. Michael Quinn Patton (1999), whose work is discussed later in this text, says that evaluators should consider the ways in which concepts of race may affect their understandings and action. He also suggests that researchers and evaluators should search for "methods and measures (that) fairly capture and communicate the experiences of people of color and the poor" (p. 438).

Rodney K. Hopson (1999) believes that definitions of minority issues in evaluation may be part of the problem. There are constant struggles about the ways in which people of color define themselves, as well as changes in the nomenclature that defines minority groups of color. He proposes revisiting all these definitions and issues, as well as finding ways to better involve underrepresented groups in evaluation research.

Hopson (1999) points out that the very structure of American education relies on concepts that are inherently prejudicial against minority groups, especially people of color. These have impact, too, on the ways evaluations are conducted. He writes, "An inherent part of the problem with the way that minority issues in evaluation are conceptualized and constructed has to do with the inevitable contestation of issues surrounding race, power, and hegemony in the social organization and structure of American institutions. Our educational system is replete with historical instances where diverse cultural groups have been affected by the deepseated beliefs by those who dictate educational policy and evaluation" (p. 446). Those deep-seated beliefs are, of course, that race is a reality, not a myth, and that skin color has consequences—ideas that Stanfield and others have determined are untrue. Hopson advocates the revival and support of efforts by the evaluation profession to recruit and retain more people of color.

Ernest R. House (1999) agrees that racial categorizations infect evaluation and social research. He also suggests that American society is much more racist than is ordinarily assumed and that the situation may be even worse than Stanfield concludes.

Ethical evaluation research requires careful attention to ethnic differences, and those differences probably should be considered in developing evaluations, especially those dealing with minority communities.

Technology Ethics

The American Evaluation Association has published a collection of essays dealing with several of the issues, including ethics, associated with the use of information technologies in evaluations (Gay and Bennington, 1999). These editors note that evaluation activities are increasingly mediated through various forms of technology. In the area of ethics, they point to the new obligations of evaluators to "reconceptualize traditional ethical concerns such as anonymity, confidentiality, prevention of harm, and disposition of data" (p. 2). This premiere evaluation organization provides guidance, through publication, to evaluators in a heightened atmosphere of technological applications.

Types of Evaluations and Evaluators

Figure 2.1 outlines some of the evaluations that may be conducted and the evaluation personnel who may be selected, based on the authority under which the evaluations were initiated.

Much depends upon the kind of evaluation being conducted and the authority under which it was established. For example, accreditations are almost always designed to be conducted at arms length by persons who have little or no prior contact with a program being evaluated or its personnel. The accreditation is conducted to determine whether or to what degree a program complies with the standards of the accrediting body. Therefore, the accrediting body, which promulgates the accrediting standards, builds in some ethical constraints on the process.

When a funding agency requires an evaluation to determine the extent to which a program is achieving its objectives (in the case of a summative evaluation)

FIGURE 2.1 *Purposes of Evaluations and Choices of Evaluators*

Purpose	*Commissioning Body*	*Types of Evaluators*
Program improvement	Board or executive staff	External evaluators Internal evaluation team Internal/external combination
Accreditation	Agency board and staff	Chosen by accrediting body under established policies
Summative (Is it achieving objectives?)	Funding sources, agency board or staff	External evaluators, internal or combination
Formative (Is it performing properly?)	Funding sources, agency board or staff, or other authority	External reviewers, such as auditors
To justify changes in program or leadership	Typically, board or other authority	External evaluators
In response to press or public criticisms, inquiries, or concerns	Board, staff or other authority	External evaluators or internal specialized staff

or conforming to a project plan or standards (in the case of a formative evaluation), it may choose to independently employ an evaluator or evaluation firm from outside the program to conduct the evaluation and report. In some cases, however, funding agencies prefer to allow a program to design and conduct its own evaluation, which, after it is completed, is forwarded to the funder. Such evaluations are becoming increasingly common. Until the 1980s, many human services programs funded by the U.S. Department of Health and Human Services and other agencies were monitored, audited, and evaluated periodically by federal officials. However, when block grants replaced categorical programs in 1981, the rules changed so that programs employed their own auditors and conducted their own evaluations, which were then shared with the federal agency. The new approach cost less and was less cumbersome. It also allowed the federal agencies to reduce the size of their staffs—a high priority in the federal government since the election of President Ronald Reagan.

At times, agencies decide that they want to evaluate all or part of a program or to determine how effectively its top staff members perform. In such cases, external evaluators typically are employed. This is especially true when the authority figures in the agency—usually the board of directors or, in public situations, a higher level of government—have negative feelings toward all or part of a program or its key personnel. The evaluation is used to verify—or refute—their suspicions or, in some cases, to justify making programmatic or personnel changes. In those situations, of course, internal evaluations typically are not used.

At other times, agency leaders, including top staff, want a fresh look at what they are doing and how they are doing it. In such cases, again, they use agreed-on evaluators from outside the agency because it would make little sense to use the staff currently carrying out the program that will be evaluated.

There are also times when public pressure, press inquiries, and client complaints raise questions about the efficacy of an agency and its performance. Under such circumstances, the agency or those responsible for it such as a government organization or a board of directors may call for an evaluation to determine the validity of the complaints and concerns.

Kettner, Moroney, and Martin suggest that the primary purpose of any program evaluation is the provision of feedback on the results of a program's activities, so those who fund the program and make policy for it can determine its efficacy (1999). They also provide several suggestions on the kinds of data that are needed in order to conduct a sound program evaluation. Included are items such as coverage, which deals with the extent to which the program meets the community's needs; equity, which examines the extent to which the program meets the needs of minorities, persons with disabilities, women, and others who might be left out of the services; process, which evaluates the extent to which the program is being implemented as it was originally designed; effort or output, which examines the extent to which the program is producing results; cost-efficiency, which is comparable to cost-benefit analysis, discussed in other parts of this book; and results or outcomes, which are analyses of the impact of the program and the extent to which the program is achieving intermediate, long-term, or final outcomes.

They also suggest making extensive use of management information data in order to effectively evaluate programs.

Weiss (1998) explains that there are three ways in which evaluations are commissioned or initiated by an agency. One is to have an evaluator on the staff, either through a permanent position that is part of the overall agency or by hiring, perhaps for a specified period of time, an evaluator to carry out specific activities. Usually, a special evaluator reports to the agency's chief executive officer—as may the permanent staff—although in some cases the evaluation staff is part of some sort of larger system. In some cases, the evaluation staff is colocated with fraud and abuse detection units and quality control programs.

A second form of commissioning an evaluation is to hire an evaluation organization. There are many available, such as units of universities, individual faculty members, private firms that specialize in evaluation, and accounting firms. As a third alternative, Weiss (1998) notes, agencies may develop requests for proposals to which any of the organizations and individuals specified previously may respond. With requests for proposals, the procedure is tightly defined, along with the deadlines and specifications for work. Judges, often within the agency, determine which proposers or bidders agree to meet the specifications and conform to the procedural requirements. Then decisions are based on the quality of the proposed plans, the prices submitted, or a combination of the two.

It is also clear that some of the evaluation organizations discussed later in this book can be useful in designing and carrying out evaluations. The Urban Institute and the Manpower Demonstration Research Corporation are highly experienced in evaluating some kinds of social programs, especially those in financial assistance.

There are also specialized organizations that primarily evaluate such specific programs as mental health and disabilities. Such organizations also provide specific outlines, checklists, and scorecards for concretely analyzing and evaluating a program.

Those who are conducting or establishing evaluations for their own programs often need help in defining the elements of the evaluation and determining the best ways to operate it. An excellent source for doing so is *The Evaluator's Handbook* (Herman, Morris, & Fitz-Gibbon, 1987). The book talks about all the procedures for conducting an evaluation, and provides guidance on three types of studies that are discussed in this book—a formative evaluation, a summative evaluation, and an experiment. It also gives checklists for determining the best instruments and records to keep. It provides worksheets on costs, the dimensions or boundaries of the evaluation, and the ways in which to specify with an organization or a contractor the elements that are to be completed in the evaluation. A guide such as this is indispensable for developing a sound evaluation for one's organization or in planning the conduct of an evaluation for an agency that wants a social worker's services.

Several books which are part of the Sage series called the *Program Evaluation Kit* are useful in designing and contracting for a program evaluation. The authors provide practical and detailed instructions on various techniques of evaluation, and various dimensions of developing and providing a useful evaluation of a program. Included in the kit are books that specifically provide guidance on focusing evaluations (Stecher & Davis, 1987), using performance and test measurements of program achievements (Morris, Fitz-Gibbon, & Lindheim, 1987), and using qualitative methods in research designs (Patton, 1987).

All of the books in the kit are useful in understanding and carrying out evaluations of programs. However, the primary focus is on some of the designs discussed in Chapters 10 and 11 of this book rather than on such issues as accounting, quality control, licensing, and accreditation. But for the more or less traditional approaches to evaluation, there are a few sources better than those in the Program Evaluation Kit.

Accountants and Attorneys

Although it is outside the field of social program evaluation, some of the work of Thomas J. Stanley (2000) is pertinent to understanding approaches to conducting evaluations. Stanley is an expert on millionaires and has written books and articles and conducted seminars for those who are or who aspire to be millionaires. In discussing the investment decisions millionaires make about their personal funds, he suggests they check with their accountants and attorneys to determine whether a proposed investment is wise. Attorneys and accountants often have general knowledge as well as disinterested postures on the financial decisions of their clients. They are often able to provide useful advice—advice that is often more useful, Stanley says, than that provided by brokers.

The analogy may be that agencies can use those professionals to help evaluate programs. They might also assist an agency in evaluating possible evaluators or evaluation firms. Although it may not be wise to call upon these professionals for an entire evaluation of a program, they are likely to be useful correlative advisers on program evaluations. Agency leaders often fail to use the full benefits that attorneys and accountants can provide. Government officials often learn that there is great merit in regularly checking with both kinds of professionals, especially on controversial or contentious issues involving money and other resources or the law.

Conclusion

This chapter covers the parameters within which contracts for evaluations are established and carried out. It also details the ethical demands placed upon professional evaluators. Because evaluations are sensitive in so many ways, high-quality professional conduct—no matter what one's profession may happen to be—requires adherence to the highest ethical standards.

Questions for Further Study

1. Describe, in your own words, three ethical principles contained in the NASW Code of Ethics that you consider most significant for those engaging in program evaluations.

2. How would you define the issues of "racialism" raised by Stanfield and their effects on evaluations? What are some of the ways researchers and evaluators can guard against incorporating racist concepts in their research?

3. Assume you are the director of a family service agency and that your board has asked you to embark on a comprehensive evaluation of the overall program. What steps might you take in locating an appropriate evaluator or evaluation organization to carry out the board's request?

4. Prepare a brief outline of a request for proposals that might be used in carrying out the assignment discussed in Question 3.

References

Gay, G., & Bennington, T. L. (Eds.). (1999). *Information technologies in evaluation: Social, moral, epistemological, and practical implications.* San Francisco, CA: Jossey-Bass.

Herman, J. L., Morris, L. L., & Fitz-Gibbon, C. T. (1987). *The evaluator's handbook.* Newbury Park, CA: Sage.

Hopson, R. K. (1999, Fall). Minority issues in evaluation revisited: Re-conceptualizing and creating opportunities for institutional change. *American Journal of Evaluation,* pp. 445–451.

House, E. R. (1999, Fall). Evaluation and people of color: A response to Professor Stanfield. *American Journal of Evaluation,* pp. 433–435.

Humphreys, L. (1970). *Tearoom trade: Impersonal sex in public places.* Chicago: Aldine.

Jones, J. H. (1993). *Bad blood: The Tuskegee syphilis experiment* (2nd ed.). New York: Free Press.

Kettner, P. M., Morony, R. M., & Martin, L. L. (1999). *Designing and managing programs: An effectiveness based approach* (2nd ed.). Thousand Oaks, CA: Sage.

Milgram, S. (1965, February). Some conditions of obedience and disobedience to authority. *Human Relations, 18,* pp. 57–76.

Morris, L. L., Fitz-Gibbon, C. T., & Lindheim, E. (1987). *How to measure performance and use tests.* Thousand Oaks, CA: Sage.

National Association of Social Workers. (1999). *Code of ethics of the National Association of Social Workers.* Washington, DC: Author.

Patton, M. Q. (1987). *How to use qualitative methods in evaluation.* Thousand Oaks, CA: Sage.

Patton, M. Q. (1999, Fall). Some framing questions about racism and evaluation: Thoughts stimulated by Professor John Stanfield's "Slipping through the front door." *American Journal of Evaluation,* pp. 437–443.

Reamer, F. G. (2000). *Social work ethics audit.* Washington, D.C.: NASW Press.

Rossi, P. H., Freeman, H. E., & Lipsey, M. W. (1999). *Evaluation: A systematic approach* (6th ed.). Thousand Oaks, CA: Sage.

Stanfield, J. H., II. (1999, Fall). Slipping through the front door: Relevant social scientific evaluation in the people of color century. *American Journal of Evaluation,* pp. 415–431.

Stanley, T. J. (2000). *The millionaire mind.* Kansas City, MO: Andrews McMeel.

Stecher, B. M., & Davis, W. A. (1987). *How to focus an evaluation.* Thousand Oaks, CA: Sage.

Weiss, C. H. (1998). *Evaluation* (2nd ed.). Upper Saddle River, NJ: Prentice-Hall.

Approaches to Program Evaluation

Program evaluation has many different meanings and many different approaches, as this book has made clear. This chapter reviews specific evaluation approaches, as described in the professional literature. Several subjects are introduced in this chapter and expanded later in the text. Licensing, monitoring, accreditation, and accounting/auditing are not discussed here but are explained later. This chapter's focus is on several subjects that may not require as extensive treatment as the foregoing but that are, nevertheless, important components of any discussion of evaluation.

It is important to know that evaluation takes place in all kinds of social work settings. The requirements for systematic evaluation affect every kind of program and client group. Many of the examples in this text are from fields such as mental health and financial assistance. However, social services programs, adoptions, foster care, corrections, and social planning are all impacted by the demands for evaluation. Many private practitioners also use varieties of evaluation as a means of better assessing the quality and outcomes of their work.

Quantitative versus Qualitative Approaches

A basic dichotomy often followed in research and evaluation is that between quantitative and qualitative approaches, although, in some ways, the distinction may be less clear than it often seems. Most evaluations and much of the research and evaluation in the human services are quantitative. That is, the descriptive parts of studies translate observations into numbers and statistics that are presented in the forms of graphs, frequency distributions, and other statistics. In some cases, numerical data and statistics are used to infer facts about the phenomena being studied through the use of inferential statistical tests. Such tests enable researchers to draw conclusions about the correlations or associations, or the lack thereof, among the variables that are being studied. Such approaches are referred to as quantitative in nature. A later chapter on experimental design shows how these quantitative measures and tests are used to better understand the performances of programs.

On the other hand, some studies are qualitative, in that their focus is on variables and characteristics that are essentially non-numerical. Field studies and case studies, as examples, may document and describe phenomena with little reliance on numerical description or statistical manipulations. Grounded research, a qualitative method that is growing in popularity, may rely on a small number of cases if they are prototypical; whereas a quantitative researcher is highly interested in the number of subjects studied and the sizes of the samples that are analyzed. The emphasis in qualitative research is on understanding a program or assessing behavioral patterns through observation, rather than through collecting and analyzing quantitative data. Direct observation of behavior is a major technique used by qualitative researchers. At times, such researchers function as participant-observers and at others as nonparticipant-observers. Some of the best known users of qualitative research are Erving Goffman (1961) and Elliot Liebow (1999). Goffman's studies of mental hospitals, recounted in his classic book, *Asylums*, are based on direct observations of the functioning of mental hospital patients and staffs. His books *Behavior in Public Places* (1985) and *Presentation of Self in Everyday Life* (1959) are also based on direct observations and recording of those observations. Liebow studied African American men who socialized together on a street corner in Washington, D.C. He also studied homeless women (1995), again in the Washington, D.C. area.

Although much of the emphasis in evaluation is on quantitative studies, it is possible that large numbers are actually carried out in qualitative ways. For example, when a social agency employs an expert to examine, evaluate, and report on one of its programs, it is often essentially using a qualitative approach. This is especially true when the report is based on observations of the program in action and on interviews with staff, clients, and community members.

As suggested earlier, the qualitative–quantitative distinction may be more of a false than a genuine dichotomy, because qualitative studies tend to somehow convert their findings into numbers—for example: how many times did the stigmatized person turn her head away when approached by strangers; how long did the tea room sex encounters last; how many mental hospital patients behaved in specific ways? The quantitative researcher also counts behaviors and other phenomena that, in the final analysis, may have been defined qualitatively. Although it is useful to know the distinction between quantitative and qualitative evaluations, that distinction is not emphasized in this book because so many evaluations actually combine the two orientations, even though they may not always choose to do so.

For those who want to learn more about the qualitative–quantitative distinction, several texts devote extensive attention to the differential use of the two approaches. One of the better explanations can be found in Posavac and Carey (1997). The two authors devote chapters to the evaluations and settings that best lend themselves to each approach.

Patton's *How to Use Qualitative Methods in Evaluation* (1987) is a basic source on the subject. In his book, Patton discusses the uses of case studies, observations, and interviews in conducting evaluations. He contributes checklists, instruments, and record-keeping forms for qualitative evaluators. In addition, he provides guidance on selecting samples for qualitative evaluations. The book is a fundamental guide to using qualitative methods. Patton also wrote about utilization focused evaluation, which is described later in this chapter.

Cost-Benefit Analyses and Unintended Consequences

One of the primary tools used in many organizations to evaluate programs is cost-benefit analysis. Simply stated, the organization defines the costs of a program and the beneficial results that arise from the program's implementation and operation. Of course, many social goals are worthwhile, but cost-benefit analysts have to ask, "at what cost?" If the cost is unreasonable, compared with other strategies that solve the same problem or address the same need, the program, even if successful, might have to be scrapped. For example, highway safety could be achieved at a higher level if everyone drove a large van. However, the cost of producing the vehicle, as well as the cost of fuel, might make such a choice financially prohibitive. Similarly, reading and other educational problems might be resolved by providing a tutor for every child who has school difficulties. However, the cost makes such a solution unreasonable, so group educational methods are used. Chapter 12 includes a discussion of cost-benefit analysis.

A related concept is the unintended consequence. Many social programs have results that are well outside the purview of those who develop them. For example, an after-school program may provide a vehicle for young people to form anti-social gangs in their neighborhood, or an assistance program may counter the desire for employment among low-income people. These are unintended consequences of social programs—factors that must be considered in evaluating the results of such programs. A Canadian study of the unintended consequences of an income supplement program is found in Chapter 13.

Satisfaction Studies

Among some of the most common forms of evaluation is the satisfaction study. These studies can be found in the operations of most hotels, restaurants, and other public facilities. Many hospitals and social agencies also use satisfaction studies to determine the quality of their efforts.

Satisfaction studies are used in several ways. The most sophisticated use is to compile a large number of them and analyze the results to determine an overall level of satisfaction from the clients or customers of the service provider. However, one of the problems with such studies is that the responses are not random. Those that are submitted are done so at the discretion of the participant or customer. In many cases, people complete their reaction forms because they are dissatisfied with the performance of the organization. Some organizations specifically request that customers identify outstanding employees or high quality services. However, it is often doubtful that a reliable range of responses that includes the diverse levels of consumer satisfaction is available to the organization. This can be overcome by requiring participants to complete forms or by rewarding them for doing so. However, that is difficult outside the context of an institution such as a hospital, where there is a more or less specific and comprehensive discharge procedure.

Some organizations use satisfaction documents to rapidly identify serious organizational problems. If an employee is incompetent or abusive, management wants to know immediately—outside the context of a complex and reliably researched report on consumer satisfaction. These kinds of studies are covered in Chapter 9.

Needs Assessments

A major means of evaluation is the needs assessment, which does not evaluate results or the functioning of programs but instead concentrates on determining the extent to which a need exists for a program that is being considered.

Before social agencies and other institutions offer new programs for clients, they typically conduct needs assessments. Sometimes these assessments are conducted by agency staff members, but at other times they are conducted by specialists under contract. Surveys, census data, and focus groups are used to determine who may need the service, how many may need it, how it might compete with existing services, and how much it might cost. Surveys can help define the extent of interest in the program, and they can be conducted with either clients or social work and other human services professionals or both. Census data helps identify the needs of the community. For example, an analysis of age structure may help determine the number of older people who may need a senior citizens program or children who may be candidates for day care programs. Focus groups bring people together to discuss their interests in services. Krueger (1997) is a major author of works on focus groups, which are increasingly common in needs assessments. Further discussion of needs assessments can be found in Chapter 9.

Single-Subject Designs

A major interest of social work is in single-subject research designs, which assist workers in evaluating their own practice. In some cases, agencies require workers to conduct single-subject evaluations. The results are compiled and analyzed by the agency to determine how well or how poorly the staff is functioning with clients.

The basic idea of the single-subject evaluation is for the worker to use standardized instruments or instruments especially developed to evaluate a specific client or intervention and the progress in the services that are provided. The worker establishes a baseline for the client's functioning, provides treatment or services, and then assesses the client's progress after services have been provided.

Detailed procedures for using single-system evaluations as well as software for statistically analyzing progress can be found in Bloom, Fischer, and Orme (1999). Another useful source for learning about single-subject designs and procedures is Tripodi (1994). More-complete information on this approach to evaluation is included in Chapter 8.

Experimental Approaches and Models

One of the mainstays of evaluation is the experimental approach. Several texts (Gabor, Unrau, & Grinnell, 1998; Posavac & Carey, 1997; Royse & Thyer, 1996; Weiss, 1998) devote extensive attention to experimental approaches. Chapter 10 outlines the main points and provides suggestions for the best methods of using them in conducting program evaluations.

Experimental approaches are usually summative, which means that the evaluation is designed to determine how well a program is reaching its objectives. There is a variety of research designs used to establish experiments. These designs were originally developed by Campbell and Stanley (1963), who have been the source of much of the writing about experimental design in the social sciences for decades. True experiments have two groups: an experimental and a control group, each of which is randomly selected. The control group receives a treatment or intervention; the control group receives nothing. This enables the evaluator to determine the extent to which the program's services make a difference in the functioning of the subjects. Some of the most common designs are categorized as:

Preexperimental (experimental designs with no control group) designs:
> One-group, posttest only (to determine how the subjects function after the intervention or treatment)
> One-group, pretest/posttest design (which tests the functioning of the subjects before and after the intervention)

Experimental designs:
> Pretest/posttest control-group design
> Posttest only control-group design
> Four-group design (Solomon design)

Standard social science and social work research texts (e.g., Marlow, 1998; Rubin & Babbie, 1997; Yegidis, Weinbach, & Morrison-Rodriguez, 1998) cover the whole matter of experimental designs and their uses for those who want more information than Chapter 10.

Utilization-Focused Evaluation: Michael Quinn Patton

Michael Quinn Patton (1997) concentrates his efforts on the utilization of evaluation results, which is incorporated into the title of his book, *Utilization-Focused Evaluation: The New Century Text.* He concludes, as does the author of this text, that there is great diversity in program evaluation. Evaluations range from looking at a small aspect of a single organization to completing multimillion dollar, long-term, and even international comparative-evaluation research designs.

Patton (1997) explains that evaluations serve the primary purposes of making judgments, making improvements possible, and generating knowledge. He adds that evaluations can be classified as either examining the merit or worth of a program or generally making overall judgments about a program's ability to meet its goals—showing if the program should be continued, if the program did what its funding suggested it should do, and determining, overall, if the program worked.

Many kinds of evaluations, including those carried out by government auditing bodies and inspectors are judgment-oriented. However, Patton (1997) says, in order to use an evaluation for making judgments, the evaluation must be quite clear about the criteria for determining the answers to the questions of effectiveness, compliance with the rules, and whether the program is worth continuing. The function of an evaluation is to help inspectors, government officials, and funding agencies to determine whether to continue a program. Judgment-oriented evaluations may enable decision makers to determine how and under what circumstances, if any, a program is to be continued.

Evaluations that Patton (1997) describes as oriented toward improvement are somewhat different than the judgment-oriented evaluations. They gather more data about strengths and weaknesses, they focus on ways to improve programs rather than on simply evaluating their worth in general, and they do not typically attempt to determine whether programs are worthwhile for continuation. They try to find out how the staff as well as the clients perceive the program, and they try to identify efficiencies that could make the program less costly but still effective.

Patton (1997) also, comments at length on the distinctions between formative and summative evaluations, a subject that occupies the attention of many writers on program evaluation. Essentially, Patton believes that formative evaluations examine what a program is doing and how well it is doing it in line with the criteria established for success. Summative evaluations, on the other hand, focus on results such as changes in the client groups that are served by the program. For example, a formative evaluation might look at a program of community mental health care to determine whether the funds allocated for the program are being spent properly and whether the client services and visits are being made appropriately. These criteria deal with the activities of the project rather than the results. A summative evaluation of a similar program would deal with the length of time clients remain out of institutional care and how well they become integrated into the community.

Patton (1997) also focuses on what he calls knowledge-oriented evaluations, which are not designed either to evaluate how well a program is operating within the prescribed rules or whether the program is achieving its results. Instead, the knowledge-oriented evaluation focus is on understanding a program a bit better, determining what it is actually doing, and being able to report data to funders and responsible persons such as board members. The focus of the knowledge-oriented evaluation is information that can be fed back to those who are responsible for financing or directing a program. Like other forms of evaluation, this approach studies the functioning of the program. However, it is best used for capturing information about the nature and function of the program. Patton and Carol Weiss (1998) both refer to this sort of evaluation as focusing on "enlightenment." The goal is to facilitate understanding, not to determine the proper operations of the program, as in the classically defined formative evaluations, or to evaluate the extent that the program meets its objectives, as in the typical summative evaluation.

Patton's (1997) utilization-focused evaluation is structured to find a problem-solving approach designed to make the evaluation effective. The emphasis is not on looking for problems and reporting on them or on simply educating others about the program. Instead, it is a way to evaluate a program in ways that will become useful to the recipients of the evaluation. The emphasis is on the information that is sought by those who will use the evaluation. It is the intent of Patton's approach to make it possible for users of evaluations to either make judgments or to improve the program—or both—with the evaluation results, therefore the emphasis is on the usability of the evaluation material in any number of contexts.

The idea of utilization-focused evaluation seems simple enough: to provide the kinds of data and results that those who pay for the evaluations or those who are responsible for the organization being evaluated can and will use. However, it is not always clear that evaluators understand that element of evaluation or that evaluations, in general, always meet the needs of those who pay for them.

Empowerment Evaluations

Another approach to program evaluation has been called empowerment evaluation. Fetterman, Kaftarian, and Wandersman (1996) edited a book discussing a variety of approaches to empowerment evaluation, which they describe as "the use of evaluation concepts, techniques, and findings to foster improvement and self-determination." It employs both qualitative and quantitative methodologies. Fetterman et al. says that the approach focuses on programs, although it can be applied to other entities such as individuals, organizations, communities, and even larger systems such as societies and cultures. Carol H. Weiss (1998) is another advocate of empowerment evaluation.

Essentially, empowerment evaluation involves recipients of service in defining the design and implementation as well as the analysis of a program evaluation. Participants in programs are involved from the beginning and are collaborators with the professional evaluators, rather than serving only as the subjects of evaluations.

Advocates of empowerment evaluation say the process is democratic because it promotes the participation of those who are involved in programs in the evaluation of those programs. Some proponents (Fawcett et al., 1996) suggest that there are four phases to empowerment evaluation. The first is setting the agenda, the second is planning, the third is implementation, and the fourth is the outcome of the evaluation. Participants are involved at each phase of the evaluation. In some ways, empowerment evaluation is comparable to community development or community organization activities in social work—macro social work, in particular. In fact, community psychologists, whose intentions and efforts often seem comparable to those of social work macro practice, are among the founders and major supporters of the empowerment evaluation approach.

There are many examples of empowerment evaluation projects in Fetterman et al. (1996). The approach has been the theme of the American Evaluation Association, which is the primary organization involved in human services evaluation programs.

Fraud and Abuse Detection

Although not often discussed as part of the evaluation of programs, many social programs are evaluated regularly for fraud and abuse. Action is taken to eliminate problems, and efforts are typically made to punish those who commit inappropriate acts. One major example is the monitoring of medical care programs for inappropriate billing. Medicaid, the program funded by the U.S. government and the states, is one of the largest social welfare programs. It is also subject to abuse by providers of services. States have detection and enforcement units that examine such programs in a variety of ways, sometimes by checking records and audits and other times operating on tips received from citizens.

Typical of the kinds of abuses encountered are pharmacies that bill governments for providing name-brand prescription medicines while actually dispensing much lower cost generic formulas. That is one of the most frequently found forms of Medicaid abuse. Another is charging the owner's personal expenditures as actual expenses for the operation of a nursing home. Cases have also been detected of physicians seeing whole families—treating only one family member, but charging Medicaid for examining and treating all of the family. These kinds of cases are also discussed in Chapter 4.

Design Evaluation

Fiona Gardner (2000) provides an example of design evaluation from her experiences working at St. Luke's, a large voluntary agency in Victoria, Australia. During the past two decades, Gardner explains, the agency has begun working in different ways with the individuals and families it serves. They "introduced a solution-focused, competency-based approach as well as an integrated model of services delivery. . . . Families were able to access a range of resources through a generalist worker rather than seeing a different worker for each service" (p. 177). However, this was not a single program initiative that was introduced all at once. Instead, it gradually evolved over years, and there was little documentation of the changes and their implementation. When the agency wanted an evaluation, Gardner called on John Owen, an evaluation specialist from the Centre for Program Evaluation at Australia's University of Melbourne. Owen had written about the importance of developing procedures for evaluating designs. Gardner defines design evaluation as documenting what is happening or what is hoped will happen in implementing a program. Owen believes that design evaluation will help connect the idea behind a program and its eventual implementation. In large measure, this approach to evaluation analyzes the logic behind a program and the validity of that logic. In design evaluation, as Gardner discusses it, the evaluator works closely with the program managers and the staff who deliver a program.

The design evaluation at St. Luke's was conducted by an outside evaluation expert who interviewed selected families who received services, workers in the agency, and workers in other agencies. After the interviews were completed, analyzed, and assembled, the results were shared with staff members and discussed in team meetings. Some changes were made in the program and its design, such as determining that families would make decisions about their services to the extent that was possible rather than simply saying that families would make decisions. Gardner (2000) believes that design evaluation works well to clarify and refine services that have evolved over time.

The design evaluation approach, unlike summative evaluation, is geared toward evaluating the system of providing services instead of the results of that system.

Case Studies

Some evaluations are more narratives about programs than experiments or surveys of programs. Those kinds of evaluations are called case studies. In a typical case study, some examples of which are included in this book, researchers devote their time to interviewing program operational staff, community leaders, and clients, as well as looking at program statistics and records. In such evaluations, the task of the evaluation researchers is to document exactly what was done and how it was done. Then the evaluators describe the results with vignettes, examples from clients and workers, and performance statistics.

Generally, the case study method of evaluation falls under the rubric of qualitative rather than quantitative research. The methodology is description, but it is description from which principles may be distilled. The complete description of the program makes it possible for others to replicate it in their own environments. Of course, any sound research—evaluation or otherwise—should be replicable in other situations. That, more than the specific approach to evaluation that is used, helps distinguish a sound evaluation from one that is less than sound.

Journalistic Evaluations

Although they are not commonly discussed in the evaluation literature, the publications of popular magazines, books, and newspapers, as well as popular public affairs television programs, are probably among the most prevalent and influential of all the sources of evaluation materials. Television programs such as *20-20*, *60 Minutes*, and *Dateline* often cover social services and social work issues such as child welfare, financial assistance, and medical care. Mental health services, day care, and programs for the elderly have all been subjects of televised reports. In addition, popular news magazines such as *Time*, *Newsweek*, and *U.S. News and World Report* frequently report on social programs. Many of these journalistic critiques are negative. The focus, in other words, is often on scandals identified by reporters and included in their journalistic outlets.

Although the subject has not been extensively studied, it is possible that such journalistic reports are the impetus for program evaluations that might otherwise have not been conducted. Public concern about scandals uncovered by reporters often leads to extensive public discussion of programs which, in turn, lead to the conduct of formal evaluations. Journalistic reports on social programs also often capture the attention of public officials, including legislators, who may conduct public hearings and who may either modify programs or request reliable evaluation information from the public agencies that are mentioned.

A current and prototypical example of such work is Martin L. Gross's (2000) book, *The Government Racket: 2000*. Gross authored 10 earlier books on public scandals dealing with the inefficiency of large institutions, especially governments. Physicians, hospitals, teachers, and psychologists are among the targets of his work. In his newest book, an update of an earlier work with a similar theme—the wastefulness of government—Gross deals with a number of subjects close to social workers and other human services personnel, although he is not a foe of human services or welfare. In fact, he writes positively about the programs that serve people who are in need. On the other hand, he is strongly opposed to services provided to those who do not need them. The author has appeared before congressional committees to express his concerns.

One of the targets in his current book is the federal government's practice of providing free food to day care centers, even those who provide care to middle- and upper-income children. Through a program of the U.S. Department of Agriculture, day care programs receive free food—or the money to buy food—so that all participating families benefit. Characteristically, Gross has no difficulty with providing such help to low-income families but he is a opposed to such help being given without a means test. Of course, the Department of Agriculture is not a welfare program—even though its food and nutrition programs, which include food stamps, often dwarf everything provided in some states. However, its major objective is support for the agriculture industries, and by providing free food, it stimulates the use of food and, therefore, the financial success of farmers, food processors, and food distributors.

Gross further condemns the federal and state governments for:

1. Spending more on welfare than any other program (about 17 percent of the federal budget, he says)
2. Providing the Earned Income Tax Credit benefit, which can be as much as $4,000 per year, to people with savings and Social Security payments
3. The legal payouts of Supplemental Security Income, designed for aged, blind, and disabled people, to many who, in his opinion, do not need it

Clearly, journalistic reports of welfare scandals and human services programs that, on their face, make little sense to most observers, are a powerful form of evaluation of which social workers must be aware.

Conclusion

This chapter has introduced a variety of approaches to and definitions of evaluation. Some of the subjects are covered more specifically and in greater detail in subsequent chapters. These brief interpretations and discussions lay the basis for further exploration.

Questions for Further Study _____

1. Describe a situation from your personal or professional experience that might lend itself to cost-benefit evaluation.

2. The author suggests that the difference between quantitative and qualitative evaluation may not be as great as sometimes assumed. Do you agree or disagree? Justify your position.

3. What would seem to be the relationship between studies of satisfaction and needs assessments? Are they distinct or, in some ways, different perspectives on a similar process?

4. How are single-subject designs and experimental designs different from one another?

References _____

Bloom, M., Fischer, J., & Orme, J. G. (1999). *Evaluating practice: Guidelines for the accountable professional* (3rd ed.). Boston: Allyn & Bacon.

Campbell, D. T., & Stanley, J. C. (1963). *Experimental and quasi-experimental designs for research.* Boston: Houghton Mifflin.

Fawcett, S. B., Paine-Andrews, A., Francisco, V. T., Schultz, J. A., Richter, K. P., Lewis, R. K., Harris, K. J., Williams, E. L., Berkley, J. Y., Lopez, C. M., & Fisher, J. L. (1996). Empowering community health initiatives. (1996). Empowering community health initiatives through evaluation. In D. M. Fetterman, S. J. Kaftarian, & A. Wandersman, *Empowerment evaluation: Knowledge and tools for self-assessment and accountability* (pp. 161–187). Thousand Oaks, CA: Sage.

Fetterman, D. M., Kaftarian, S. J., & Wandersman, A. (Eds.). (1996). *Empowerment evaluation: Knowledge and tools for self-assessment and accountability.* Thousand Oaks, CA: Sage.

Gabor, P. A., Unrau, Y. A., & Grinnell, R. M., Jr. (1998). *Evaluation for social workers: A quality improvement approach for the social services* (2nd ed.). Boston: Allyn & Bacon.

Gardner, F. (2000, March). Design evaluation: Illuminating social work practice for better outcomes. *Social Work,* pp. 176–182.

Goffman, E. (1959). *The presentation of self in everyday life.* New York: Doubleday.

Goffman, E. (1961). *Asylums: Essays on the social situation of mental patients and other inmates.* New York: Doubleday.

Goffman, E. (1985). *Behavior in public places: Notes on the social organization of gatherings.* New York: Free Press.

Gross, M. L. (2000). *The government racket: 2000.* New York: Avon.

Krueger, R. A. (1997). *Focus groups: A practical guide for applied research.* Thousand Oaks, CA: Sage.

Liebow, E. (1995). *Tell them who I am: A study of the lives of homeless women.* New York: Penguin.

Liebow, E. (1999). *Tally's corner: A study of Negro streetcorner men.* Boston: Little, Brown.

Marlow, C. (1998). *Research methods for generalist social work* (2nd ed.). Pacific Grove, CA: Brooks-Cole.

Patton, M. Q. (1987). *How to use qualitative methods in evaluation.* Newbury Park, CA: Sage.

Patton, M. Q. (1997). *Utilization-focused evaluation: The new century text* (3rd ed.). Thousand Oaks, CA: Sage.

Posavac, E. J., & Carey, R. G. (1997). *Program evaluation: Methods and case studies* (5th ed.). Upper Saddle River, NJ: Prentice-Hall.

Royse, D., & Thyer, B. A. (1996). *Program evaluation: An introduction.* Chicago: Nelson-Hall.

Rubin, A., & Babbie, E. R. (2001). *Research methods for social work.* (4th ed.). Belmont, CA: Wadsworth.

Tripodi, T. (1994). *A primer on single-subject design for clinical social workers.* Washington, DC: NASW Press.

Weiss, C. H. (1998). *Evaluation* (2nd ed.). Upper Saddle River, NJ: Prentice-Hall.

Yegidis, B., Weinbach, R., & Morrison-Rodriguez, B. (1998). *Research methods for social workers.* Boston: Allyn & Bacon.

Part II

Classic Evaluation Processes for Social Work Programs

Well before the advent of some of the more sophisticated evaluation procedures described here, social work programs and agencies used a variety of methods to guarantee the quality of their work and to demonstrate effectiveness and competence to the public. Some of those longstanding evaluation processes are the subject of this part of the text.

Accounting and auditing, the subjects of Chapter 4, are fundamental management and evaluation tools in almost every part of American enterprise and service delivery. Professional accountants help agencies and individual practitioners maintain careful records of their work. Most agencies are subject to periodic audits of their finances and programs. This chapter covers the accounting and auditing procedures and describes some of the standards and tools used in these processes.

For a long time, accreditation has been used as a yardstick for measuring the quality of programs. Family Service America and the Child Welfare League of America maintained active accrediting programs. Accreditation by one or the other—or both—of these national organizations was an indication of a high-quality program. The two merged their efforts into a single accrediting body for family and children's programs, which is described in Chapter 5. The accreditation of hospitals and other health care facilities, as well as the accreditation of education and, especially, social work education, also is explored.

Social agencies, especially those providing residential and day care, have required licenses in most states. More recently, individual practitioners also have been licensed to practice social work in most states. Before that, voluntary credentials, such as those regulated by private organizations, were available, as they still are, to social workers. The licensing process is described in Chapter 6.

In all, these three processes—auditing and accounting, accreditation, and licensing—encompass the traditional approaches to evaluating social work programs. They are still fundamental evaluation modes to which social work practice and social agencies are committed, and they dominate much of the activity in the human services.

4

Accounting, Auditing, and Budgeting

Perhaps the most common forms of evaluation of social work are auditing, accounting, and budgeting. Virtually no agency can function without careful financial planning and supervision. Those who play management roles in social welfare agencies evaluate their own performances and the functioning of their organizations largely by these financial tests and measures. How well the organization is performing, what it really does, what its priorities and plans for the future are, how close it comes to being legitimate and forthright in its operations—all can be determined, at least in part, from financial information.

The Importance of Financial Evaluation

Most managers of social agencies and alert staff members can cite multiple examples of the importance of financial accountability. Human services and religious and educational organizations are far from immune from financial crimes. In fact, they are sometimes not scrutinized as closely as they should be because of their humane objectives and nature. However, human services organizations handle billions of dollars every year—bundles of money that are as attractive to dishonest people as the money in banks and businesses. Nothing can so readily destroy a human services organization and its credibility with clients, funders, and the larger public as financial fraud and other money difficulties—a point made several times in this chapter. Some typical kinds of cases, all of which the author has encountered in his own work and in reading reports from others, are:

1. A financial clerk in a rural public welfare office was responsible for receiving and depositing children's Social Security checks for youngsters in the office's care. They were foster care clients whose parent or parents had died. The children received survivor payments from their parents' accounts. For years, the clerk

managed to deposit large numbers of those checks in her personal account in a local bank. The office records clearly showed that the checks were deposited to the accounts of the children—including copies of deposit slips. However, the clerk destroyed those slips before the checks were deposited and placed the money in her own account with new deposit slips. The office was regularly audited, but the state agency auditors relied on the records in the office. Eventually, an alert auditor went a step further and checked the actual bank records, which showed that the money was deposited in the clerk's account. The clerk had taken tens of thousands of dollars and was prosecuted for the crime.

   2. An assistant pastor of a prestigious religious organization visited several local banks in his city and asked for loans—on the basis of his administrative position. The banks assumed the requests were legitimate and had the support of the wealthy members of the board. However, the board and pastor knew nothing about the loans. The assistant pastor pocketed the money and used it for his own purposes.

   3. A major university experienced financial problems constituting mismanagement rather than crime or fraud. The president made frequent suggestions and requests for funds to carry out special projects to the director of the university's voluntary foundation, to which supporters made major donations every year. After two years of foundation compliance with suggestions, auditors discovered that the foundation had overspent its funds by millions of dollars. The university had to quickly cut back on its foundation-funded programs and essentially seized and reduced the accounts of several university departments in order to balance the budget.

   4. A large and highly regarded school district discovered, when a new superintendent came into office and initiated audits, that the assistant superintendent for fiscal affairs for years had appropriated school district money for himself and other district employees. About $3.5 million had been diverted from the school system to lavish personal vacations (sometimes with traveling companions to whom they were not married), for the fiscal chief, football coaches, a choir director, principals, and travel agency owners (Roberts, 2000).

   Those with many years of service in social work can usually cite many cases like these. It is probably not necessary to say that the overwhelming proportion of agencies and their employees are honest and do an excellent job of managing funds. That is also true of banks and other businesses. However, the possibilities of fraud and abuse are such that a careful evaluation program requires extensive attention to auditing and sound accounting.

Innumeracy—Number Illiteracy

For reasons that are not always clear, fiscal and accounting information is probably emphasized less in human services professions than it probably should be, based on its importance in the operations of services. Emphasis in the social work curriculum is on matters such as human behavior, social work practice methods, social welfare policy, and social research methods and procedures. Some observers suggest that social work students have phobias about mathematics, based upon poor experiences with the subject matter in public schools, but that may be true for much of the U.S. population. One popular writer on mathematical issues (Paulos, 1988) suggests that innumeracy is a critical problem that exceeds illiteracy as a source of nonfunctional skills among students and much of the rest of the population.

The author of this text is a "recovered innumerate" and has devoted some of his teaching to helping students overcome the lack of knowledge innumeracy implies. Of course, there are daily examples of the ways in which commercial enterprises take advantage of what they know is a fundamental problem. Each year, auto manufacturers offer very low interest rates for new car purchases—1, 2, perhaps 3 percent—when everyone knows that the usual rate is several times any of those. However, the "small print" says that the buyer, instead, could have a discount of $1,000 or more. Of course, the low interest rate is simply a reflection of charging more than the company's lowest acceptable price for the car. If the buyer takes long enough to pay, the overall profits to the company are greater with the low interest rate than they would be if normal interest were charged for a cheaper price.

Also, of course, U.S. financial matters are complicated. Try explaining auto insurance coverage to someone unfamiliar with it, or attempt to describe the federal or state income tax systems to someone new to the tax system. Its complexity, which is designed to help equalize the tax burden for people of various income groups—in some cases the poorest citizens—is so confusing that Americans who would suffer from them often endorse schemes such as flat taxes, and national sales taxes, which place unequal burdens on the poorest citizens and have proportionately poor consequences for the middle-income groups.

One more example is credit card schemes that provide low introductory rates that quickly go up to rates much higher than the prime rate. Many Americans spend a fortune on interest because of their credit cards and other charge accounts. Banks and retail establishments often make more money from their interest on credit purchases than they earn in profit on their products.

These issues of financial operations, auditing and accounting, and budgets are not widely discussed in the social work literature, despite the fact that few elements of agency operations and evaluation criteria are more important than these monetary matters. Practitioners of social work, especially those with managerial responsibilities, devote much of their time to fiscal concerns. However, they are rarely educated in detail about such matters in their social work or other human services studies. Most have to learn the material on their own or rely on the consultation of the fiscal experts in their agencies. In too many cases, social welfare administrators abandon their agency's fiscal operations to other staff members. If those staff members are expert and honest in their dealings with the manager, the manager can exercise his or her influence over the financial matters. In too many cases, however, managers fail to learn enough to ask intelligent questions of the fiscal staff, who become, in effect, the top agency managers because they control the organization's resources. Of course, most of a social agency's accounting functions are routinely handled by support staff. Accountants and auditors assist them in setting up systems and in periodically examining and reporting on their work. However, the top agency management is responsible for everything, perhaps especially finances. If one does not manage the resources, one is not managing the organization, because all the program and its activities can be is translated into resources. In other words, nothing happens unless there are funds to make it happen. Over the years, the author has seen agency executives defer to the decisions of their fiscal managers, even when they dislike the outcomes, simply because they fear the consequences of failing to do so. Some accountants ascend to top power positions when they should function instead as specialized and technical staff, helping the manager and board make the appropriate decisions. It is also often true that managers fail in their social agency work because of fiscal errors or incorrect decisions. Fiscal problems probably are the source of terminations of the largest numbers of agency social executives who lose their jobs. The author has, for decades, advised social work graduate students who have management aspirations to take an elective course or two in accounting. To his knowledge, none has ever done so—except for those who pursue dual degrees in social work and fields such as business and public administration, which require much more fiscal education than social work programs.

Budgets

Even modestly well-organized organizations have budgets. Essentially, budgets are the fundamental plans of any organization. They reflect the amount of money the organization will have available for a specified period, usually a year. They also reflect the sources of those funds. For social agencies, fund sources are government contracts and grants, foundation grants, contributions, fees, interest on investments such as endowments, and allocations from central funding organizations such as United Way. The budget is prepared to reflect the planned expenditures. Ideally, budgets are prepared and presented in two ways: as line items (or "objects"), which specify expenses in categories such as personnel, rent, equipment, and travel, and as program (or functional) budgets. Figure 4.1 shows a line item budget, and Figure 4.2 shows program budgets. The program budget delineates expenditures for the agency's activities and combines all of the expenses from the appropriate line items. It reflects what the agency does with its money in terms of its objectives and clientele, rather than the item-by-item expenditures. Some organizations divide their functional budgets into program activities and supportive services, which enable all the program activities to operate and which include such elements as rent, utilities, and accounting services.

One source (Budak et al., 1998b) says that financial accounting standards require nonprofit organizations to prepare and make available both line-item budgets and program budgets. Those who review budgets know that they can tell little about what an organization actually does from a line-by-line list of expenditures

FIGURE 4.1 *Common Natural (Object) Expense Classifications*

Natural (Object) Classification	Types of Expenses That May Be Included
Salaries	Salaries Bonuses Vacation and compensated absences
Employee Benefits	Employee insurance Contributions to defined benefit pension or contribution plans Other employee benefits
Payroll Taxes	Employer portion of FICA Unemployment insurance Workers' compensation insurance
Professional and Other Contract Service Fees	Accounting and auditing fees Legal fees Consulting fees Actuarial fees Outside data processing services Investment management fees
Supplies	Program supplies Office supplies Copying supplies
Telephone	Telephone Long distance Fax charges
Postage and Shipping	Postage Shipping Other delivery expenses
Occupancy	Rent Utilities Janitorial and maintenance services Building and grounds maintenance supplies
Interest Expense	Interest expense
Rental and Maintenance of Equipment	Equipment rental Equipment maintenance
Printing and Publications	Printing Advertising Informational materials Technical journals and books

Source: Reprinted with permission of Practitioners Publishing Company, Fort Worth, Texas, from PPC's *Guide to Audits of Nonprofit Organizations*, 1998 edition. To order or for further information, call 1-800-323-8724.

FIGURE 4.2   *Program Budgets*

Examples of Determining an Organization's Programs Determining an organization's programs requires judgement and knowledge of the organization's operations. Therefore, programs presented for functional reporting purposes may depend on an organization's individual facts and circumstances. To illustrate, each of the following scenarios are based on the same organization programs and amounts.

An organization separately tracks costs related to the following seven programs

Alcohol abuse prevention	$ 184,000	12%
Alcohol abuse treatment	386,000	25%
Drug abuse prevention	167,000	11%
Drug abuse treatment	425,000	28%
Group counseling	223,000	14%
Evaluation	69,000	4%
Education	85,000	6%
	$1,539,000	100%

Example #1. The organization's four alcohol and drug abuse programs are separately administered and viewed as separate major services of the organization. Group counseling and other services are secondary operations. The organization's program services for functional reporting purposes might be:

Alcohol abuse prevention	$184,000
Alcohol abuse treatment	386,000
Drug abuse prevention	167,000
Drug abuse treatment	425,000
Group counseling and other	377,000
	$1,539,000

Example #2. The organization administers the alcohol and drug prevention programs together in the same facilities and evaluates them as one program. The organization's alcohol and drug treatment programs are separate major activities, as is group counseling. Other services are secondary. The organization might choose to group its program services for functional reporting purposes as follows:

Alcohol and drug abuse prevention	$351,000
Alcohol abuse treatment	386,000
Drug abuse treatment	425,000
Group counseling	223,000
Other	154,000
	$1,539,000

FIGURE 4.2   *Continued*

Example #3. The organization considers its three primary services to be alcohol abuse services, drug abuse services, and group counseling. The organization's program services might be presented as follows:

Alcohol abuse prevention and treatment	$570,000
Drug abuse prevention and treatment	529,000
Group counseling	223,000
Other	154,000
	$1,539000

Source: Reprinted with permission of Practitioners Publishing Company, Fort Worth, Texas, from PPC's *Guide to Audits of Nonprofit Organizations,* 1998 edition. To order or for further information, call 1-800-323-8724.

alone. That is the reason for the requirement of program budget information. An explanation of and some examples of program budgets are found in Figure 4.2.

One authoritative accounting source says "The budget of a not-for-profit organization is a strategy for financial operations that provides a basis for the planning, controlling, and evaluating of its activities" (Bailey, 1998, p. 33.12). Although not all such organizations are required to present budgets to comply with accepted accounting and auditing principles, "the use of a budget is a recognized method of controlling a(n) organization's expenditures and evaluating the effectiveness of its management" (p. 33.12).

Budget preparation and management are complex processes and are fundamental interests of effective agency managers. Normally, a budget must be approved by an agency's governing board, and, almost always, the funders and potential funders of an organization want to see a budget before making decisions about providing resources. Of course, a budget normally can be modified to reflect changes in circumstances and new priorities. However, budget changes are usually not made lightly. An organization's stability is often considered synonymous with the stability of its budget.

In most agencies, periodic (usually monthly) budget reports are prepared to show how well the organization is following its plan in the form of a budget. Is the budget on target? Behind the plan? Overexpended for the length of time the budget has been in effect? These are data that governing bodies such as boards of directors and executive directors want and need. Generally, it is not proper for an organization to end a year having spent more than it budgeted, unless it has an endowment or reserve fund from which money can be transferred to make up any deficit. Even that is a formal process that requires an end-of-the year formal action.

Although some organizations view budgets narrowly, Kettner, Moroney, and Martin say that there are three purposes for budgeting—control, management, and planning (1999). They say that many agencies do not fulfill all those purposes with their budgeting processes. Kettner and his co-authors are concerned that control is more likely to be a purpose of budgeting than the other two. They also point out that accounting and budgeting are very different activities. Accounting is strictly a financial activity, they suggest, while budgeting is a programmatic as well as a financial activity.

Of course, for evaluation purposes, control is one of the main uses of finance and budgeting and the control function helps an evaluator, for example, determine the financial condition of the agency and its programs.

Budgets and their management are significant criteria in the evaluation of social agencies. Some might suggest they are the most important criteria. There is no surer way for an agency to lose its financial and other public support—or for an agency executive to lose that position—than ineffectively budgeting and managing the budget process.

Accounting

Accounting, in lay terms, is the process of keeping track of an organization's receipt and expenditure of funds. In its simplest form, it is the maintenance of a checking account record—entering checks when they are written, deducting their amounts from the account balance, entering deposits, and reconciling the records supplied from banks in monthly statements with one's own records.

Organizations, of course, maintain much more complex accounting systems that are keyed to the varied accounts that the organizations may maintain. These systems relate expenditures and income to the organizations' budgets and otherwise keep records of the organizations' fiscal affairs.

Many nonprofit and governmental accounting systems are more complex than many of those used in businesses. There are several different ways that social welfare organizations set up their accounting systems, an activity that usually involves consultation with and training by professional accountants. It is beyond the scope of this text to discuss those systems in detail. It is more an administrative or management set of issues than evaluation, per se. However, it should be clear to students of social welfare agency evaluation that accounting has a great deal to do with the precision with which an organization may be evaluated. Audits, which are discussed later in this chapter, are among the principal methods used to evaluate social welfare programs.

Accounting is a technical and professional enterprise of its own, and professionals in accounting are educated in colleges and universities. Those who complete appropriate studies and pass formal examinations in their states are designated certified public accountants (CPAs), who are something of an elite in the accounting profession. Many other people with various professional or pre-higher education credentials also engage in accounting activities. Few social welfare organizations have full-time CPAs, but most have someone, even if it is the executive director, who "keeps the books" for the agency. By contract or other forms of periodic payment, organizations often use the services of professional accountants to verify bookkeeping and produce financial records. Annually, in many cases, organizations also hire accounting firms to conduct audits of their financial operations.

The accounting profession, which is often represented by the American Institute of Certified Public Accountants, establishes and maintains standards for accounting and auditing practices. It also defines the classifications of organizations that are subject to accounting and auditing and establishes Generally Accepted Accounting Principles (GAAP) for those classifications of organizations. The profession promulgates, through publications and professional meetings, the GAAP for U.S. accountants, who, in turn, apply them in their work with the organizations they serve.

Public or governmental organizations operate under GAAP that are different than those applied to profit-making and nonprofit organizations. Social welfare organizations fall into all of the several categories of organizations. Some are governmental, some are proprietary or profit-making, and others are voluntary or nonprofit.

All of these concepts and classifications have many other implications and impacts beyond the definitions. For example, the tax status of an organization depends on its classification, as does the nature of the contributions it may receive. That is, whether a contribution is deductible from a contributor's income taxes depends on the classification of the organization.

The concepts that accountants apply in making those classifications are highly instructive and critical in understanding the social welfare system. Although the distinctions may seem clear, there are more and more "mixed" social welfare organizations that operate with some public, some private, and some proprietary funds. The demarcations are no longer as crisp or as well delineated as they may once have been.

Nonprofit versus Profit-Making Organizations

There are many different kinds of nonprofit organizations, although the most familiar to social workers is the 501(c) (3), which is the designation given by the U.S. Internal Revenue Service to religious, scientific, literary, educational, and charitable organizations. However, this is only one classification of nonprofit groups. Others include organizations that educate about labor, agriculture, and horticulture, civic leagues and local employee associations that work to improve human services, professional organizations, and social and recreation clubs. In fact, there are more than 25 categories of such organizations, all of which share the characteristic of being tax-exempt (Carmichael, Dropkin, & Reed, 1998). Of course, obtaining tax-exempt status requires (except for churches) the completion and approval of applications for the Internal Revenue Service and periodic reports demonstrating that the organization continues to be nonprofit.

The following criteria are used in distinguishing not-for-profit organizations from businesses. Not-for-profits have:

1. Contributions of significant amounts of resources from resource providers who do not expect commensurate or proportionate pecuniary return
2. Operating purposes other than to provide goods or services at a profit
3. Absence of ownership interests like those of business enterprises (American Institute of Certified Public Accountants, 1997 p. 1)

The CPAs also define not-for-profits by distinguishing them from profit-making organizations. Profit-making groups are those that include enterprises that are owned by investors and provide dividends or that give economic benefits directly to their owners, members, or participants, such as mutual insurance companies, credit unions, cooperatives, and employee benefit plans (American Institute of Certified Public Accountants, 1997).

Accountants rely on the definitions and standards promulgated in their literature, such as the *AICPA Audit and Accounting Guide: Not-for-Profit Organizations*, published by the American Institute of Certified Public Accountants (1997). They rely also on the works of other authors and publishers for more details on matters such as contributions. An example is Budak et al.'s *Guide to Nonprofit Contributions*, (1998a), Practioners Publishing Company. That volume deals with some of the complex issues associated with accounting for contributions to nonprofits. For example: When are membership dues and initiation fees contributions? How must organizations account for income from special events, such as a dinner that costs $100 per person but that provides a meal that ordinarily costs $35? (Usually, the dinner participants can only claim a contribution of $65 each because they have received $35 in value.) How may the organization and the donor evaluate a donated piece of property, such as land, real estate, or a work of art? How do radio and television stations account for their contributions of air time to a charitable organization?

The book contains detailed checklists and instruments to assist accountants and auditors in making such decisions and in writing their reports. For example, it includes a chart that shows how much contributed money is worth that is donated to the organization. A contributor might contribute a specific amount in a specific year at a specified rate of interest. The chart shows the value of that contribution at the time it is made. By simply referring to the chart, accountants can determine the value of the contribution for tax purposes, as well as the value to the agency that receives the contribution.

The contributions guide (Budak et al., 1998a), which is a training manual for accountants studying additional accounting information, provides forms for documenting contributions, suggested thank you letters for donors (which can serve as the contributor's documentation of a donation), and guides for budgeting contributions.

The guide also deals with such donations as those that are "in-kind," such as the services of people. Of course, specially skilled people such as medical and psychological personnel and other experts often provide their time to social welfare agencies. Some of them claim the expenses associated with their voluntary efforts as tax deductions. Therefore, there must be corresponding information in the agency showing that the services were provided. The agency also must show in its expenditures that the voluntary efforts were used. The accountants, however, suggest that ordinary volunteer efforts not be counted as contributions. That is, help with childcare, transportation, or meal preparation does not qualify as a contribution like the efforts of skilled professionals who are providing their expertise to the organization. The test is whether the organization would have purchased the services, if it could have done so, rather than the value of the effort. Therefore, regular volunteer efforts are not documented in financial reports as either contributions or expenditures.

Misrepresentation

Another area for which agency managers must take responsibility is the possible misrepresentation of donations or loans. Typically, in such cases, an agency official may ask a supporter for a special donation for a specific purpose, such as helping a client who has serious health or housing problems. The official may actually divert the contribution to his or her own purposes, instead of helping the client, who may or may not exist. In another dramatic case, a religious organization official borrowed several thousand dollars from a local bank in the name of the church that employed him, although neither his supervisor nor the board of directors authorized his action. He was able to transfer the money to his own account, and it was only months later, when the bank sought repayment and called volunteer board members, that the misrepresentation was detected.

These kinds of misrepresentations are possible because of the generally honorable ways of nonprofit organizations and their officials. Misrepresentations are few and dishonesty is minimal, therefore, donors, banks, and others trust organization officials. However, the few exceptions make careful monitoring important. Accountants and agency officials warn that they are concerned about more than an occasional loss of funds. Much more problematic is the loss of the future ability of an organization to solicit funds from the public. Even small, well-publicized losses to financial fraud and abuse damage organizational credibility and the capacity of an organization to survive.

A *Forbes* magazine article describes situations in which charitable contributions might be used for ongoing institutional expenses even though the money was donated for a specific purpose (McMenamin, 2000). In one example, a widower donated $34,000 to a health, education, and research foundation to establish a lectureship in his wife's name. A hospital that received the money encountered some critical operating expenses and used the money to cover those. The state attorney general prosecuted the hospital officials, who face up to 25 years in prison if they are convicted. The importance of following the rules on donations and clearing any changes with reliable accountants is important to the organization and the staff. Any deviations can cause serious problems.

Purchases of Services

One of the primary ways in which accounting and auditing play significant roles in human services is in the increasing use of purchase of services and contracting agreements between state governments and voluntary or proprietary organizations. Instead of carrying out, for example, full programs of services to children, many state social services agencies contract with group and family foster care organizations for the care of the children. Instead of operating homes or foster care services of their own, states may pay nongovernmental organizations a per diem or monthly fee for caring for children. The state agency sets criteria and refers children for the appropriate services. Then the government agency monitors the services that are provided. In many cases, similar arrangements are made for various social services including adoptions, nutritional programs for older adults, and counseling for clients who need professional help. Much of the work done in such contracting is fiscally centered. In addition to these efforts, state social services agencies also usually are responsible for paying for the care of indigent nursing home patients. They do so by paying directly to the nursing homes at a rate that is reasonable for both the government and the nursing homes, most of which are nonprofit or proprietary. In the case of nursing homes that are the property of local or even state governments, their financing is similar to that of nongovernmental homes. The state pays for care on the basis of costs, including food, medical services, housekeeping programs, social services, recreation, administration, mortgages of the property, and (for proprietary homes) a reasonable amount of profit. Nursing homes are part of the Medicaid program, which provides payments for medical care to low-income Americans. The formulas adopted by the states for reimbursement of prescription, hospital, physician services, and medical equipment costs are another example of cost accounting and auditing that states must consider in their operation and evaluation of programs.

Designing the scope and nature of the contracts, as well as the amounts that will be paid, are important functions of modern program evaluation. In many states, the purchases of services are based on "units of service," such as the number of counseling hours provided, meals delivered, or people participating in group dining services. The governmental agency is responsible for paying a reasonable amount for the costs of the services it purchases from others. Similarly, the nongovernmental organizations are responsible for maintaining and publishing detailed information on their costs. In some cases, this process becomes a kind of contest between the governmental agency, which wants to spend as little as possible without compromising the quality of services, and the contractor, which wants to maximize the amount of money it obtains for its services.

The whole range of human services is involved in the contracts described here. For example, many states now contract for the incarceration of prisoners, including youth inmates of correctional facilities. In some cases, new facilities are built in and belong to the state. In others, states contract with facilities in other states that provide secure custody or specialized programs such as health care for prisoners who are ill. States also may contract with specialized corrections firms and turn over the operation of the facilities to those firms for a fee—per year, per month, per inmate, or by some other measure. Again, the figures are based on the cost of care plus a reasonable profit for the firm, if it is proprietary.

Conflicts about reimbursement or contract levels are often contentious, sometimes leading to legal battles in the state or federal courts. Battles between the nursing home industry and state governments are often common. Federal statutes and regulations require the states to pay for nursing home care on the basis of the costs of that care. However, determining what is a reasonable cost may be the source of disagreements. When administering a Medicaid program several years ago, this author was confronted with a lawsuit charging that the state was not fully reimbursing the costs of one chain of nursing homes. The Medicaid program used the services of a complex cost-accounting organization, which developed a program for calculating costs based on the average costs in the state. After an administrative hearing, in which the nursing home firm's petition was denied, the case was taken to federal court, with a suit against the state agency. Ultimately, the federal judge dismissed the case and said the state had the constitutional right to set reimbursement standards.

Handling Cash

Accounting experts need to help organizations handle donated money, so the contributions guide (Budak et al., 1998a) provides suggestions for the ways in which cash contributions should be received and monitored by an organization (two employees are involved in seeing and documenting the contributions), as well as some clues for controlling fraud and theft. The accountants suggest that the duties of receiving cash, processing deposits, recording transactions, and reconciling bank statements should be segregated from one another so that errors and misuses of funds do not occur.

Although most fiscal experts suggest that cash contributions be avoided, there are still many. The church collection plate, the spontaneous passing of the hat at a civic club luncheon or agency board meeting, the staff donations of funds for flowers for colleagues who are ill, and the voluntary agency coffee fund all have potential for abuse. Wise managers know that all fiscal operations must be carefully monitored and controlled.

Of course, the way an agency handles its contributions is a major element that is evaluated by boards, external groups, and, especially, auditors, whose work is described later in this chapter.

Expenses

According to Budak et al. (1998b), the handling of nonprofit organization expenses is also a significant matter. As mentioned earlier, the expenses an organization incurs should be organized and reported in both line item (object) budgets and program (functional) budgets. The examples earlier in this chapter show the ways in which such budgets may be organized and presented.

The accounting of expenses is, of course, a complicated procedure. Many times expenses must be allocated across a number of functions. For example, a single office rental expense in some cases may be accounted for as a supporting service for the agency. However, in other cases the rental expense may have to be allocated over several of the organization's functions or programs. That can be important in understanding the full cost of, for example, an alcohol and drug counseling program. The program could not take place without office space, and the amount spent for that space for that function is critical in describing the real cost. In other cases, various funding sources may have allocated money for different functions. A foundation or government grant program may require information on the expenditure of funds for rent for that specific program. Therefore, although the organization may pay a single amount for rent, the amount taken from the specific source for that program's rent must be identified. The expense report may show rental expenses in several different places, although they should all add up to the composite rental costs of the organization.

Similarly, Budak et al. (1998b) use an example of a performing arts organization that charges membership dues of $100. If $80 of the dues is used for tickets and other member benefits such as a magazine, then $80 of the dues should be allocated to the costs of those programs and $20 to the costs of fund-raising (to solicit and process memberships). Similarly, the members are able to use only $20 as a tax deduction because $80 is spent on services and products of value to them. The guide contains detailed checklists that accountants use in setting up an organization's bookkeeping records and procedures.

Governmental Agency Accounting

Local and state government agencies, which are traditionally the major social welfare programs in the United States, also follow specific accounting principles, which may be similar to those used for nonprofit organizations but also may be substantially different. Bailey (1998) points out that some governmental organizations are often similar to voluntary organizations. That is, they may receive donations and grants from individuals, foundations, and other governmental entities. At times, they may also be similar to commercial, business activities. There are whole sets of rules that apply to governmental organizations as well as several levels of accounting in many cases. For example, a local human services department may maintain its own accounting procedures and staff; it may also be subject to the accounting functions of its larger local or state government; it may be responsible for providing accounting information to the federal government, which supports parts of its activities; and it may also be required to provide accounting information to a foundation or central fund-raising body such as a United Way. Of course, a voluntary organization that receives funds from multiple sources may have similar multiple accounting obligations. Also, even though a department is part of the executive branch of government, it may be responsible to a legislative financial group that conducts studies of the agency's finances and periodically audits all or part of it.

Governmental agency accounting is often based on projected revenues from appropriations, expected caseloads, and governmental financial procedures. The author, who was a state government official for ten years, recalls not only the complicated budget requests and procedures but also the significant accounting and financial monitoring requirements of state governments. For example, the state legislature passed eligibility standards for programs such as Medicaid, based upon projected caseloads. However, when the caseloads actually experienced exceeded those projections, the appropriated money was insufficient to meet the costs of those who were eligible. Reductions had to be made in programs or additional funds had to be allocated for the activity. In another difficult situation, the state's tax revenues appeared to be falling short of projections. An order was passed to all the state's agencies to reduce their annual expenditures by a total of 5 percent. However, the order came with only six months remaining in the fiscal year. Therefore, expenditures had to actually be reduced by 10 percent for the remainder of the year. In such situations, agencies are quickly and decisively evaluated by government fiscal authorities and by the press. Charges are leveled of "overspending," which is illegal in most states. That is, if an agency obligates more money than it has available during a fiscal year and ends the year with a negative balance, someone—often the director—may be charged with a criminal act. Such consequences are stark examples of agency evaluation. In this particular case, which happened several times, the agency explained the reductions it would be required to make to conform to the budget shortfalls. Those were onerous because they required removing patients from nursing homes. Only certain activities were options under federal regulations, and, of course, only optional programs could be reduced. Eventually, the legislature allocated additional funds to the agency to prevent the reductions.

Some agencies find themselves publicly evaluated because of the choices they make for dealing with fiscal reductions. Some critics call these "Washington Monument" threats. That is, if the agency that manages the Washington Monument were faced with a fiscal reduction and was asked how it would implement the necessary savings, it might say it would close the Washington Monument—a highly visible and unpopular choice that might be designed to persuade Congress to appropriate more money. Some state legislators considered the reduction of nursing home services a form of the Washington Monument threat. It wasn't, but the criticisms of observers are understandable.

The standards and procedures for government accounting are specific and have been promulgated in a variety of ways by the accounting organizations. However, each governmental entity establishes its own procedures and rules and these take precedence.

It is probably sufficient to say that government accounting is as central to the evaluation of public social welfare agencies as is the foregoing, which focuses more heavily on non-profit organizations.

Proprietary Social Welfare

Although the typical social welfare service has historically been governmental or nonprofit in nature, an increasing number of human services programs are proprietary. That is, they earn profits in the fees they charge and distribute them to owners. Such organizations include home health care services, adult and youth correction services and facilities, child care programs, and nursing homes. Another example is the private clinical practice, a pervasive form of social work for many years. Many times, these organizations' largest customers are governments. The primary distinction between them and nonprofits is that they are set up to earn profits.

The accounting procedures in such organizations are the same as for any other business enterprise, of course. As discussed earlier, part of the government's accounting responsibility with proprietary organizations is to determine the amounts that are paid for the services that are purchased.

As has been discussed in this chapter, most small- to medium-sized organizations cannot afford to employ full-time qualified accountants, especially CPAs, whose salaries are high and whose services are in great demand. More typically, an organization employs an accountant or accounting firm to establish an appropriate fiscal record-keeping system, to periodically review its procedures and records, and to periodically audit its complete records. Perhaps one of the most important functions of the accountant or accounting firm is to train the organization's fiscal personnel and to consult with the agency management about fiscal matters. Such training and consultation are essential for any organization in modern social welfare practice. The demands for correct and detailed fiscal records are fundamental for organizations that want to operate with donated funds from foundations or individuals or to receive grants from government bodies.

Auditing

The examination of records and accounts to evaluate their accuracy is called auditing. It is likely that audits are the most pervasive form of program evaluations. Social agencies that would never consider conducting experimental studies of their programs or even engaging in single-subject design analyses still would likely be audited, often annually. Fund contributors and central fund-raising organizations such as United Way typically require audits. Guides for nonprofit auditing are available from the American Institute of Certified Public Accountants (AICPA, 1994a, 1994b).

Audits are typically conducted by CPAs or CPA-supervised accountants. Auditors are independent; that is, although their services are paid for by the organization being audited, their opinions are their own and they are bound by their professional ethics to provide opinions based upon the facts they find. Sometimes their findings are negative, but, especially when they are, they are bound to call attention to those negative findings. For example, an auditor who finds fraud but does not report it can be found partially responsible for the fraud when it is later identified and acted upon by the agency or by legal authorities.

Auditors examine the records of an organization and analyze all or a sample of the organization's transactions. Although the focus is heavily on financial data, other kinds of materials are also studied to find out if the organization is performing properly. For example, if an organization is supposed to devote a specified number of dollars from a granting organization to a specific activity, such as marital counseling, the auditors may examine documentation that the service was provided. They may look at the time sheets of the employees and supervisors who were engaged in the counseling to determine if the required resources were devoted to the activity. Auditors compare data on contributions with records of contributors and look for proper notification and acknowledgment to those who have provided funds.

Of course, the complexity of an audit is a result, at least in part, of the quality of the organization's accounting. If records are clear and complete, the auditors have less difficulty in their work than if records are poorly kept or not kept at all. In such situations, auditors often have to reconstruct the income and expenditure reports to collect enough information to make a thorough audit report.

In many cases, auditors use sampling techniques, not unlike those used in research methods, to examine one part of an agency's programs or processes. If an audit is supposed to determine the day-to-day functions of an organization, the auditors may not want to spend the time necessary to analyze every work day of the staff since the last audit. Instead, they examine a few randomly selected days and project their results onto the whole year's efforts. They also may study the agency's financial transactions by examining only a relatively small sample of a year's transactions.

Auditors collect all sorts of information by looking at records, interviewing staff, and often directly observing processes within an organization. A series of manuals on auditing nonprofit organizations (Carmichael et al., 1998) provides guidelines, forms, and checklists to make it possible for auditors to do their work satisfactorily.

The final step in the audit process is a report from the auditors to the agency, often with a draft submitted for comments and clarifications before it becomes official. The audit generally will include observations about the organization's functioning and may also make a variety of recommendations that the auditors think will improve the record-keeping and accounting processes. These comments and recommendations are often included in a document called a "management letter," which is provided to be helpful and which does not suggest any discrepancies within the organization. According to Carmichael et al. (1998), management letters are not a requirement of audits but often are provided as an additional service. Such letters tend to point to:

1. Weaknesses in accounting practices and controls that are not significant
2. Weaknesses and inefficiencies in controls not related to financial data
3. Operational inefficiencies, such as inefficient inventory management controls

4. Opportunities to increase revenues by using assets more effectively, such as by investment of idle cash
5. Suggestions for increasing personnel motivation or performance
6. Comments about data processing hardware or software
   (Vol. 1, pp. 850.05–850.06)

When there are no fiscal or accounting problems uncovered in the audit and no discrepancies between what the organization is supposed to have done and what the auditors have found, the auditors attest to the proper functioning of the organization by providing an audit that has no exceptions noted. The common description of an audit that notes no exceptions is a "clean" audit.

When there are problems encountered in the audit, the auditors may provide an audit with "audit exceptions." Sometimes these are serious and require corrective action within a short period of time. Of course, effective agency managers work throughout the year to ensure that an audit will be clean and that the agency's processes and records are satisfactory. An audit with several serious exceptions is, perhaps more than anything else, a negative evaluation of a program that can raise questions about the organization's ability to use donated or contracted funds properly, about the agency's ability to carry out its mission, and about the skills of the agency management. Therefore, ensuring that the audited functions of the organization are operating satisfactorily is a critical element for agency leadership.

Government Agency Audits of Service Providers

As discussed earlier, state government agencies are often responsible for providing help to their clients through purchasing services. The purchase of services agreements allow the state agency to audit the service providers. Some examples demonstrate the difficulty of carrying out such audits in all circumstances:

1. A state agency contracted with a low-income legal services provider so assistance clients and others with insufficient incomes would not have to pay attorneys. The legal services provider was asked to submit a report on every case for which it sought payment, with details of the problems addressed and the services given. The agency, however, balked at providing such information because it would constitute a breach of their commitment to provide services confidentially. The legal profession often follows more-stringent ethics in their services than some other professions. After lengthy negotiations, the agency and the legal services provider were able to develop a system that documented the fact that services had been provided without being specific about the ways in which help was given or the problem that was addressed.

2. Although health services providers are generally scrupulously honest, occasional examples of fiscal misconduct arise. Every Medicaid program has an investigative unit that audits health care providers who are affiliated with Medicaid and that works to reconcile any discrepancies. In one situation, an auditor found suspicious coding and accounting of expenditures. A private nursing home had mislabeled several items that seemed personal—trips to resorts, a daughter's wedding costs, and similar expenditures—as if they were legitimate expenses such as laundry, food, and housekeeping. An investigation demonstrated that these were likely examples of fraud—a fact that was presented to law enforcement authorities and that ultimately led to a federal court conviction of the owners of the facility.

3. Other cases of health care improprieties are also well known to those who operate and audit Medicaid programs. For example, a physician who was treating a child billed for those services, but also for examinations of the child's mother and two siblings who had accompanied the child to the physician's office. The physician was dismissed from Medicaid and fined by the courts. In another case, a pharmacist was billing Medicaid for name-brand prescription medicines but dispensing much lower-cost generics. Because the patients did not pay for the prescriptions, they had no idea that there was a discrepancy. The pharmacist was dismissed from participation in the Medicaid program.

Most auditing matters are much less dramatic than these examples. Service providers willingly provide data on their services while maintaining the confidentiality of their work. Although there may be regular disagreements between auditors and health care providers, they are usually honest disagreements and not examples of fraud. Differences of opinion are resolved amicably, compromised, and otherwise addressed. The larger policy issues of low reimbursements by governments for services provided to clients are sources of tension that are often resolved by lobbying legislatures for better reimbursement formulas and more money for the social services budgets. The examples given previously are unusual exceptions to the day-to-day auditing functions and the more typical relations between governments and those who provide services to government clients.

Conclusion

This chapter has covered some of the most crucial elements of program evaluation in the human services—budgeting, accounting, and auditing. Although they have not been dealt with extensively in much of the social work literature, these activities are central to the operations of any social welfare agency. In social work practice, management personnel carefully attend to these matters because failing to do so may cause more difficulty for an organization than any of the other kinds of evaluation processes and measures discussed in this text.

Perhaps the critical lesson from this information is that effective social welfare agencies employ and capably and knowledgeably supervise their fiscal specialists. Not keeping up with an agency's resources is a potentially disastrous error for social welfare managers. Of course, it is not simply concern with potential criticism that is significant for the agencies. Audits can uncover genuine problems of performance, noncompliance with the rules of funding organizations, and possible fraud and abuse—much more common problems than is generally acknowledged—among the organization's personnel. The solution is obviously to direct an organization, in every element of its operations, as it should be directed. Doing so should guarantee not only clean audits but also effective services to the agency's clientele.

Questions for Further Study

1. Distinguish between a line item (objects) budget and a program (functional) budget. What is the rationale for developing each for a nonprofit organization?

2. This chapter suggests that audits are the most pervasive kind of evaluation in social agencies. Do you agree, based on your experience in social work programs? If so, what evidence do you have that this is correct? If you disagree, justify your response.

3. Provide some examples of the ways in which social agencies may be financially defrauded.

4. What are two or three of the reasons Medicaid is more subject to financial abuse than other social welfare programs?

References

American Institute of Certified Public Accountants. (1994a). *Audit and accounting guide: Audits of certain nonprofit organizations.* New York: Author.

American Institute of Certified Public Accountants. (1994b). *Industry audit guide: Audits of voluntary health and welfare organizations.* New York: Author.

American Institute of Certified Public Accountants. (1997). *AICPA audit and accounting guide: Not-for-profit organizations.* New York: Author.

Bailey, L. P. (1998). *Governmental GAAP guide: A comprehensive restatement of currently promulgated governmental generally accepted accounting principles for state and local governments.* New York: Harcourt, Brace and Company.

Budak, S. W., Cline, B. A., Eason, S. B., Hartfield, C. A., Burns, J., & Fransen, K. W. (1998a). *Guide to nonprofit contributions.* Fort Worth, TX: Practitioners Publishing Company.

Budak, S. W., Cline, B. A., Eason, S. B., Hartfield, C. A., Burns, J., & Fransen, K. W. (1998b). *Guide to nonprofit expenses.* Fort Worth, TX: Practitioners Publishing Company.

Carmichael, D. R., Dropkin, M., & Reed, M. L. (with Milito, V. R., Eason, S. B., Fransen, K. W., & Holland, S. E.). (1998). *Guide to audits of nonprofit organizations* (11th ed., Vols. 1–3). Fort Worth, TX: Practitioners Publishing Company.

Kettner, P. M., Moroney, R. M., & Martin, L. L. (1999). *Designing and managing programs: An effectiveness based approach* (2nd ed.). Thousand Oaks, CA: Sage.

McMenamin, B. (2000, May 15). Creative giving: Donor's intent. *Forbes,* p. 78.

Paulos, J. A. (1988). *Innumeracy: Mathematical illiteracy and its consequences.* New York: Hill and Wang.

Roberts, C. (2000, January 16). How a school district's top financial officer stole millions and hid the scam in plain sight. *The State* (Columbia, SC) pp. A1, A10–A11.

5

Licensing of Social Work Agencies and Social Workers

The powers of state governments allow them to regulate the health and safety of various kinds of institutions. Most powers over those programs that deal directly with citizens are powers of the states, rather than powers of the federal or local governments. Most law enforcement is based on state laws, including prison sentences, probation and parole, and juvenile justice. Similarly, public education is a state function, and the standards for schools and their financing are state government matters.

All this is true, too, of social welfare programs. State governments control such programs and services as public assistance, mental health, developmental disabilities, services to older adults, and almost everything else in social welfare because the U.S. Constitution strictly defines the roles of the federal and state governments. When the United States was created, the nation's founders specifically chose to have a national government that was limited in its scope and powers; they were people who had fought to escape what they considered a tyrannical British government. For several years after the American Revolution, the United States was governed under the Articles of Confederation. The nation operated within a loose set of agreements about the ways in which the central government would operate. When the Constitution was written, it was a basic principle that the states would have significant power, whereas the federal government, the U.S. Congress, and the president would have limited authority to deal with a money system, international relations, and matters of wars and peace. The federal government would also regulate interactions between the states (interstate commerce).

Matters have changed significantly since the origins of the nation, partly because of social welfare initiatives taken during the Great Depression of 1929 and the 1930s. Modern welfare systems in the United States, such as those encompassed in the Social Security Act of 1935, specifically defined the roles of the federal and state governments. Under the Social Security Act, the states operate the social welfare programs with funds provided, in part, by the federal government. Similarly, the states began giving food stamps to low-income people in 1961, but the cost of the stamps is paid for with federal funds. The administration also is paid, in part, by federal funds. Prior to the election of Franklin Delano Roosevelt as president in 1932, there were no federal welfare programs. All social welfare was handled by the states because of the limited role of the federal government.

Students of social welfare history will remember that during the presidency of Franklin Pierce, Dorothea Dix, the greatest of the nation's mental health advocates, proposed, and Congress granted support for, state mental hospitals. However, President Pierce vetoed the act and the federal government largely remained removed from social welfare until the Roosevelt presidency.

There were always modest exceptions. The federal government provided services to freed slaves after the Civil War. It also gave assistance to war veterans, which was an obvious federal responsibility. In addition, it supplied some education and welfare services for Native Americans, who were also a federal responsibility.

However, health and safety matters and social welfare fundamentally remain state responsibilities. There is no such thing as a national fire or police department. Federal law enforcement personnel such as members of the Federal Bureau of Investigation deal only with federal criminal acts, which are quite limited. There are federally employed social workers, but they are either administrators or consultants to joint federal-state programs or they work in the military or in federal establishments in Washington, D.C., which is a federal city not affiliated with any state. The other exceptions are those already mentioned: veteran and Native American services.

It is useful for social workers to understand the powers of the states in social welfare matters. States have powers over affairs that are not specifically federal because the U.S. Constitution mandates that all powers not taken by the federal government are left to the states.

Most states operate their social welfare programs through a variety of state government agencies or, in many cases, through a single umbrella agency that incorporates several different kinds of social programs. Many will notice that social welfare programs are not all operated directly by states. Even state offices have county or multicounty offices to operate their programs. Some welfare offices are operated by counties and local governments. A relatively large number are centered in counties, but they are called county-administered but state-supervised. Under the federal laws governing joint federal-state programs, the states retain responsibility for social welfare. However, each state can give its counties major responsibility for the programs while retaining authority and exercising supervision of them. In a few cases such as New York City, which operates one of the world's largest welfare programs, the state authorizes the local program and delegates its power to it. States can, of course, delegate program authority while retaining responsibility.

This is not to suggest that the federal government simply supplies money to the states. It is responsible for ensuring that the money is spent in the ways intended. Therefore, the federal government requires audits, conducts a certain amount of monitoring, and demands detailed reports on how federal resources are used.

Many states are also increasingly devolving their provisions of direct human services to local governmental and proprietary programs. Through contracts and purchases of services, states may delegate their foster care programs, food stamp distribution, or virtually any other activity to other entities while retaining responsibility for what goes on in those programs. For example, few states operate homes for children or day care centers. Instead, they contract with and pay private or local government organizations to provide the services.

One of the primary ways in which state governments maintain quality control over programs is through licensing. The authority to issue or withhold a license is often sufficient power to exercise authority over and control programs of human services.

It is also interesting that states sometimes exempt themselves from their own licensing requirements. For example, all hospitals other than state hospitals for persons with mental illness may require licenses to operate. All children's homes, except for the few that are state-run or the state's own institutions for children in difficulty with the law, may require licenses. This is often a state's policy, which is designed to avoid the unusual circumstance of a government licensing or failing to license one of its own institutions.

State governments also have and use the authority to regulate the practice of professions through licensing. The practice of medicine, law, nursing, teaching, social work, and other professions is, to some extent, under the authority of the states. This chapter describes some of the ways in which states regulate the operation of human services agencies and the social work profession.

Licensing of Group Care Facilities

The licensing of group care facilities and services is a function of governmental bodies. In most states, the law requires that group facilities that care for people be licensed under the specific laws of the state. The facilities include group homes for children, nursing homes for people who are ill or disabled, child day care facilities, health and mental health facilities and services, and others identified by the state. Some states, as mentioned, exempt government owned and operated facilities. They may also exempt group facilities such as children's homes and nursing homes that are owned and operated by religious organizations.

Of course, the rationale for public licensing of such services and facilities is the protection and guarantee of the well-being of those who live in them. Unsanitary conditions can lead to epidemics of illnesses, which spread rapidly in large facilities that house numerous people. Poor food-preparation practices can also lead to widespread illnesses among residents. The physical facilities and practices, too, can physically endanger residents. For example, unsafe floors, stairs, and bathrooms can lead to falls and other injuries that endanger residents. Fire hazards are also a serious problem. Unsafe fire prevention and control activities can lead to fires, which will often take multiple lives among people who are living in close quarters. Fire-safe doors, fire alarms, sprinkler systems, and fire extinguishers, are crucial in group care facilities. This author recalls from his participation in licensing activities a well-meaning community group that paid for an expensive child day care facility, which had not yet opened. The building design was unsatisfactory for fire safety. A small fire could have spread rapidly throughout the building and probably would have taken many lives. Unfortunately, the design was such that the facility could not be modified to comply with fire safety standards. Ultimately, the building had to be almost completely torn down and reconstructed.

This example illustrates the significance of licensing not only for the state government and residents but also the operators of facilities. By and large, although some programs are owned and operated by governments, most group care facilities are not government property. Instead, they are owned by nonprofit community groups or private entrepreneurs who build and operate them and who are reimbursed by the state or insurance companies for caring for residents. However, government agencies and insurance companies are unwilling, in most cases, to pay for care in unlicensed facilities. Therefore, whether a facility is deemed to comply with licensing standards is a crucial issue for the owners and operators of the programs. The facilities range from converted orphanages that have shifted their care to serving foster children to national child-care and nursing-home business chains that are part of multibillion dollar, publicly owned enterprises. In all cases, the failure of a facility to gain a license may prove to be an economic disaster for the owners, whether volunteer board members or private business persons.

Licensing Bodies

Although the licensing function is generally given to a committee or board designated by state law or to an agency of state government, the law also usually provides for the involvement of state and local law enforcement agencies in carrying out licensing inspections.

Some states place the responsibility for licensing on a special interdepartmental committee or board. Although the licensing organizations may be different for different functions, most are interdisciplinary in nature. It is possible for one licensing organization to evaluate a broad range of facilities, but it is also possible for different organizations to analyze different programs such as nursing homes, residential child care facilities, and child day care programs. The licensing organization typically consists of representatives of the state welfare agency, the state public health department, and fire control or fire safety representatives, and it can include persons from the mental health program and education. Some states may include operators of facilities and community representatives who are not part of government to provide input from professionals and consumers of services on the operation of programs.

Often, when states authorize a department of government to take responsibility for licensing, they also create an advisory or supervisory board that is more broadly representative to offer guidance and advice on the overall licensing activity.

Operations of Licensing

Generally, public laws give the licensing group wide latitude and power over the facilities that are evaluated. The South Carolina law, which is similar to the laws in most other states, gives the state's Department of Social Services responsibility for licensing child day care facilities. The law makes it clear that the department has wide latitude and authority to investigate and inspect:

> In exercising the powers of licensing, approving, renewing, revoking, or making provisional licenses and approvals, the department shall investigate and inspect licensees and approved operators or applications for a license or an approval. The authorized representative of the department may visit a child day care center or group day care home anytime during the hours of operation for purposes of investigations and inspections (South Carolina Department of Social Services, 1993, p. 19).

The South Carolina law gives authority to a specific agency of state government, but it also mandates that other agencies assist with specific aspects of the licensing investigation and approval process:

> In conducting investigations and inspections, the department may call on political subdivisions and governmental agencies for appropriate assistance within their authorized fields. The inspection of the health and fire safety of child day care centers and group day care must be completed upon the request of the department by the appropriate agencies (i.e., Department of Health and Environmental Control, the Office of the State Fire Marshal, or local authorities).

Of course, there are some general rules followed in licensing that are found in most states. For example, persons convicted of crimes may not be issued licenses. In some states, administrators of group care facilities are subject to separate licensing regulations; that is, they must apply for and receive licenses as nursing home administrators or child day care operators. In those cases, one of the criteria for licensing the facility is that the chief executive officer of the facility must have the appropriate license. The length of licensing and the specific regulations vary from state to state. In most cases, facilities are required to post their license in a conspicuous place. Being licensed is an agency responsibility along with providing proper care, a subject that is monitored by the licensing agency or one or more other agencies.

Licensing of Individual Practitioners

Thus far, this chapter has discussed the quality control of services through licensing of human services programs. That is one direction in which licensing applies. Another form of evaluation of professional human services practice is through the licensing and other kinds of certification of professionals.

Licensing is a form of credentialing. It establishes that a person who is performing a task is qualified to perform that task and is someone who subscribes to and is bound by a code of ethics and other commitments to quality professional services. Licensing is a form of permission to do something with authorization by law; therefore, the term licensing might apply to the practice of a profession but also to such activities as to marry, to operate a program, or to drive an automobile.

In social work, professional licensing or some other form of legal regulation is part of the law in every state and has been for several years. There are two basic kinds of licensing or regulation for social work. One is the title protection license. Under that license, a state makes it a violation of the law for someone to call himself or herself (to hold oneself out to the public) a social worker if that person does not hold a social work license. People cannot say they are social workers without first qualifying for and obtaining licenses. The other kind of license is one that regulates practice. Such a license protects the community from anyone carrying out social work functions who does not hold a social work license. Even if someone calls himself something other than a social worker, performing the tasks of a social worker requires a license.

The National Association of Social Workers Code of Ethics (1999) admonishes social workers to only represent their competence within their preparation, experience, and their license status. In other words, ethics demand that social workers avoid claiming levels of abilities that are not certified by their state license.

Each state sets its own licensing procedures and criteria; however, almost all states are associated with the licensing or certification work of the Association of Social Work Boards (ASWB). That board, which is headquartered in Culpeper, Va., maintains procedures and standards for licensing, collects data on the licensing regulations and board structures in every state that is affiliated with ASWB, and helps develop and administer social work licenses. (In March 2000, *NASW News* [National Association of Social Workers] reported that the former American Association of State Social Work Boards was changing its name to the Association of Social Work Boards because the old name was unwieldy and because some of its members such as Washington, D.C., the Virgin Islands, and Alberta, Canada, are not states. In this text, reference remains to states because those are the entities that provide most social work licenses.)

Social work licenses exist at several levels, depending on the jurisdiction. There is bachelor-level licensing for people who have completed bachelor's social work degrees, usually at schools of social work accredited by the Council on Social Work Education. There are also master's certifications and licenses, again associated with graduates of master of social work programs accredited by the

Council on Social Work Education. Some states have special licenses for clinical social workers or independent social workers, a term that is often used synonymously with clinical. Performing private social work practice often requires a social work clinical license. Of course, there are variations. Some states give special recognition to those who hold doctoral degrees in social work, and others grant licenses to graduates of unaccredited baccalaureate programs or social work concentrations within sociology, human services, or related degrees.

Every state is different in its licensing approaches. For example, in some cases, employees of public social or human services agencies can receive licenses without meeting the formal requirements that employees of other kinds of agencies might have. In many states, when licensing began, those who met certain criteria were "grandfathered" into licenses; that is, they were granted licenses even though they did not meet the criteria or pass the examinations required of new licensees.

Persons who are interested in specific licenses and state regulations are able to contact their own state licensing agencies or the ASWB: The mailing address for the organization is 400 South Ridge Parkway, Suite B, Culpeper, Virginia, 22701. Information on the association is also available on the world wide web at www.aswb.org. The group also maintains a toll-free telephone number.

ASWB creates the license examinations that are used in most states. It does so with the involvement of professional social workers from various fields, who help write the exams. For many states, the association schedules the examinations, which can be taken at specified test sites several times each year. In other words, exams do not have to be taken at specific sites at only a few times each year. The association also arranges for examinations to be given, usually on an individual, on demand, basis, through contact by the candidate for license with the ASWB.

Each state chooses its categories for licenses, the examinations that will be used, and the passing scores for the examinations. However, the examinations are established with procedures that equate the scores so that each candidate, no matter what the passing numerical score may be, reflects the same level of competence. That is, if a required test score result is 70 in one state and 75 or 80 in another, all three are roughly comparable because the number of correct answers for each score must be essentially the same. Therefore, all candidates reflect the same level of ability (American Association of State Social Work Boards, 1996). The examinations follow a percentage breakdown, depending on the area of licensure that is sought.

For example, the basic examination, which is largely for baccalaureate-level social workers, requires 15 percent of the content in human development and behavior, 7 percent on effects of diversity, 23 percent on assessment in social work practice, 23 percent on practice with size systems, 7 percent on interpersonal communication, 4 percent on professional social worker/client relationships, 7 percent on professional values and ethics, 3 percent on supervision, 3 percent on practice evaluation and using research, 7 percent on service delivery, and 3 percent on social work administration. The examinations progress from the basic level to the advanced and the clinical with different emphases. For example, the clinical examination content requires 12 percent on diagnosis and assessment and 19 percent on psychotherapy clinical practice, substantially more in those areas than for other examinations.

Some states have reciprocity, which means that someone who is licensed in a particular state can automatically receive a license in another state. In states without reciprocity, participants must take the new licensing examination and meet other requirements for the new state.

The examination questions developed by ASWB are based on detailed job analyses with social workers of the levels for which the examinations will be administered so that the licensing is connected with the actual tasks that social workers have to perform (American Association of State Social Work Boards, 1997).

In addition to licensing, there are several voluntary credentials that social workers may earn to demonstrate their ability to practice. These include: membership in the Academy of Certified Social Workers, which is administered by the NASW; two private-practice credentials, one administered by NASW and another by the clinical social work societies; credentials for social work managers, administered by the National Network for Social Work Managers; a special certification for school social workers, sponsored by NASW; and certifications that apply to social workers as well as other professionals, such as certification by the American Association of Marriage and Family Therapy (Ginsberg, 2001).

There are also efforts to develop licensing or other kinds of certification programs for the evaluation field. The American Evaluation Association Task Force developed plans in the late 1990s for programs of certification for program evaluators. The intent was to find ways to certify and provide credentials to evaluators of programs who conduct the kinds of work described in this book. The task force report, which is discussed along with several other articles on certification of evaluators, is in the *American Journal of Evaluation* (Altschuld, 1999).

Although it is clear that a number of professions and institutions contribute to the evaluation profession and to program evaluations of various kinds, it is also clear that a movement is developing to establish specific quality controls for those who wish to conduct program evaluations.

At this point, it appears that the major impetus would be voluntary credentialing, like the approach of the Academy of Certified Social Workers. The academy is a voluntary organization sponsored by NASW. Social workers who want to receive ACSW certification must serve two years as professional social workers under the supervision of an ACSW certified social worker. In order to obtain the ACSW qualification, they must take and pass an examination, maintain membership in NASW, and pay a fee in addition to national NASW dues.

It is somewhat doubtful that a field as broad and diverse as evaluation would come to the point of requiring a common license for all those individuals and organizations who provide evaluation services. However, voluntary participation in a credentialing program could establish a corps of evaluators who meet a set of standards that could be promulgated and understood by those who employ evaluators for their programs. Thus, there would be some additional quality control for those interested in providing evaluative services, as well as some starting point for those who are interested in employing evaluators or evaluation organizations with qualified employees.

Conclusion

This chapter focuses on licensing and credentials for social workers and other professionals. It also provides information about and the reasons for licensing of some kinds of institutions and services. As the chapter suggests, there are many different types of legal and voluntary regulations in the human services with which social workers should be familiar. Learning about and participating in credentialing and licensing is an essential feature of a professional social work career. Regulation is a central issue in the evaluation and enforcement of high standards within the human services.

Questions for Further Study

1. In your own words, describe U.S. society's rationale for requiring licenses for (1) group care facilities and (2) individual practitioners of social work.

2. Distinguish between legal regulation requirements and voluntary credentials. In your opinion, what is the significance of each? Why would social workers choose to qualify for voluntary credentials even in a state in which they would be required to secure licenses?

3. What are some of the reasons that specialists in evaluation should, in the opinions of some, be required to obtain professional credentials?

4. Do you believe that states should provide reciprocity for those who have licenses in other states? Explain and justify your answer.

References

Altschuld, J. W. (1999, Fall). The certification of evaluators: Highlights from the reports admitted to the board of directors of the American Evaluation Association. The *American Journal of Evaluation*, 481–493.

American Association of Social Work Boards. (1996). *Social work job analysis in support of the American Association State Social Work Boards and Examination Program*. Culpeper, VA: Author.

American Association of Social Work Boards. (1997). *Information for social work regulator board members*. Culpeper, VA: Author.

Ginsberg, L. H. (2001). *Careers in social work* (2nd ed.). Boston: Allyn and Bacon. In press.

National Association of Social Workers. (1999). *Code of ethics of the National Association of Social Workers*. Washington, DC: Author.

National Association of Social Workers. (2000, March). Social work boards' group changes name. *NASW News*, 13.

South Carolina Department of Social Services, Family and Adult Services. (1993). *South Carolina child day care licensing law*. Columbia, SC: Author.

6

Accreditation of Social Work Programs

Among the most common forms of program evaluation currently used, especially in the United States, is accreditation. The formal definition of accreditation is "the acknowledgement and verification that an organization (such as an educational institution, social agency, hospital, or skilled-nursing facility) fulfills explicitly specified standards" (Barker, 1999). One of the dictionary author's examples is educational accreditation by the Council on Social Work Education, which accredits bachelor's and master's programs in social work and which is discussed later in more detail.

Accreditation is sought and recognized by many organizations in the human services field. It is a way to ensure their own quality and to ensure that they are comparable to similar organizations in other places. It is also a condition for receipt of some funds and, in some places, for the legal right to provide services.

Inputs, Outputs, and Outcomes

Accreditation is different than some of the other evaluation methods and approaches described in this book. It evaluates programs and services for compliance against specific standards established by the accrediting bodies whose sanction the organizations seek. As Barker (1999) suggests, accreditation involves an agreement on a sort of ideal model of an organization against which individual organizations can be compared. An organization that seeks accreditation must demonstrate that it is in compliance with some of the more important standards or benchmarks of quality established by the accrediting body. It must also, in most cases, show that it complies with or is moving toward compliance with *all* the standards in the accreditation documents. However, an organization may, under some circumstances, meet the accreditation requirements without necessarily producing results or outcomes that are also excellent. For example, a family counseling organization may meet or exceed all of the accreditation requirements to which it is subject and still perform poorly in providing counseling services. Clients may be no better off after receiving the organization's services than they were before they came for help. However, the counselors may be well qualified, the supervisors may have top quality skills and credentials, the offices may be attractive, and the ethical and other consumer protection guarantees may be inviolate. These benchmarks of accreditation may or may not indicate high quality results of services. Basically, such organizational efforts reflect emphases on the organization's resources or "inputs," rather than their results.

Increasingly, however, accrediting organizations are placing great emphasis on the quality of the candidate for accreditation's outcomes. Among the earmarks of an organization that is of sufficiently high quality for accreditation is the degree of success that the organization's consumers experience from the services they receive. Counseling clients are evaluated for improvement in the conditions that brought them to the organization. Educational organizations are evaluated according to the extent of the learning of their students, the graduates' success in finding professional work, and the degree of their success in that work. Child care organizations also may be evaluated according to their successes. For example, in the 1997 standards of the Council on Accreditation of Services for Families and Children (1996), each of the kinds of services evaluated in an organization include an outcomes requirement. For adoption services, each organization is required to demonstrate the extent to which the children it serves are legally free to be adopted, are placed in adoptive families, are adopted with subsidies when they qualify for such help because they have special needs, and are provided with services after being placed in adoption.

The Council on Accreditation's services are described in detail later, along with those of other accrediting bodies, but the importance of results is clearly indicated in that organization's standards as well as the standards of most accrediting organizations. Other chapters of this book also discuss outcome and results measurement. Accrediting bodies follow set procedures in evaluating the success of the organizations that seek accreditation.

Voluntary Nature of Accreditation

In many parts of the world, accreditation is not the process that is followed to control the quality of educational programs. Instead, governments authorize, monitor, and provide the authority for educational programs to exist.

Accreditation in the United States is voluntary, and the organizations that carry out accreditation functions are voluntary, too. Governments do not control accreditation, and agencies need not seek accreditation to offer services, in most circumstances. The accrediting bodies have only voluntary memberships. They are not, in other words, official, governmental entities.

In practical terms, however, accreditation is virtually required for some kinds of efforts to be feasible and worthwhile in many parts of the United States.

Accreditation may be a licensing requirement, making accreditation a virtual requirement for effective and publicly sanctioned operations. For other organizations, however, accreditation reflects a degree of excellence or quality to which many agencies might aspire but which they are not required to attain.

For example, many government bodies rely on accreditation as a quality assurance process when they determine whether to provide financial support, licenses, and contracts to organizations. Therefore, accreditation has serious and significant consequences for human services practitioners and educators in many fields and many places.

The funding guidelines of many governmental and voluntary community financing groups (United Way organizations, for example, which are also discussed in Chapter 12) and foundation grant programs demand that agencies applying for financial assistance demonstrate that they meet accrediting requirements. So many organizations are dependent upon external funds that it is almost required that they achieve accreditation if they are to compete with other service agencies and survive. Consumers may be steered away from unaccredited organizations. Lawsuits may be filed against unaccredited service providers for failures in their efforts. Suits may be filed against accredited organizations, as well, however, an effective legal defense may be that an organization meets the high standards of its accrediting body. Whether it succeeds or fails with consumers, the organization can at least show that it tries to meet the criteria for excellence of the pertinent accrediting organization.

One of the best examples of the need for accreditation is social work education. State governments do not often require that baccalaureate and master's programs in social work be accredited. However, as a practical matter it is unlikely that unaccredited social work programs are viable in some states, whether in public or private colleges and universities. A state's higher education governing body may mandate that all social work programs be accredited by the Council on Social Work Education, (which is discussed later) or be in the process of seeking accreditation. In such cases, intentionally unaccredited programs are not likely to be offered. Similarly, a state's licensing board may require that all those who seek full professional social work licenses be graduates of accredited social work programs. Again, offering an unaccredited program under such circumstances may not be a reasonable choice.

How Accreditation Works

Accreditation often seems, especially to those seeking it, to be something of a mysterious process over which the subjects of the process have little control. In fact, the procedures and guidelines, as well as the standards, for accreditation are typically spelled out in detail in writing and are readily available to any individual or organization seeking them. The process is generally quite open, although the materials about individual organizations seeking accreditation are, understandably, at least in part confidential. The release of details about an organization's budgets, salaries, and operations could put it at a disadvantage in its whole field of services, but the procedures followed and the standards used in accreditation are widely available and promulgated publicly to keep the process open and accessible to all.

As mentioned, accreditation bodies are private and voluntary, not governmental. However, because accreditation has significance for organizational success or failure, the bodies must perform fairly. Civil court suits may be brought against them if they fail to treat all those who seek accreditation with equal attention and criteria.

Governance of Accreditation

In accreditation processes, a voluntary organization establishes standards for performance of various activities. The rules, regulations, and standards for accreditation are determined by the organization's board of directors or accrediting council or commission, whose members are selected from among organizational members and who are often, in large measure, officials and employees of the kinds of organizations that are to be accredited. Usually community representatives, volunteers, and other persons who are not necessarily professionals in the field are included in the accrediting decision-making body.

In some fields, the accrediting body and its governing board are associated directly with the professional association that is central to the program or service being evaluated. In others, the accrediting organization is separate from the professional association. Some organizations have modified their relationships with professional organizations. The Council on Accreditation of Services for Families and Children (called the Council on Accreditation in this chapter) was established in 1977 as an outgrowth of the accrediting efforts of the Child Welfare League of America and the Family Service Association of America (now called Family Service America), which had each conducted their own accreditation processes. The new council replaced the accrediting efforts of the two standard-setting and advocacy organizations and made accreditation of affiliates a process that is separate from the two groups. The Council on Accreditation now evaluates and accredits a large variety of organizations, so the children's and families fields have established an organization separate from the organizations that deal with family and children's services. Similarly, social work education's accrediting body is different than the professional association, the National Association of Social Workers.

The various accrediting bodies establish policies, statements, and standards, which the members or those who are seeking accreditation learn about through formal mechanisms such as newsletters, meetings, the Internet, and published documents. Also, in many cases, interested organizations visit or communicate by mail with an accrediting body to learn the details of the process. The organizations that are affiliated with the accrediting bodies and subject to their accreditation have opportunities to comment on and, therefore, influence the standards that are established, especially when they are revised.

Self-Studies

The standards and the criteria for achieving accreditation vary significantly between accrediting bodies. Generally, however, the entity that seeks accreditation (or reaffirmation of an existing or established accreditation) submits a self-study and an explanation of how it complies with the standards that are in effect. These typically are extensive documents dealing with facts and statements about every aspect of the organization's operations. Usually the accrediting body provides a detailed outline that the organization seeking accreditation follows in preparing its self-study. Matters of budget, personnel, services provided, facilities, and all the other elements included in the accrediting body's standards are reported in narratives and on specific forms provided by the accrediting group.

It is significant, however, that the applying entity is responsible for describing itself and for showing how it meets the required standards. Much of the accreditation process—both preparing reports and complying with the standards—is the responsibility of the organization seeking accreditation rather than solely a process by which an external organization evaluates and acts on an agency.

Site Visits

Ordinarily, as part of the accreditation process, a team of site visitors travels to the organization that seeks accreditation and makes direct observations of its compliance with the standards. The selections of teams vary from body to body. In virtually all cases, however, site-visiting-team members cannot have obvious conflicts of interest such as being employed as a staff member with or consultant to the organization under review. Also, if they have or have had a competitive or close, complementary relationship of some other kind, potential site visitors are eliminated from teams. The accrediting organizations typically expect the potential site visitor and the program being visited to identify problematic relationships. For example, a person who has been a consultant to the agency in the relatively recent past would not necessarily be an impartial site visitor. In other cases, persons from the same city or state are not permitted to make a site visit. Under the rules of some accrediting bodies, team members are selected in consultation with the organization being evaluated. In other cases, the selection of team members is solely a function of the accrediting body staff.

In some accrediting procedures, each team makes recommendations or decisions about the accredited status of a program. In others, a team renders a report to the accrediting body, which, in turn, evaluates appropriate materials, including the site team report, and makes a decision about the status of the organization.

In some accrediting bodies, decisions about accredited status are made by volunteer members of committees or commissions. Those members are typically appointed by the organization's board of directors, who seek a balanced commission or committee membership—for example, that people from all regions, both genders, various ethnic groups, and professional specializations are selected.

In addition to the volunteer decision-makers, accrediting bodies have professional staff members, most of whom have experience in the profession or the field of practice that is being accredited. Staff members review and organize materials for the volunteer committees and, in some cases, make decisions themselves. Some staff members, when they are dealing with factual, not judgmental, issues, render decisions about an organization's compliance with accreditation standards.

Agency Accreditation

Education, whose accreditation is discussed later, is the most pervasive kind of human services effort that is accredited, but many social agencies and services are accredited by professional bodies, as well.

Council on Accreditation

In some programs that employ many social workers, the Council on Accreditation accredits family service and child welfare agencies, as has been discussed. The Council on Accreditation enlists and trains evaluators, requires site visits and reports, and has a volunteer body that acts on the accredited status of family service and child welfare agencies throughout the United States. The council also has a series of advisory boards with membership from various professional groups.

Because the Council on Accreditation, with its headquarters in New York City, is one of the best developed of the human services accrediting bodies, its procedures and standards are described here in some detail as an example of how agency accreditation operates. However, it is only one of several accrediting bodies for social services organizations.

Two documents govern the Council on Accreditation's procedures for voluntary organizations: the *Manual for Peer Reviewers* (Council on Accreditation of Services for Families and Children, 1997) and the *1997 Standards for Behavioral Health Care Services and Community Support and Education Services* (Council on Accreditation of Services for Families and Children, 1996). In addition to these, the council publishes a set of Canadian standards and separate volumes for public-sector organizations and child and family service networks.

Although this organization was formed by the Child Welfare League of America, and Family Service America, it is now also sponsored by a variety of other secular and sectarian groups, including the Association of Jewish Family and Children's Agencies; Catholic Charities, USA; the Foster Family-Based Treatment Association; Lutheran Services in America; the National Association of Homes and Services for Children; the National Committee to Prevent Child Abuse; the National Council for Adoption; the National Foundation for Consumer Credit; and the National Network for Youth. It also has seven "supporting" organizations: the American Association of Children's Residential Centers, the American Network of Community Options and Resources, Child Welfare League of Canada, the

EAGLE Program of the United Methodist Association of Health and Welfare Ministries, the National Alliance for the Mentally Ill, the National Association of Psychiatric Treatment Centers for Children, and the National Community Mental Healthcare Council.

The Council on Accreditation (1997), in explaining an accreditation's purposes, says:

1. It provides an external, objective marker for the organization's "public" that the organization meets national standards of organizational strength and quality of service; and
2. It results in a detailed analysis, a charting of specific strengths and weaknesses in most areas of the organization's governance and operation (p. i).

Basic Procedures.   The first step in the process is for an organization to complete an application form and send it to the council. If the application is satisfactory, the organization is notified of its acceptance, and the staff decides from the application information which of several specialized services are offered by the applicant organization and, therefore, must be evaluated. These services, which cover almost everything imaginable provided by direct-services agencies, are outlined in the accreditation manual (Council on Accreditation, 1996). They include the services shown in Table 6.1.

When an organization determines that it wants to seek accreditation for one or more of its services, it usually follows a series of steps with the Council on Accreditation.

1. The organization's leadership determines that it wants to seek accreditation.

2. The organization contacts the Council on Accreditation and notifies it of its intent to seek accredited status.

3. The organization receives a self-study manual that outlines the material necessary for completing the study, which is then conducted according to a schedule and timetable agreed to by the organization and the council.

4. A copy of the self-study is sent to the council, and copies are also sent to the review team members who are appointed by the council staff.

5. The review team members study the documents provided and make judgments about compliance with the standards.

6. The review team leader arranges a site visit and then conducts the visit with at least one other site visitor.

7. After the visit, the team submits its report to the council. For any standard that it rates as partial or noncompliance, the team provides written justification.

8. The council sends a preliminary report on the organization's accreditation to the organization, which returns a response within 30 days. This report includes preliminary ratings, which are based on a 4-point rating scale for each standard.

TABLE 6.1   *Accreditable Services*

Counseling and mental health services for individuals, families, and children

Home-based, family-centered casework or treatment

Psychosocial rehabilitation service/psychiatric rehabilitation service

Employee-assistance programs

Case management services

Substance abuse treatment; addiction or chemical dependency counseling; codependency counseling; diagnostic, assessment, and referral service

Methadone maintenance treatment service

Emergency shelter service

Short-term care

Runaway children and youth service

Crisis intervention service

Child protective service

Adult protective service

Domestic violence counseling service

Rape crisis service and/or battered women's service

Pregnancy counseling and supportive service

Adoption service

Intercountry adoption service

Home visitor service

Homemaker/home health aide service

Early intervention services for infants and youth children

Family life education/family support programs/support group service

Intensive family preservation service

Foster care services (foster family care; therapeutic foster care; foster care for medically fragile infants and children; foster or group care for unaccompanied minors)

Respite care

Independent living for youth/adult supported living; community supported living day treatment service/social adjustment service/treatment-oriented day care service/partial hospitalization service

Adult day care service

Group home service/transitional residence service/residential center for adults/residential center for children and youth

Residential treatment

Therapeutic residential wilderness camping service/adventure-based therapeutic outdoor service

Person and family-centered assessment and planning

Person and family-centered service delivery processes

Social advocacy/community organization service

Information and referral service

Refugee resettlement service

Immigration and citizenship assistance service

Group service for social development and enrichment

Employment and vocational services

Financial management service/debt counseling service

Volunteer friendship service/volunteer relationship service

Group child day care for children; family child day care for children; child day care center service/early childhood education service

Supportive services to the aging

Emergency telephone response service

(1 = full compliance; 2 = substantial compliance; 3 = partial compliance; 4 = noncompliance.) (Council on Accreditation action involves a four-year cycle. Agencies are accredited for four years and are reevaluated at the end of that time.)

9. The site team report and the organization's response, as well as comments on the response by the site team, are given to the Accreditation Commission, but the applicant is not identified; that is, the commission does not know the organization it is reviewing.

10. The commission reviews the documents, makes any changes it chooses in the ratings, and decides on the organization's accredited status.

11. The organization is notified of the accreditation decision.

12. The Council on Accreditation Board of Trustees is given notification of the decision and takes final action to ratify that decision.

13. When accreditation is denied, there is an appeals process.

Generic Standards.   In addition to the specific services outlined, the Council on Accreditation applies a list of "generic" standards that are applicable to all organizations seeking accreditation. These include statements about and evidence of compliance for:

1. Organizational purpose and relationship to the community
2. Continuous quality improvement processes
3. Organizational stability
4. Management of human resources
5. Quality of the service environment
6. Financial and risk management
7. Professional practices

For each of these generic standards, there are multiple substandards dealing with matters such as codes of conduct, payroll procedures, protection of research subjects, physical accessibility of facilities, and other details of operation. Standards that are promulgated are weighted, in some cases, and count for more in the accreditation process than others. The distinctions and definitions are provided in the organization's publications.

Although the Council on Accreditation standards and procedures are specific to its functions, they are sufficiently comprehensive to provide an idea of how accreditation operates. Each accrediting organization has its own arrangements and documents, but most are similar to those outlined for this group. Both public and private agencies may be accredited by the council and, in some cases, divisions of large agencies may seek accreditation, such as the social services or child services of a state department of social services.

Joint Commission on the Accreditation of Health Care Organizations

In the health field, the Joint Commission on the Accreditation of Health Organizations (JCAHO) is an important entity in accrediting hospitals and other organizations. Of course, accreditation is required for hospitals that seek reimbursement from third parties such as insurance companies and from government programs such as Medicaid and Medicare.

JCAHO is also involved in the accreditation of some other kinds of health care facilities, many of which involve social work practitioners. These include health care networks, programs of home care, long-term care, behavioral health care, ambulatory care, and others. In all, the organization accredits about 20,000 facilities and programs.

Like other accrediting organizations, JCAHO, which was founded in 1951, is nonprofit. It has a 28-member board, which includes consumers of health care services, physicians, medical directors, ethicists, labor representatives, and others.

JCAHO maintains a complete directory of the health care organizations it accredits. Interested persons can obtain information about the status of those organizations by reviewing information on its web site or by contacting JCAHO, which is located in Oakbrook Terrace, Illinois. Its telephone number is (630) 792-5000. The organization establishes outcome measurements and provider performance indicators. The best source of detailed information on the organization is its web site, www.jcaho.org.

An accreditation by the Council on Accreditation costs an average of $8,000, based on the agency's annual revenues plus the expenses incurred by site visitors. The Child Welfare League of America pays the costs of accreditation for its member agencies. An accreditation by JCAHO costs an average of $9,000, and the Child Welfare League reimburses its member agencies that seek JCAHO accreditation for a portion of those costs (Boehm, 2000).

Commission on the Accreditation of Rehabilitation Facilities

Some organizations and agencies, especially those involved in rehabilitation, are accredited by the Commission on the Accreditation of Rehabilitation Facilities (CARF), along with some community mental health programs and other such services. In all, CARF accredits about 25,000 programs in the United States, Canada, and Europe. Among the kinds of functions it accredits are adult day care services, assisted living programs, medical rehabilitation services, and employment programs.

CARF, a nonprofit accrediting organization, was established in 1966 and has headquarters in Tucson, Arizona. Its telephone number is (520) 325-1044. It has a Rehabilitation Accreditation Commission that makes decisions about its applicants for accreditation.

Although its sponsoring organizations are different than those of the Council on Accreditation and are more likely to be medically oriented, there is a clear possibility that agencies could and do affiliate with both the council and CARF. For example, some aging organizations are sponsors of CARF. Several developmental disability groups and mental and behavioral health groups also affiliate. Health care programs such as those accredited by JCAHO could also affiliate with CARF. A basic source of information about CARF is its web site, www.carf.org.

CARF operates through three manuals of standards: behavioral health, employment and community services, and medical rehabilitation. The organization has four different accrediting options: three-year accreditation, one-year accreditation, provisional accreditation, and nonaccreditation.

Other Accreditation Examples and Functions

There are other kinds of accreditation that may be equally familiar to readers. For example, the American Automobile Association has standards for hotels and other accommodations. Camping organizations may be accredited by the American Camping Association. Health departments have standards for day care centers, residential facilities for children and elderly people, and restaurants. Failure to comply with the standards leads to the loss of the license to operate the program. These governmental functions are often a matter of licensing, not simply services provision. Local health departments also are involved in the regular monitoring and licensing of hospitals and nursing facilities.

In addition to studying and dealing with accreditation, accrediting bodies provide educational programs for site visit members and for organizations seeking accreditation. They also maintain rosters of accredited groups and provide information about them to the public. These kinds of standard-setting and compliance organizations are among the most common evaluative experiences of social work organizations and are the subject of much of the time and effort put into evaluation by human services organizations and their managers. Periodic evaluation is often a time of great anxiety and flurries of activity in social welfare agencies and social work education programs.

Education Accreditation

Education is an important example of accreditation because it affects most public and private education organizations in the nation. The United States is divided into regional accrediting associations, each with its own headquarters, professional staffs, and standards. The organizations are supported by grants and contracts but also largely by dues from the associated institutions. Each state or other government such as the Commonwealth of Puerto Rico, the Virgin Islands, and Guam, are affiliated with one of the regional accrediting bodies. The associations accredit schools and higher education institutions. The state affiliations follow historical patterns in which states became part of one or the other association. The following are the regional accrediting bodies for education in the United States:

Middle States Association of Colleges and Schools
New England Association of Schools and Colleges
North Central Association of Colleges and Schools
Northwest Association of Schools and Colleges
Southern Association of Colleges and Schools
Western Association of Schools and Colleges

Some of these groups are divided into separate bodies for different levels of education.

In addition to regional accreditations, many professions have specialized or professional accreditation of their educational programs. Social work is one of the professions that has its own specialized accreditation process. Law, medicine, nursing, public health, education, and many other fields also follow accreditation processes with organizations that evaluate them.

In some cases, the professional accrediting body requires full compliance with all the standards established for its field. In other cases, programs that seek accreditation must be in substantial compliance with a percentage of the standards, although not all of them. Still others have some standards that are mandatory and others that are optional or that do not require as high a level of compliance. This is similar to the discussion of accrediting procedures followed by the Council on Accreditation described earlier in this chapter.

Council on Social Work Education

In social work education, accreditation is provided by the Council on Social Work Education (CSWE), a voluntary association of baccalaureate and masters programs in colleges and universities. A special division of the council, the Commission on Accreditation, handles the accreditation function. The standards followed by CSWE's Commission on Accreditation, as well as its most recent curriculum policy statement, constitute the bases for which accreditation decisions are made (Council on Social Work Education, 1994; 1995).

The Commission on Accreditation is one of the organizations that requires full compliance with all its accreditation standards. It has two basic kinds of standards: eligibility and evaluative. The eligibility standards deal with absolute, minimum requirements such as:

The college or university must have regional accreditation;

The social work program must be authorized by the institution's chief executive officer (usually a president or chancellor);

The social work program must demonstrate that its status is sufficient for it to carry out its objectives and that it is treated in a manner comparable to other professional programs in the institution;

There must be evidence that the catalog or bulletin shows that the social work program prepares students for professional social work practice and that it is accredited by the Council on Social Work Education;

The program must have a full-time chief executive officer such as a chair, dean, or director in the case of master's programs or a full-time employee of the institution with a principal assignment to the social work program, in the case of bachelor's programs;

The program must require two full-time years of study for master's programs;

The program must have an institutional affirmative action plan; and

The program must show a fully implemented curriculum plan.

There are eight social work education evaluative standards by the CSWE (1994), which all have series of substandards for both bachelor's and master's programs. They include:

1. *Program Rationale and Assessment.* Programs must present a set of objectives as well as a mission statement. The mission and goals must be in consonance with the professional purposes, ethics, and values of professional social work. The program must demonstrate the ways in which it implements its mission and goals. It must also show that it carries out regular self-study and evaluation of its program and that its evaluations are considered in carrying out the program.

2. *Organization, Governance, and Resources.* The program must show how it is organized, how it fits into the institution, and how it is governed. Faculty rights and responsibilities over the curriculum and other aspects of the program are discussed, along with the budget, facilities, and other resources.

3. *Nondiscrimination.* The program must document the ways in which it works to guarantee that it operates without discrimination against faculty, staff, and students. Issues such as grievance and appeals procedures regarding perceived discrimination, sexual harassment, and program policies preventing discrimination are discussed.

4. *Faculty.* The program must show evidence of sufficient numbers of faculty members with a sufficient breadth of education and experience to operate the program. Full-time faculty to student ratios are detailed, as are the responsibilities of faculty for teaching, scholarship, and community service. Bachelor's programs must have at least two full-time faculty members with master of social work degrees, and it is recommended that master's programs have sufficient numbers of faculty to maintain a ratio of one faculty member per twelve master's students. There are special requirements for faculty members who coordinate field practicum activities and who teach professional practice courses.

5. *Student Development.* The program must explicate its procedures for admission, its student-advising procedures and policies, policies and procedures for evaluating student performance, and its statements and regulations on student rights and responsibilities.

6. *Curriculum.* The program must detail its curriculum and show its compliance with the appropriate curriculum policy statement (for either baccalaureate or master's social work programs), which is a separately developed document that deals only with curriculum matters.

7. *Alternative Programs.* The program must explain any alternative activities—educational activities that deviate from the full-time on-campus curriculum. The Commission on Accreditation must give advance approval for such alternatives, but they are also reported on and evaluated at the time of accreditation. A program offered, in part, by computer is an example of an alternative program. The establishment of an off-campus program is another. Essentially, anything that is offered that differs from the described educational program requires approval and evaluation.

8. *Experimental Programs.* Programs are free to propose experimental activities—new ways of educating—for approval by the Commission on Accreditation. These are reported on and evaluated at the time of accreditation. An evaluation design is required, along with the experimental design. Time limits are also expected for experimental alternatives.

Under the procedures of the accreditation commission, educational programs that do not meet all the standards—that are, in other words, out of compliance with one or more standards—may be given conditional accreditation for up to one year while the program works to meet the required standard.

CSWE's Commission on Accreditation has several actions that it can take when dealing with a program. For example, with a newly initiated social work education program, the commission may grant a status called candidacy, a condition that gives the program three years to meet the standards for accreditation. During that time the program can work with consultants and its own faculty to develop its activities in ways that it hopes will comply with the accreditation requirements.

The Commission on Accreditation may send a member to the program once every year for up to three years to help evaluate work and offer guidance.

The professional staff of the Commission on Accreditation, which is called the Division of Standards and Accreditation of CSWE, is available for consultation by telephone, through visits by the program to the CSWE headquarters in Alexandria, Virginia, or through visits to the college or university.

After candidacy, a school becomes eligible to apply for initial accreditation, which requires a full, detailed, and usually lengthy, self-study on all aspects of the standards and the curriculum. Matters such as admissions procedures, faculty qualifications, budgets, facilities, affirmative action procedures, and organizational structure, are included in the six broad standards under which social work education accreditation is conducted.

After the self-study is completed, a team of two to five social work educators and practitioners visits the program for the site visit and makes observations about the program's compliance with the standards. Once the self-study and site visit have been completed, the program is evaluated by the Commission on Accreditation, which determines whether the program will be granted accredited status, given conditional status for a year because it fails to comply with the programs, or granted accreditation with the requirement for an interim report in one or two years covering some aspects of the program that, although not out of compliance, are of concern to the commission.

There were 418 CSWE-accredited baccalaureate programs and 137 CSWE-accredited master of social work programs in the United States and Canada in 2000. There were also 35 bachelor's programs in candidacy and 17 MSW programs in candidacy in that year. Some social work programs are combined, with one college or university sponsoring both baccalaureate and master's programs. CSWE does not accredit the many existing community college and doctoral social work programs.

Canada has its own accreditation process, but many Canadian schools choose to have dual accreditation from their own organization—the Canadian Association of Schools of Social Work—and the CSWE.

There are several other features to the social work education accreditation process. The site visitors are selected and placed on a list by the staff of the Division of Standards and Accreditation, which also provides training and periodic updates on accreditation processes for site visitors.

The staff attempts to select teams that are balanced from various regions of the nation and, in many cases, that recognize the size or special mission of the program being accredited. For example, Puerto Rican schools invariably have Spanish-speaking site visitors. Attempts are made to provide rural programs with persons who understand rural life and rural social work education.

Programs that are seeking accreditation are given an opportunity to make rejoinders to the site visit report. They may respond to the written document prepared by the site visitors, especially when they find it necessary to clarify misinterpretations or information that is not fully correct. However, they may also disagree with interpretations and conclusions made by site visitors during the accreditation process, so the report reflects such differences of opinion or disagreements about the facts of the program.

The social work education accreditation cycle is eight years. That is, a program may be reaffirmed every eight years and for no longer. In some circumstances, programs request delays in site visits and reaffirmation decisions. However, when they do so, the delay is calculated into the cycle. A program that delays for a year, with permission of the Commission on Accreditation, then complies with another reaffirmation of its accreditation seven, rather than eight, years later.

Consequences of Accreditation

Of course, accreditation has important consequences for students. Graduates of schools whose programs are not accredited may find that they are unqualified for licensing by their profession's state licensing board. With licensing and certification (a similar process) required to practice one's profession in many states, graduating from an unaccredited educational program has very significant negative consequences. Some state licensing bodies, however, recognize programs that meet the licensing board standards, even though they may not have sought accreditation.

For funding educational programs, accreditation is also significant. Grants and contracts from foundations and from government bodies may be predicated on the program's accreditation. Many fund grantors have policies that require all applicants for their funds and all recipients to be accredited by the professional accrediting body and the regional education accrediting body.

There are not large numbers of educational institutions that are not accredited by their regional bodies, although there are a few. Some are not accredited because they do not meet the requirements of the accrediting body, whereas others are not accredited because they have ideological and religious conflicts with the accrediting group.

The consequences of operating a higher education institution or, for that matter, a public high school that is not accredited, are significant. For example, credits may not be transferable from unaccredited institutions to institutions that are accredited. Unaccredited degrees may not be accepted by graduate schools for study at the master's or doctoral levels.

Quality and Accreditation

As was indicated at the beginning of this chapter, accreditation and high quality are not necessarily synonymous. Accreditation deals with a program or organization's input of regulations and procedures as well as resources, rather than what it produces. Therefore, a program might have a curriculum, resources, and all of the other elements required by the accreditation standards that are well in compliance with those standards. However, it still might execute its program poorly. Accrediting bodies try to guard against such possibilities by including standards that deal with fairness, reactions of students and clients, and other factors that measure effectiveness. Also, one of the standards for the CSWE and most other accrediting bodies deals with the outcomes or results of programs. A social work education program might be examined for the kinds of jobs its alumni find, the evaluations of their work by their employers, their success in passing licensing examinations, and other standardized evaluations of credentials, as well as many other matters. Therefore, accreditation should be a thoroughly reliable measure not only of what a program has and what it does but also the consequences of its activities. The qualifications of its faculty and students, its library, and its curriculum are all studied for evaluative purposes.

Conclusion

Although it has not often been explicated in the professional literature of social work, accreditation is one of the most common methods used in the human services to attempt to build high quality into education and service delivery programs. Each year, millions of dollars are expended on accreditation processes, as well as untold hours of preparation by staff members and agency managers.

Those who are employed in social welfare programs that are subject to or that seek accreditation can expect to devote at least part of their work each year to preparing for and otherwise working toward accreditation.

Questions for Further Study

1. Accreditation is called a voluntary process in the United States for evaluating educational and service programs. In your opinion, what are the advantages and disadvantages of the process functioning on a voluntary basis?

2. How would you distinguish between the accrediting activities of CARF and JCAHO? In what ways do the two overlap?

3. What is the accredited status of the social work education program in your college or university? What was the date of its last accreditation? Is the self-study for the last accreditation available to you?

4. What is your college or university's regional accrediting body? When was its last accreditation? Where is the regional body's headquarters?

References

Barker, R. L. (1999). *The social work dictionary* (4th ed.). Washington, DC: NASW Press.

Boehm, S. (2000). Everything you wanted to know about accreditation but were afraid to ask. *Children's Voice*, pp. 16–19.

Council on Accreditation of Services for Families and Children. (1996). *Council on Accreditation 1997 standards for behavioral health care services and community support and education services* (U.S. ed.). New York: Author.

Council on Accreditation of Services for Families and Children. (1997). *Manual for peer reviewers* (Rev. ed.). New York: Author.

Council on Social Work Education, Commission on Accreditation. (1994). *Handbook of accreditation standards and procedures.* Alexandria, VA: Author.

Council on Social Work Education, Commission on Accreditation. (1995). *Curriculum policy statements for master's and bachelor's social work education.* Alexandria, VA: Author.

Part III

Internal Evaluations in Social Work

In many cases, social work programs evaluate themselves or those with whom they are associated for the provision of services. These kinds of evaluations are carried out to improve the organization's functioning or, in some cases, to satisfy the requirements for quality information from authorities over the agency.

Chapter 7 discusses two common means of internal evaluation, program monitoring and quality control. Program monitoring requires an agency to study in some detail its own operations or the operations of organizations it has paid to carry out programs in pursuit of the agency's objectives. There are many varieties of such monitoring and some are explained here.

Quality control, or quality assurance (both terms are found in the literature), is a scientific, statistical process used to assess the functioning of an agency or program. At times, it has been a major device in government evaluation of public programs. Total Quality Management, a different and advanced form of quality control that was created by W. Edward Deming, is a method of assessing and improving an organization's operations. It is a popular and increasingly pervasive method of quality guarantee and improvement that was developed in Japan after World War II and is credited with Japan's industrial success.

Chapter 8 discusses single-subject designs, the primary way in which social work practitioners are encouraged to evaluate their own professional practice. It became popular when social workers were urged to find ways to determine whether their work with clients was making changes in the functioning of those clients. Some of the methods and concepts of single-subject design are explained in this chapter.

Assessments of need and studies of satisfaction constitute the content of Chapter 9. Needs assessments typically precede the development of new programs or changes in old programs. They are commonly used in many kinds of human services program development and social work practice, as well as in business and industry. Studies of satisfaction help organizations determine the degree of satisfaction their customers or clients have with their programs. They are widely used in social work, as well as in many retail and hospitality businesses, such as restaurants and hotels.

Together, the chapters in Part III describe ways in which social workers and the agencies in which they work attempt to evaluate and improve their programs and services.

7

Program Monitoring and Quality Control

Programs that are in operation frequently use a process called *monitoring* to consistently evaluate their activities. Monitoring would be classified as a formative evaluation process by some students of evaluation, although Weiss (1998) would call it an example of process evaluation, as discussed in Chapter 1. Although the monitoring process may not assist in determining how well a program achieves its objectives, it serves to show the efficiency, quality, and competence with which the program is being operated. As Chapter 5 mentions, monitoring is one of the ways the federal government maintains control and assesses the quality of the work it does with the states in providing funds for social services.

Quality control is a specialized form of monitoring programs. It statistically analyzes specific components of a program to determine the degree, if any, of errors the program staff commit in their activities.

Monitoring

Rossi, Freeman, and Lipsey (1999) define program monitoring as: "the systematic documentation of key aspects of program performance that are indicative of whether the program is functioning as intended or according to some appropriate standard. It generally involves program performance in the domain of service utilization, program organization, and/or outcomes" (p. 192).

The authors suggest three areas of program monitoring: (1) service utilization, which measures how well the target population receives the services; (2) program organization, which compares what the program is really doing with what it was designed to do; and (3) program outcomes, which determine how the participants have changed after receiving the program services.

Gabor, Unrau, and Grinnell (1994) view monitoring as one of two approaches to program evaluation. Their distinction is somewhat like the classic difference between formative and summative evaluations or, as Weiss (1998) describes, between process and outcome evaluations. The Gabor et al. concept is that evaluations of completed programs are project evaluations, whereas those that study programs that are in process are monitoring approaches.

Weiss (1998) says that monitoring is a less formal but similar form of process evaluation. She distinguishes between process and formative evaluations, although she agrees that both take place during the development of a program, rather than after it is completed, frequently to help improve the program's operations. Often it is the agency that has provided money for a program that institutes monitoring—to determine that its funds are being appropriately used. Agencies that monitor want to understand what a program is doing and what is happening to the clients, Weiss (1998) suggests, and they want to help identify the kinds of assistance the program may require. State legislatures, which often require monitoring, want to find out if the intent of their legislation is being carried out.

Kettner, Moroney, and Martin discuss in their book, which is primarily about the management of social programs, that monitoring and program evaluation are major parts of the effective management system (1999). They define monitoring as an "assessment of the extent to which a program is implemented as designed and serves its intended target group" (p. 218). They note that monitoring comes from a Latin word that means "to warn." Therefore, they suggest that effective monitoring examines the functioning of an organization and warns when it is not performing effectively. They also define monitoring as part of the formative evaluation process because it occurs when programs are being implemented.

Monitors, Weiss writes, know in advance the standards that they will analyze, such as the people who should be served, the services that should be provided, and how program funds should be used. Specific measuring instruments are used to determine how closely an agency comes to complying with the standards. Rossi et al. (1999) add that evaluative standards are implied in monitoring. That is, the kinds of questions that are asked by monitors usually involve value terms such as *"appropriate, adequate, sufficient, satisfactory, reasonable, [and] intended"* (p. 193). Therefore, monitors are placed in the position of deciding whether various elements of a program meet the standards they are examining.

Monitoring is often carried out by specified staff of either the funding agency or the operating agency, and it is typically an internal process closely associated with the organization that sponsors or runs the program. Monitoring is usually ongoing, continually analyzing and evaluating a program. Reports of results may go to the monitoring agency's chief executive officer, perhaps in addition to another structure. That other structure may combine functions such as monitoring, quality control, and fraud and abuse control and detection.

Elements Monitored

The basic issues that are monitored depend on the nature of a program and the plan for implementing it. Therefore, program monitoring elements are predicated on the specific program's objectives and services. Here are common questions asked in monitoring:

1. What is the effectiveness of the program in reaching its *target populations*? Many human services programs are designed to reach specific population groups or targets of service. For example, the funding for the program may be focused on attracting low-income preschool children, such as in a Head Start project. If the program, instead, involves middle-income children, the monitoring may reveal that the target is not being reached. In the case of a community mental health center, the target may be people who have been released from mental hospitals or who have the possibility of being hospitalized and who now need community care. If the program's primary emphasis is on clients who seek counseling but who have never been hospitalized for serious mental illness and who do not seem likely candidates for hospitalization, the program may not be meeting its target clientele. A correlate may be learning that there are people who need such outpatient mental health services but are not receiving them.

2. Is there evidence that equal employment opportunity and affirmative action are applied in the program? In many cases, depending on the community's ethnic composition, monitors would expect a program to include a complement of minorities of color, such as Hispanic, African American, and Asian American clients. Similarly, a diverse staff should be characteristic of most human services programs in most parts of the United States.

3. How much does the program cost per unit of service provided? How much does the program spend on administration compared with its expenditures on services to clients? Is the program operating efficiently within its budgets? If the program has spent two thirds of its allocated funds in the first six months of the program, monitors may have serious questions. Do cost-benefit analyses demonstrate that the benefits of the program tend to outweigh the costs?

4. How do employees spend their time? Monitors may inspect time sheets and calculate the amount of time spent with clients rather than in staff meetings or planning functions. Although some nonclient time is necessary to develop and provide quality services, a disproportionate number of staff hours used for nonservice-related purposes may raise questions for the monitors. How well do employees work together and how satisfied are they with their managers and supervisors?

5. Are clients satisfied with services? Monitors may check agency satisfaction studies that are completed by clients. The degree to which clients and their families believe the program is effective and delivered in compassionate and friendly ways is a subject for analysis in the monitoring process.

6. Are clients improving because of the program? Evaluations of outcomes, which programs should conduct and report, are necessary for determining the degree to which the program is meeting its objectives. Ideally, monitors would have information not only about those who recently completed the program but also about clients who left services within the past several years. These would show if the results of the program were sustained over a period of years.

7. Are the agency facilities safe and accessible? Can people with disabilities enter and leave the program quickly and safely? Can people in wheelchairs and others who have disabilities comfortably enter and use the agency facility? Are fire safety standards observed and enforced? Are dangerous products such as caustic cleaning materials stored safely and out of the reach of children?

Agency Responses to Monitoring

Effective monitoring does not pose a threat to agency management and employees whose goal is to improve the quality of the program through evaluation. Although many organization employees and leaders prefer working without outside persons scrutinizing their work, capable monitors and improvement-oriented agency personnel view monitoring as free advice and consultation. In fact, sound monitoring can improve the functioning of a program with little cost to that program—in the same ways that employed consultants might help at the invitation and expense of the monitored organization.

Grinnell (1997) suggests that monitoring, as a type of formative evaluation, is replacing the summative evaluations that are most typically associated with analyzing the success of completed projects. He says, "The monitoring approach is more congruent with the principles of feedback, development, and integration than the project approach. This approach uses data that are continuously collected, synthesized, and analyzed to provide solid data on which practice and program decisions are based" (p. 594).

That continuous process of collecting and analyzing information can be fed back to agency management, providing it with information it can use to improve the program. Many of the same kinds of issues one encounters in summative evaluations (how well a program's population targets are involved, how well the services delivered match the ideals that are desired, and how close a program is to meeting its objectives) are included in monitoring. However, the time differences are significant. Instead of evaluating a program after it is completed, the monitoring approach evaluates while the program is in progress. That concept lends credence to Weiss's (1998) suggestion that process evaluation is a better description than formative evaluation of evaluations that take place while a program is developing. Weiss uses the term outcome evaluation for what much of the literature calls summative evaluation.

Grinnell (1997) asserts that monitoring, as a form of ongoing evaluation, is different in many ways than outcome or summative evaluation. Most important, perhaps, is that it does not interfere with the operations of a program because it is designed to improve that program. As such, it can become an integral part of a program's operations and implementation. Monitoring also provides opportunities, he says, for staff to make suggestions for small but immediate changes in a program to improve their work, the work of the organization that employs them, and the program's sponsors.

Monitoring Instruments

Monitoring typically is carried out through the use of monitoring instruments such as checklists or forms that a monitor can complete. In many cases, the forms are based on specialized computer programs. Database software programs are often used in larger-scale monitoring programs. For example, if a state government agency is monitoring all of the group child care facilities it uses for children who cannot live with their own families, programs are designed to create a database on those services. Often, standard software programs can be used to create such monitoring data.

Some agencies establish "information systems," which are regularly updated and provide managers with constant information on costs, clients, services provided, and other data they want for evaluating and improving their services. These management information systems are an important element in many kinds of evaluations.

Elements of an Effective Monitoring Program

An effective monitoring program needs several elements that have been discussed. These include:

1. Clear ideas of what the program is designed to achieve through the preparation of specific goals, outcomes, and objectives
2. Careful orientation of the program's managers to monitoring so they will have information readily available and complete
3. A well-trained and supervised monitoring staff
4. Appropriate monitoring instruments or forms on which monitoring notes may be entered (these instruments outline the criteria for the program's success)
5. Data analysis equipment and programs that will allow comprehensive and effective use of the monitoring results

Monitoring Savings in Individual Development Account Programs

One of the more interesting and innovative social welfare ideas of recent times is the promotion of Individual Development Accounts (IDAs). Professor Michael Sherraden (Sherraden et al., 2000), of the Center for Social Development of the

George Warren Brown School of Social Work at Washington University in St. Louis, Missouri, originally proposed the idea of providing avenues for low-income people to develop assets rather than simply receiving assistance that they are expected to expend, in total, each month. The development of assets allows for low-income families to invest in the purchase of homes, home repairs, education, training, and their own businesses. In 2000, the center reported on its monitoring of 14 IDA programs sponsored by 13 organizations around the United States. The organizations agree to match individuals' savings deposits with organization funds for people who are participating in their programs at a ratio determined by the organization and with a specified maximum annual amount. All of the participants have low incomes. The matching amounts range from one dollar provided for each dollar saved to seven dollars matched to each dollar saved. Some programs have variable rates of matching. The maximum amounts the sponsors are willing to match also vary from $360 per year to as much as $9,000 over a four-year period.

Staff members from the center monitored the participants' deposits for two years to determine how much the participants saved and to learn about any problems with the approach. This form of evaluation—regular monitoring—provides opportunities to examine precisely how a program is operating and to identify and terminate any cases of fraud. It also gives ongoing information about the patterns of saving of the participants.

After the monitoring was completed, the study showed that the average participant, based on the 1,326 who saved funds, deposited about $33 per month and thereby accumulated $100 each month in assets. Ninety percent of the participants had incomes 200 percent below the poverty line. The average match provided by the organizations was two to one.

The monitoring demonstrated that there was no difference on the basis of income of the participants' accumulation of assets. Perhaps lower-income people in the group saved less regularly and uniformly than those who had greater incomes, but the accumulation of assets did not seem to be affected. In fact, those who were quite "income poor" saved at a higher rate than those who were not as poor. Those with 50 percent of the poverty level income saved an average of 8 percent of income. Those with incomes between 50 percent and 125 percent of the poverty level saved 4 percent. Households with 150 percent of the poverty level income or more saved 2 percent in their IDAs.

Interestingly, those who received assistance such as Aid to Families with Dependent Children or Temporary Assistance for Needy Families appeared to save more and to save more regularly than those who had not been assistance clients. The older participants saved more than the younger. Although African American participants saved a bit less than White participants, the differences between White and African American savings were much smaller than the differences between White and African American net worth in American society (4:3 for savings and 10:1 for net worth) (Sherraden et al., 2000).

Of special interest for this text is the utility of program monitoring for evaluating a program of this sort. The center's experience seems to show that program monitoring can keep the details of a program in sight so that quick corrective steps can be taken, and it can provide meaningful evaluative information about processes and outcomes overall.

Quality Control and Quality Assurance

A system of evaluating and monitoring that began in manufacturing but that is now applied to human services is called quality control, or in some situations, quality assurance. Barker's *Social Work Dictionary* (1999) says that quality assurance (which he says is synonymous with quality control) is "the processes and measures an organization takes to determine that its products or services measure up to the standards established for them" (p. 393). Barker classifies many of the evaluation measures discussed in this book as examples of social work efforts to implement quality assurance. He includes licensing and certification, continuing education requirements, adherence to codes of ethics, peer review, and other measures as the ways in which social work uses quality control and assurance concepts.

Quality control actually began with the inspection of each item to come off an assembly line—something that continues in the 2000s. Open a new shirt or check the pockets of new pants or other clothing articles and you'll find a slip of paper that says "inspected by 16," or something of the sort. Similar documentation is included with many manufactured products such as electrical appliances. In other words, quality is controlled by examining every product produced by the manufacturer, but that is not the only way to determine quality. It also is often a much more expensive procedure than is necessary, and it often fails to provide the feedback that manufacturers need to maintain and improve the soundness of their products.

Ledolter and Burrill (1999) note that quality efforts began with the concept of quality control, which they say was originally designed to "identify faulty products and prevent their being shipped to customers" (p. 3). However, the efforts to assure quality shifted from the product itself to the processes used in producing the product, and that led to statistical quality control, which is the more commonly used system today.

Over the years, the scientific processes of research (especially sampling) led to new methods of conducting studies and making judgments about human behavior and public attitudes, as well as physical matters such as water, land, food, and construction. Using statistical methods to analyze and improve quality has grown as the major form of quality control, although it has not replaced inspection.

Sophisticated research and sampling techniques make possible some quality evaluations that would be impossible if a complete "census" or 100 percent sample were required. For example, testing water quality would be impossible without sampling methods. Samples of public water supplies are taken from a number of sources and are thoroughly analyzed for safety, levels of pollution, and the effectiveness of treatment procedures. The analysis can lead to additional treatment procedures or, in extreme cases, warnings to the public to avoid ingesting the water unless it is boiled. Similarly, some food supplies are also evaluated, graded, or inspected by government employees.

A familiar example of the ways in which inspection has been replaced by sampling and quality control measures is that of international travel, especially travel to the United States. Customs officials in U.S. airports once inspected the luggage of virtually all arriving passengers, whether or not they were citizens. This took an inordinate amount of time and large numbers of employees. When large jet airplanes and a shrinking world made international travel more common, customs agencies made major adjustments in their procedures—through sampling. Now, arriving passengers complete declaration forms and are free to pass through an exit that says "nothing to declare." Those with something to declare, such as purchases that might require the payment of duty, alcohol in excess of the allowable limit, or more money than passengers are allowed to bring into the country, may exit through another gate. Of course, all passengers' passports are screened before they reach customs. If there is suspicion that they might be carrying illegal drugs or weapons, they are "flagged" to the customs officials, who then carry out an inspection, no matter what exit they may have chosen. Some ports of entry use dogs to sniff luggage for illegal substances, but it is rare for any entering passenger's luggage to be inspected. Sampling—including stratified sampling—has replaced the earlier procedures.

Statisticians also have developed quality control methods that provide sampling procedures in which only a few products are thoroughly inspected. From those procedures, the quality of a whole enterprise is judged by the quality control staff. However, the modern focus is less on finding and dealing with errors and more on improving processes and products.

To best understand the application of statistical quality control to human services programs, it is important to look at such programs as the results of production processes, just like physical objects. Ledolter and Burrill (1999) suggest that there are four stages of production processes: analyzing, designing, building, and testing. In the human services, the analysis step is in the form of needs assessment or satisfaction studies. Is the program established to meet the needs of the client or client system? Is a new system of services needed to make the services more satisfactory? That first phase is complicated for social workers and other human services providers because the "customer" who defines the needs and enunciates the degree of satisfaction is not always as distinct as in manufacturing or other kinds of services. For example, a public assistance program may be more satisfactory to its clients or recipients than it is to those who define and finance the program, such as the U.S. Congress and state legislatures. The former Aid to Families with Dependent Children program was not especially satisfactory to anyone. However, the members of Congress in the late 1990s were especially offended by what they thought were program characteristics that discouraged work, encouraged unmarried adolescent pregnancies, promoted long-term dependency, and cost more than they should. Therefore, in 1996 they passed and the president signed a new program under the Personal Responsibility and Work Opportunity

Reconciliation Act of 1996. The reconstructed assistance program—Temporary Assistance for Needy Families—set time limits for receiving assistance, as little as two years at the state option but with a five-year maximum in all states. That new program is the subject of intense evaluations to determine how well it is achieving its objectives and how well it serves the needs of clients. Some of the evaluations of the program are discussed in a later chapter. In an industrial analogy, an automobile manufacturer would analyze the market for vehicles as well as learning about the characteristics of vehicles most desired by the automobile-buying public.

The design phase of the assistance act is the legislation that was signed into law, and, of course, the design was accomplished by professionally and technically qualified employees of Congress and the executive branch, along with members of Congress and senators and their professional staff. The design is essentially all the details of the program: the work requirements, the time limits, and the services provided.

The building phase of production can be described as the preparation of regulations and policies and the implementation of the program. Such building and implementation of approved legislation is comparable to the actual production of parts for a car and the assembly of that vehicle, based on the design specifications developed by engineers.

The last, testing, phase is what this book is about—evaluation of programs. The evaluations of the new (5-year-old) welfare program are some examples of testing. In the automobile example, there would be an analysis of the actual operation of the vehicle.

Quality Control and the Human Services

In the 1970s and 1980s, there was great interest in quality control because of evaluation methods imposed by Congress on agencies such as state departments of welfare or social services. The book's author was commissioner of Human Services in West Virginia from 1977 to 1984, a time when the heavy focus on examining aspects of social welfare programs led him to his interest in program evaluation methods.

Over the years, Congress had become disenchanted with public welfare programs and it began to use a quality control mechanism to check on the number of overpayments and payments to people who were ineligible and to examine the numbers of people who were qualified for assistance who did not receive it. They established units in the Department of Health and Human Services to set standards for quality control activities and to monitor the state quality control programs. There were financial penalties attached to states that exceeded the error tolerance, which ranged during that time period from zero to a few percent of cases.

The essential feature of the operation was that when a state was found to have given help to people who were not eligible, the state paid back the federal government (which had financed 50 percent to as much as 80 percent of the program, depending upon the per capita income of the state) the money that was spent incorrectly. However, because this was statistical quality control rather than a 100 percent analysis of the entire case load, even if the quality control efforts located only a handful of cases that were in error, it was assumed that the same percentage of error applied to the thousands or tens of thousands of cases in the state. Therefore, the penalty was the percentage of the error applied to the whole state expenditure on the program.

Of course, these kinds of issues led to great controversies, appeals, and challenges between the states and the federal government. Not surprisingly, the states argued that those areas that were the most urban had the highest error rate. The volatile living styles in urban communities meant that people relocated often and that the family life of welfare recipients was less than stable. It was also true that many rural areas had better quality control records than metropolitan areas, even within the same states.

West Virginia, where this author was working at the time, used a special system for quality control called "error prone." In its system, the sample chosen for quality control evaluation was more likely to be in error than the case load at large. Cases in which there was family income, for example, traditionally were more likely to have errors than those in which there was no income and, therefore, the error prone sampling process focused on those that had the more likelihood of errors. The federal government did not conduct the quality control efforts but simply monitored and supervised the states' quality control programs.

One of the problems with quality control was that it often focused on a number of issues that appeared to be relatively minor—at least to the workers in the offices. For example, a typical error was discovering that infants had not been registered with Social Security. That seemed to make little sense to many workers because infants were not going to be employed and would not need a Social Security number. Of course, a Social Security number is simply a system for documenting that American people really exist, so signing infants up for Social Security was a way of assuring that there would be no fraudulent children claimed as a means of increasing welfare checks.

Another common error was a failure to refer clients for employment. Of course, many clients were ineligible for employment for many reasons. However, it was required that everyone be referred for employment services and, if they could not be employed, that determination would be made later. Another error was failure to refer parents to the agency service that sought child support payments. In many cases, child support was unlikely to be available because the absent parent could not be located, because the absent parent was unlikely to pay child support, or for any number of other reasons. However, the absolute requirement was to refer people to the child support services program, which would then make a reasonable effort to obtain child support payments. If it was unable to do so, that was not an error—only a problem with the child support program, which might become another difficulty for the agency but not a quality control error.

This author's investigations of why errors were being committed and where they were being committed showed that almost all the errors in the sample came from a few large city offices, which would normally be brought into the sample because of their large number of cases. The agency found that by sending a team of monitors and consultants and trainers into those offices for a brief period of time that they could improve the performance of the workers and virtually eliminate the errors. It was also possible to pinpoint exactly who committed the errors and to institute training, better supervision, and even reassignment to eliminate the errors.

Of course this kind of quality control was not the sort that is designed to improve operations as they go along. It was really a form of summative evaluation that determined how effective the program was in carrying out its objectives.

A panel sponsored by the National Academy of Science, under contract with the U.S. government studied quality control issues in the Aid to Families with Dependent Children, Food Stamp, and Medicaid programs. The panel consisted of experts on statistical quality control and welfare administrators. Reports on the findings of the panel were disseminated by the National Academy of Science (Affholter & Kramer, 1987; Kramer, 1987).

Total Quality Management

The theories behind quality control and the use of quality control have been effective and widely used in other elements of social work and human services agency practices.

Perhaps the system that has caught on best in social work is Total Quality Management. The notion of Total Quality Management comes from the works of W. E. Deming, one of the early developers of quality control. Deming, an American, was an expert in statistical analysis, and he developed many of the ideas of studying the process of production rather than the final outcome. He is most famous for going to Japan after World War II and helping the Japanese develop quality measures as they rebuilt their industry after the war.

According to Halberstam (1986), Deming embraced the Japanese industries, which were suffering after World War II. He was courteous and gentle with them. At the same time, he was disdainful of American management and industry because he thought it was becoming wasteful. And, of course, he and his ideas became prominent in the United States only after they faced the aggressive competition of Japan, which succeeded in part because of their following of Deming's ideas.

One excellent example of the ways in which quality processes made a difference to the Japanese is in the automobile industry. Many readers will recall that Japanese automobiles were an unusual innovation in the 1960s in the United States. Japanese products, both before and shortly after World War II, were considered inferior. Saying that something was "made in Japan" was an indication that the product was without very much merit and that it was probably cheap compared with something made in the United States.

When the Japanese decided to try marketing their automobiles in the United States (a subject about which there is extensive literature), they were faced with a variety of problems in addition to the poor reputation of Japanese products

(Halberstam, 1987). The Japanese at the time did not have a network of repair services, which American automobile manufacturers had in connection with all the dealerships they had acquired over the years. The solution was to build automobiles of such quality that there would be little need for repairs and services dedicated to those Japanese vehicles. Of course, the system worked rather well. The Japanese cars suddenly developed a reputation that was opposite the traditional reputation of Japanese products. Now they were considered exceptionally reliable and of very high quality.

The author recalls that in the early 1960s an independent sports car dealer became the company that sold Datsun automobiles in Norman, Oklahoma, where the author was living at the time. Datsun was the name that Nissan used in its early days because Japanese marketers thought Nissan sounded too foreign for the American market. One of the automobiles on the lot was called the Fair Lady, which sounded American. According to Halberstam (1986), Yukata Katayama, one of the first Japanese auto manufacturing executives, came to the United States on behalf of Nissan Motors (then called Datsun in the United States) and was highly successful in understanding the American automobile market and the desires of American consumers. He thought the name Fair Lady, which was chosen because a Nissan executive liked the musical My Fair Lady, was horrible. So Katayama and his staff pulled the Fair Lady labels off the cars and replaced them with the company's internal designation for the car—240 Z. Using the company's internal name avoided his being insubordinate but also provided a potentially popular substitute for the original name.

Halberstam (1987) also pointed out that the initial Japanese car manufacturers who sold in the United States were trying to sell their cars to Americans—people who had very different patterns of automobile care than the Japanese. In cold weather for example, Japanese automobile owners would cover their cars with blankets. That was not a pattern that Americans would follow, therefore, the Japanese cars had to be adapted to the U.S. standards, with stronger batteries and systems that would help cars start in cold weather.

Deming came up with 14 points that are the essence of his plan (Table 7.1). Unfortunately for social workers, his ideas, which are highly applicable to human services, have been primarily applied to businesses and manufacturing rather than to human services issues. However, some efforts have been made to apply his work to the interests of social workers and others in the human services. For example, Morrissey and Wandersman have written about the application of his theories in health care (Ginsberg, 1995). They make a strong case for the utility of the Total Quality Management approach in the health care industry.

Dale and Cooper wrote specifically about the uses of Total Quality Management in the human resources field in their 1992 book, *Total Quality and Human Resources: American Executive Guide*. Maintaining quality assurance in long-term care settings is the subject of a human services guide by Ammentorp, Gossett, and Euchner-Poe (1991) called *Quality Assurance for Long-Term Care Providers*.

One author (Engel, 2000, p. 123) summarizes the works of Deming by writing that the Total Quality Management movement's goal is "constant customer satisfaction, the level of which provides feedback needed to adjust the system." He points out that organizations that have adopted the Deming approach try to achieve cooperation, rather than internal competition, and democratic processes in the organization's behavior and management style.

Of course, the Deming approach is not simply for evaluation but is a total approach to improvement of an organization.

Deming's own book, *Out of the Crisis* (1986), is an excellent guide to many of his ideas. Dobyns (Dobyns & Crawford-Mason, 1994) is a more current interpreter of the works of Deming and their application. Other authors have explicated the charts and control systems used in the Deming method, which include flowcharts, cause and effect models, and Pareto diagrams (Ledolter & Burrill, 1999).

Quality Control Tools

Flowcharts.   Among the primary methods used in quality control are flowcharts. These charts show the processes followed in producing the product or delivering the service. Such charts are common in many fields. An example in Ledolter and Burrill (1999) on the simple issue of making appointments for patients shows how flowcharts can be used. (See Figure 7.1.) Their specific chart refers to U.S. Navy procedures for setting dental appointments at the San Diego Naval Dental Center. For a human services enterprise, the appointment process is also applicable. Making appointments in community mental health centers or family counseling agencies should have similar steps and outcomes. The process can also be applied to determining eligibility in public social welfare services

---

TABLE 7.1   *Deming's Fourteen Points*

1. Create constancy of purpose	10. Eliminate slogans, exhortations, and numerical targets
2. Adopt the new philosophy	11. Eliminate work standards (quotas) and management by objective
3. Cease dependence on mass inspection to achieve quality	12. Remove barriers that rob workers, engineers, and managers of their right to pride of workmanship
4. End the practice of awarding business on price tag alone	
5. Improve constantly	
6. Institute training on the job	13. Institute a vigorous program of education and self-improvement
7. Institute leadership	
8. Drive out fear	14. Put everyone in the company to work to accomplish the transformation
9. Break down barriers between departments	

Source: Adapted from *Thinking About Quality: Progress, Wisdom and the Deming Philosophy,* by L. Dobyns and C. Crawford-Mason, 1994, New York: Random House Times Books.

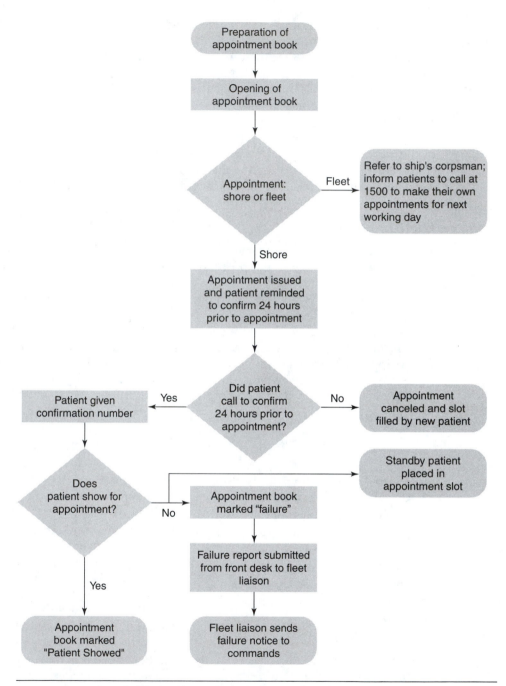

FIGURE 7.1   *Flowchart of a Patient-Appointment Procedure*

Source: Statistical Quality Control: Strategies and Tools for Continual Improvement, by J. Ledolter and C. W. Burrill, 1999, New York: John Wiley & Sons. Copyright © 1999. Reprinted by permission of John Wiley & Sons, Inc.

simply by defining the steps involved, the branches that follow, and—based on what the patient does or fails to do—the eventual outcome.

A specialized kind of flowchart, developed in honor of Kaoru Ishikawa, the developer of the concept, is the Ishikawa cause-and-effect diagram (Ledolter & Burrill, 1999). In such a diagram, all possible causes of an effect are identified, along with possible subcauses. Then the diagram is drawn to show the impact on the effect of the causes. The example shown in Figure 7.2 can be adapted to the eligibility determination process simply by specifying some of the variables such as the work methods and workers involved in the process, the equipment and measurement tools they use, and the ultimate determination of eligibility or non-eligibility. The figure could easily be adapted to work placements of temporary-assistance act recipients, with the effect being the work placement or lack of placement for a client.

Pareto Diagrams.   Another quality control analytic tool is the Pareto diagram, named for an Italian economist, Vilfredo Pareto (Ledolter & Burrill, 1999). The graph created from the Pareto approach shows the frequencies of the categories of quality problems, which are arranged in terms of the frequency of the occurrence of the problems. Figure 7.3 shows a Pareto diagram describing difficulties students have in understanding the material from a statistics course. These quality control tools attempt to understand and resolve problems through visual presentation of the problems, causes, and effects.

A simplified and clear explication of the Deming theories (which was even endorsed by Dr. Deming shortly before his death) is given in Latzko and Saunders's *Four Days with Dr. Deming* (1993). The book explains all of the theories in clear and direct language, and it also provides illustrations of the flowcharts and statistical processes developed by Deming for his Total Quality Management approach. For example, the book covers the issue of inspection, noted earlier in this chapter as a precursor of quality control. Deming says that inspection is necessary but that it should not be the process on which managers depend. Most defects and mistakes are never found, therefore, the purposes of inspection are never achieved. Also, the Deming approach is to improve the process of production so that mistakes, errors, and defects, are prevented—rather than resolved after they

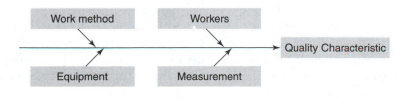

FIGURE 7.2   *A Generic Ishikawa Cause-and-Effect Diagram*

Source: Statistical Quality Control: Strategies and Tools for Continual Improvement, by J. Ledolter and C. W. Burrill, 1999, New York: John Wiley & Sons. Copyright © 1999. Reprinted by permission of John Wiley & Sons, Inc.

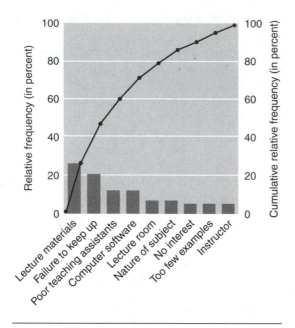

FIGURE 7.3   *A Pareto Diagram: Causes of Difficulties in Understanding Course Material*

Source: Statistical Quality Control: Strategies and Tools for Continual Improvement, by J. Ledolter and C. W. Burrill, 1999, New York: John Wiley & Sons. Copyright © 1999. Reprinted by permission of John Wiley & Sons, Inc.

are made. That approach, with its focus on the production processes, would seem to be a formative approach to program evaluation rather than summative. It works as a means to improve the organization's functions, thereby reducing errors.

In the social services, with the error rate descriptions discussed earlier, the contrast is between finding errors and charging governments with financial penalties for committing them and examining the ways in which services are delivered and improving that process. Staff training, clarifying and simplifying procedures, and other such process-oriented efforts, are examples of using the Deming method instead of a more harsh seeking of errors and punishment of organizations that allow them to be committed. Deming goes further by suggesting that most errors and flaws are built into a system. Therefore, reducing or eliminating errors requires that the system change.

In recent years, quality control and quality assurance, especially Total Quality Management, have been concepts applied to the evaluation of human services programs. Many social program managers are well trained in these methods and find them helpful in the analysis and improvement of their work.

Conclusion

This chapter has dealt with two broad evaluation approaches that are widely used in social work. Monitoring of several kinds is a pervasive method used to evaluate the ongoing operations of many human services activities. Positions in monitoring for social workers are common, and monitoring units are a regular part of many human services organizations, especially those in the public sector.

Increasingly, quality measures such as Total Quality Management are influential methods for evaluating and improving human services organizations. These two distinctive methods are important elements of evaluation in the modern assessment of human services programs.

Questions for Further Study

1. The use of monitoring and quality control has two traditional functions: evaluating programs and program improvement. Cite two ways in which each of these evaluation methods might be used to evaluate and improve a program providing treatment services for substance abusers.

2. Visit with the staff of a local human services agency, preferably a local office of a large agency. Ask for an opportunity to meet a monitor and, if you are able to do so, interview that monitor about his or her professional work in monitoring programs. If you cannot locate a monitor, ask the staff to tell you about their monitoring activities or their experiences of being monitored.

3. Determine whether your college or university uses or has used quality control, quality assurance, or Total Quality Management approaches in its administration of the institution. If so, ask to see the charts and other forms it uses in applying quality control. If not, visit with faculty or graduate students in the business school or department and determine what they learn about quality as part of their professional curriculum.

4. In what ways does the study of Individual Development Accounts differ from traditional evaluation methods discussed in other chapters of this text?

References

Affholter, D. P., & Kramer, F. D. (Eds.). (1987). *Rethinking quality control: A new system for the food stamp program.* Washington, DC: National Academy Press.

Ammentorp, W., Gossett, K. D., & Euchner-Poe, N. (1991). *Quality assurance for long-term care providers.* Newbury Park, CA: Sage.

Barker, R. L. (1999). *Social work dictionary* (4th ed.). Washington, DC: NASW Press.

Dale, B., & Cooper, C. (1992). *Total quality and human resources: American executive guide.* Cambridge, MA: Blackwell.

Deming, W. E. (1986). *Out of the crisis.* Cambridge, MA: MIT Press.

Dobyns, L., & Crawford-Mason, C. (1994). *Thinking about quality: Progress, wisdom and the Deming philosophy.* New York: Random House Times Books.

Engel, M. (2000). *The struggle for control of public education: Market ideology vs. democratic values.* Philadelphia, PA: Temple University Press.

Gabor, P. A., Unrau, Y. A., & Grinnell, R. M., Jr. (1994). *Evaluation for Social Workers: A quality improvement approach for the social services* (2nd ed.). Boston: Allyn & Bacon.

Ginsberg, L., & Keys, P. R. (Eds.). (1995). *New management in human services* (2nd ed.). Washington, DC: NASW Press.

Grinnell, R. M., Jr. (1997). *Social work research and evaluation: Quantitative and qualitative approaches* (5th ed.). Itasca, IL: F. E. Peacock.

Halberstam, D. (1987). *The reckoning.* New York: Avon.

Kettner, P. M., Moroney, R. M., & Martin, L. L. (1999). *Designing and managing programs: An effectiveness based approach* (2nd ed.). Thousand Oaks, CA: Sage.

Kramer, F. D. (Ed.). (1987). *From quality control to quality improvement in AFDC and Medicaid.* Washington, DC: National Academy Press.

Latzko, W. J., & Saunders, D. M. (1993). *Four days with Dr. Deming: A strategy for modern methods of management.* New York: Addison-Wesley.

Ledolter, J., & Burrill, C. W. (1999). *Statistical quality control: Strategies and tools for continual improvement.* New York: John Wiley and Sons.

Rossi, P. H., Freeman, H. E., & Lipsey, M. W. (1999). *Evaluation: A systematic approach* (6th ed.). Thousand Oaks, CA: Sage.

Sherraden, M., Johnson, L., Clancy, M., Beverly, S., Schreiner, M., Zhan, M., & Curley, J. (2000). *Saving patterns in IDA programs: Downpayments on the American dream policy demonstration, a national demonstration of Individual Development Accounts.* St. Louis, MO: Center for Social Development, George Warren Brown School of Social Work, Washington University.

Weiss, C. H. (1998). *Evaluation* (2nd ed.). Upper Saddle River, NJ: Prentice-Hall.

8

Single-Subject Designs

Single-subject designs are a type of evaluation method that helps social workers evaluate their own practice. Evaluation of one's own work is a current top priority in social work education and practice. Agencies that employ social workers may also use single-subject designs to evaluate the work of their agency. Single-subject designs measure client reactions and growth, and they are critical to understanding quality of work. Those who contemplate using single-subject designs with clients who are experiencing personal or family difficulties may want to look carefully at some of the works mentioned here in preparing to implement the methodology.

A related type of evaluation is the satisfaction study, something that helps an agency understand the extent to which its clients are pleased with the services they have received or continue to receive from the agency. Studies of and instruments for measuring satisfaction are extensively used in businesses, especially businesses that deal directly with the public. They will be examined in Chapter 9.

Does Social Work Work?

In Chapter 1, this text identified a lack of evidence that social work worked as one of the reasons for the greater interest in evaluation that developed in the latter part of the last century. Joel Fischer (1973), Blythe and Briar (1985), and others examined existing evaluations of social work interventions with clients and found that few could document that social work services helped. That line of scholarship, which was an example of evaluating evaluations, led to something of a crisis in the profession. There are, of course, many rejoinders to the suggestion that social work is ineffective. For one, social workers often deal with involuntary clients in drug abuse and alcohol programs and in corrections systems, and with parents who abuse or neglect their children. It would not be surprising to find that many of these resistant recipients of service do not allow the service to work. It is also difficult to discover immediate benefits for social work services. Some results are apparent only in the long term, well after any evaluations are conducted.

Nevertheless, the critique is important and worthy of careful consideration. Those who question the effectiveness of social work also note that workers often feel very positive about the results of their work, even when there is no evidence that a client has changed. As a result, efforts have been made—and continue—to encourage social workers to regularly and objectively evaluate their own practice. Schools of social work include such content in their curricula. Increasingly, agencies are building the single-subject design evaluation method into their ongoing operations.

Basic Concepts

A few somewhat different terms are used in the literature to deal with single-subject design. Bloom, Fischer, and Orme (1999) refer to the process as "single system" designs. Others write about "single case" designs. Tony Tripodi (1994), one of the other major writers on the topic, prefers the term single-subject designs. However, his concepts are specifically focused on clinical work, which is part of the title of his book. For this chapter, the terms single-subject design and single-system design are used interchangeably.

Bloom et al. (1999) write that "The phrase *single-system designs* refers to a set of empirical procedures used to observe changes in an identified target (a specified problem or objective of the client) that is measured repeatedly over time," (p. 5). It is noteworthy that although these authors, like Tripodi, focus on clinical work, the idea of a single system is potentially much broader. An individual, family, or group may be the single system for intervention. However, an organization, institution, board of directors, staff group, or any other entity could be defined as a single system, therefore, the changes pursued and observed are not necessarily clinical. In practical terms, the method is usually used in clinical situations, but it may also be applied to other kinds of client systems. Thus, single-subject design is not limited to clinical interventions. Social work managers, community organizers, and social group workers can and sometimes do make use of the method.

The key element of definition, however, is that the unit for intervention is a single system rather than a group of systems. Some researchers make the distinction between single-subject and group designs, although there have been studies of clinical interventions that grouped a number of single-subject designs together for purposes of generalizing about various forms of providing service.

Usually, however, the method is used to evaluate one's own practice with one's own clients. The purpose is to determine whether a client is improving while the service is being provided. No claims are made that the type of service is being analyzed to document its general effectiveness. Studies to validate a treatment or intervention process may be experiments with control groups and experimental groups, as described in Chapter 10. In single-subject design, the purpose is providing authentic feedback to workers so they can work more effectively.

Single-subject or single-system design approaches to social work practice are also sometimes referred to as empirical practice, research practice, or scientific practice (Reid & Zettergren, 1999). Reid and Zettergren (1999) note that the subject is widely taught in social work schools, although they say that it is not clear how much impact the approach has had on the practice of social work in social agencies.

Although it often appears to be new, they also point out that single-system or single-subject work is a logical outgrowth of the work of one of social work's founders, Mary Richmond. She suggested some similar objective approaches to understanding and assessing the development of change among clients of social workers—who were to be studied, assessed, and served—in ways that helped the worker understand the nature and degree to which those clients changed over time.

Although the original approaches to empirical practice were originally associated with the methods of behavior modification, as Reid and Zettergren (1999) note, it became clear that some forms of objective assessment could be applied to all sorts of intervention, and that the basic concern was to systematically set goals and evaluate movement toward their achievement.

Bloom (1999), the author of several works dealing with single-system design, suggests that the approach is nothing new in social work—that social workers have long systematically and consistently evaluated their practice and the progress of their clients. He identifies as the basic elements of effective work of this kind the identification of a target for change, awareness of clear interventions so workers will know what does and does not work, and some form of consistent and objective monitoring that can be used in appraising client change. In his work, Bloom also relates systematic evaluated work with clients to even earlier efforts to evaluate social programs. He clarifies that single-system design work is part of the larger continuum of social program evaluation and results orientation.

Bloom refers to single-system design as a fairly simple matter, although he acknowledges having coauthored a book that is 681 pages long (Bloom, Fischer, & Orme, 1999) on the subject.

Modern thinkers and writers about social work practice insist that there is no discontinuity between effective practice and empirical evaluation. Good evaluation suggests good practice and sound practice should be able to withstand the most rigorous kinds of evaluation. So, in many ways, systematic and empirical evaluation are very much in the tradition of professional social work.

However, there is also some tradition of resistance to empirical practice and the systems and instruments that go with it. Bloom (1999) suggests that many writers and practitioners warn about "hellfire and damnation" (p. 201) for those who consider and use single-system evaluation.

Some of the professional social work resistance to such methodologies is centered on concern that it is overly mechanistic and too lacking in humanism. However, proponents insist that there is no contradiction between good practice and systematic documentation of its effects. In fact, many would argue that it is unethical to practice without careful specification of goals and empirical monitoring of client progress. Why waste a client's time and money on rambling and non-specific interventions that lack evidence of efficacy?

Single-Subject Processes and Procedures

Bloom et al. (1999) write that single-system work is not yet a fully developed science; therefore, there are varied approaches to using such interventions and no definitive answers to many specific questions. However, data are being developed regularly that will make the single-subject orientation more fully understood and standardized. The Bloom et al. book is, at the time of this writing, the most comprehensive and detailed book published on single-subject or single-system designs. Although the authors say that the science of single-subject designs is not yet fully developed, their volume comes closer than any other source to dealing with the most important questions and suggestions about the process.

One key element in single-subject design is the use of instruments for measuring client change. Using instruments that have been statistically validated is the most widely accepted practice. That is, the scales that many want to use, as well as those that are recommended by many single-subject theoreticians, have been shown to actually measure the behaviors they are intended to measure in clients. Validated scales are also tested for reliability—showing that people with similar problems will score similarly on the scales used to measure client progress. Tripodi (1994), however, offers the alternative of "self-anchored" scales in which the client and the social worker together define the objectives of the treatment or intervention and develop a scale of client objectives that is meaningful to them. Some examples of instruments are shown later in this chapter.

The A-B Design

Research designs are generally described by letters. In single-subject design, the basic structure is A-B, with A standing for the baseline or preintervention phase, and B standing for the intervention phase. This is comparable to the concept of a pretest and posttest, although the B phase occurs during treatment or intervention, not only after that phase is completed. During the baseline, there is no intervention designed to hit the target for that treatment, according to Bloom et al. (1999). It is a phase during which attempts are made to fully understand the client or client system and the problem, and, perhaps, to choose what is perceived to be the most effective intervention.

Practitioners often want to know how long a baseline should be. Some think one reliable preintervention assessment of the client, clients, or system should be sufficient. Others continue the baselining for several sessions. Bloom et al. (1999) suggest that a baseline should be continued while it is useful, although that will vary situationally. They also note that some believe a baseline ought to be continued until it is stable—until there is little change in it. In other words, if the score on a standardized instrument during a first baseline measure is 35 but then changes to 20 during the next measurement, the baseline evaluations should continue until the scores are relatively similar. They also suggest that three baselines are probably the minimum for effectively understanding the subject of an intervention. Royse and Thyer (1996) say the more data points provided, the better the assessment. However, they also cite data showing that four is the most common number of data points in each phase. Gabor, Unrau, and Grinnell (1998) say that the A-B design is useful when an agency or worker can afford the time to carefully assess a client. Tripodi (1994) accepts the idea of a minimum of three baseline measurements as the number necessary to achieve stability.

Bloom et al. (1999) agree, however, that there are times when a baseline either is not possible or there is insufficient time to conduct the baseline phase. Time constraints are not the only basis for forgoing a baseline. These authors suggest that when a client is in obvious danger that a baseline may be waived and interventive treatment may immediately begin. A third reason for forgoing a baseline is when a specific problem that is the subject of the client-worker relationship does not occur. The worker may want the problem to occur, and if it does not, a baseline may be beside the point.

Of course, the realities of current treatment in social agencies, mental health centers, and private practice, is that many clients will accept only time-limited service. Six or eight sessions may be all they agree to use in dealing with their problems. Therefore, anything more than one baseline or a baseline during the early parts of the first session may be unrealistic. Ideally, much more baseline assessment would be used. Workers who want to test their skills on one or more treatment modalities may find it useful to apply single-subject design approaches to only a few cases that are available for the time periods required. This would provide the opportunity to use the methodology in the recommended ways while still being able to serve other clients along the lines usually followed in the agency.

Bloom et al. (1999) also pose the realistic possibility that clients may improve during the baseline and before the use of the planned intervention. This could be a product of reactivity—of the situation improving because the client has contact with the worker or therapist. Even without specific intervention, the situation may improve because there is a relationship with someone who can help. However, that improvement may not be long lasting, so workers try to guard against reactivity so that the planned interventions can be used.

Workers may also use a different design such as ABC or even ABCD. That would imply a baseline followed by two or more different kinds of interventions. A client's progress may be evaluated after each of the interventions to determine which, if any, was more successful than others. Royse and Thyer (1996) say that using an alternative intervention is not a matter of starting over but is simply the use of another approach beginning at the point the earlier approach ended.

Time Series Design and Statistics

In single-subject design work, the typical statistical measure is the time series design. Such designs are based on multiple observations, interventions, and post-intervention observations. However, single-subject interventions are only one, perhaps small, example of the ways time series statistics are used. There are many kinds of phenomena that are subject to study using the time series approach. Anything that occurs over a period of time and in which change in those phenomena is significant may be subject to time series analysis. For example, weather patterns, stock market changes, social problems that grow and decline—almost anything can be analyzed in terms of time series.

Single-subject efforts are typically graphed or charted and those graphs or charts are based on time series. What was the client's functioning at the baseline? What is it now? What was the evolutionary pattern of the change? What occurred at various points on the chart to make the significant changes in addition to the intervention or treatment? For example, a social worker who is dealing with a troubled adolescent in a community mental health agency may find that the boy has a significant decline in his instrument score at about the same time a successful intervention session appeared to have occurred. In a subsequent interview, the worker may find that the boy was suddenly rejected by his closest friends at the time of the decline in the score, or that he was called to his school's principal's office because of some misconduct of which he did not believe the school was aware. Sophisticated time series analyses can look at multiple factors that cause change in a client's scores.

Instruments and Scales

There are many scales and instruments used in single-subject design, many of which are familiar to social workers, psychologists, and others who provide treatment to individuals, families, and groups. There are also many instruments for assessing larger systems such as organizations and even communities. There is some similarity between these kinds of instruments and assessment "score cards," which deal with indicators and are mentioned in Chapter 12. However, single-subject design instruments are intended for use over periods of time to determine the progress of a client's treatment.

For social workers, the most popular and highly regarded instruments are those developed by the late Walter Hudson, in some cases with other scholars. Hudson was a social work educator and researcher with a long career as a teacher in schools of social work. His instruments are referred to as Hudson Scales, and the company that distributes these copyrighted materials is called Walmyr Publishing. It has offices in Tallahassee, Florida. It can be reached by telephone at (850) 383-0045 or by fax at (850) 383-0970. The scales and instructions can be purchased from Walmyr. A computer scoring program that was once provided is no longer available.

The collection of Walmyr instruments deals with any number of social and personal problems and behaviors, and some are designed to provide general assessments of functioning. There are also scales that measure marital satisfaction, children's attitudes toward their parents, peer relationships, and attitudes toward homosexuals, as well as nonclinical subjects such as evaluations of classroom teachers. There are catalogs or lists of the Hudson scales available in several books, including Bloom et al. (1999). Figures 8.1 through 8.10 show some examples of Hudson scales.

The analysis of single-subject designs is specified in materials available from Walmyr, along with these copyrighted materials. As should be noted, the scales use numerical values for a subject to indicate the strength of his or her agreement or disagreement with the statements. In the bottom left corner of each scale are numbers designating items that should be reversed. The reversals are used to prevent the rote completion of the instrument—someone entering the same number for each item without thinking about the responses. Using the same numbers for all items would show a rather unusual set of attitudes that actually conflict with one another. A statement such as No. 8 in Figure 8.10—"I get along well with my family"—is positive rather than negative. Someone who responds with "1—None of the time" is making quite a negative statement, therefore, 1 should be given a 7 instead. If the selection was 7, that score should be reversed to 1.

The higher the score on one of these scales, the more serious the problems facing the person responding to the instrument. The scoring instructions provide information on the cutoff scores and other elements that determine the overall degree of a client's problem. Subsequent administration of the instrument will demonstrate the degree of change, if there is any, in a client's condition. A significant reduction in a client's score means that the client is improving.

In addition to the Hudson materials, other writers and researchers have developed or disseminated a variety of popular instruments. Corcoran and Fischer (1999a, 1999b) have written two books that include scales and instruments that can be used for single-subject design work. One deals with measures for couples, children and families and the other with adults.

Another excellent source of information on single-subject scales and their use in evaluating practice is Nurius and Hudson's 1993 book, *Human Services: Practice, Evaluation, and Computers: A Practical Guide for Today and Tomorrow.* The book includes detailed information on the use of the scales and the maintenance of data on clients, as well as other information. It also incorporates software that can be used to print out some of the instruments and other materials provided by Walmyr.

Another popular and widely used scale for depression is called the Beck Depression Scale, which is part of the work of psychologist Aaron T. Beck (Irwin & Beck, 1972.) His work provides the scale, which can be used in assessing degrees of depression, along with concepts of cognitive therapy.

A search in a library or through the Internet also can yield many possible instruments for evaluating one's practice. For using single-subject designs with larger systems such as organizations, one available resource is Miller's (1991)

GENERALIZED CONTENTMENT SCALE (GCS)

Name: _____ Today's Date: _____

This questionnaire is designed to measure the way you feel about your life and surroundings. It is not a test, so there are no right or wrong answers. Answer each item as carefully and as accurately as you can by placing a number beside each one as follows.

1 = None of the time
2 = Very rarely
3 = A little of the time
4 = Some of the time
5 = A good part of the time
6 = Most of the time
7 = All of the time

1. ____ I feel powerless to do anything about my life.
2. ____ I feel blue.
3. ____ I think about ending my life.
4. ____ I have crying spells.
5. ____ It is easy for me to enjoy myself.
6. ____ I have a hard time getting started on things that I need to do.
7. ____ I get very depressed.
8. ____ I feel there is always someone I can depend on when things get tough.
9. ____ I feel that the future looks bright for me.
10. ____ I feel downhearted.
11. ____ I feel that I am needed.
12. ____ I feel that I am appreciated by others.
13. ____ I enjoy being active and busy.
14. ____ I feel that others would be better off without me.
15. ____ I enjoy being with other people.
16. ____ I feel that it is easy for me to make decisions.
17. ____ I feel downtrodden.
18. ____ I feel terribly lonely.
19. ____ I get upset easily.
20. ____ I feel that nobody really cares about me.
21. ____ I have a full life.
22. ____ I feel that people really care about me.
23. ____ I have a great deal of fun.
24. ____ I feel great in the morning.
25. ____ I feel that my situation is hopeless.

5, 8, 9, 11, 12, 13, 15, 16, 21, 22, 23, 24.

FIGURE 8.1

Source: Reprinted with permission of Walmyr Publishing Co. Copyright © 1993 by Walter W. Hudson.

INDEX OF SELF-ESTEEM (ISE)

Name: _____ Today's Date: _____

Context: _____

This questionnaire is designed to measure how you see yourself. It is not a test, so there are no right or wrong answers. Please answer each item as carefully and as accurately as you can by placing a number beside each one as follows.

    1 = None of the time
    2 = Very rarely
    3 = A little of the time
    4 = Some of the time
    5 = A good part of the time
    6 = Most of the time
    7 = All of the time

1. ____ I feel that people would not like me if they really knew me well.
2. ____ I feel that others get along much better than I do.
3. ____ I feel that I am a beautiful person.
4. ____ When I am with others I feel they are glad I am with them.
5. ____ I feel that people really like to talk with me.
6. ____ I feel that I am a very competent person.
7. ____ I think I make a good impression on others.
8. ____ I feel that I need more self-confidence.
9. ____ When I am with strangers I am very nervous.
10. ____ I think that I am a dull person.
11. ____ I feel ugly.
12. ____ I feel that others have more fun than I do.
13. ____ I feel that I bore people.
14. ____ I think my friends find me interesting.
15. ____ I think I have a good sense of humor.
16. ____ I feel very self-conscious when I am with strangers.
17. ____ I feel that if I could be more like other people I would have it made.
18. ____ I feel that people have a good time when they are with me.
19. ____ I feel like a wallflower when I go out.
20. ____ I feel I get pushed around more than others.
21. ____ I think I am a rather nice person.
22. ____ I feel that people really like me very much.
23. ____ I feel that I am a likeable person.
24. ____ I am afraid I will appear foolish to others.
25. ____ My friends think very highly of me.

3, 4, 5, 6, 7, 14, 15, 18, 21, 22, 23, 25.

FIGURE 8.2

Source: Reprinted with permission of Walmyr Publishing Co. Copyright © 1993 by Walter W. Hudson.

INDEX OF CLINICAL STRESS (ICS)

Name: _____   Today's Date: _____

This questionnaire is designed to measure the way you feel about the amount of personal stress that you experience. It is not a test, so there are no right or wrong answers. Answer each item as carefully and as accurately as you can by placing a number beside each one as follows.

1 = None of the time
2 = Very rarely
3 = A little of the time
4 = Some of the time
5 = A good part of the time
6 = Most of the time
7 = All of the time

1. ____ I feel extremely tense.
2. ____ I feel very jittery.
3. ____ I feel like I want to scream.
4. ____ I feel overwhelmed.
5. ____ I feel very relaxed.
6. ____ I feel so anxious I want to cry.
7. ____ I feel so stressed that I'd like to hit something.
8. ____ I feel very calm and peaceful.
9. ____ I feel like I am stretched to the breaking point.
10. ____ It is very hard for me to relax.
11. ____ It is very easy for me to fall asleep at night.
12. ____ I feel an enormous sense of pressure on me.
13. ____ I feel like my life is going very smoothly.
14. ____ I feel very panicked.
15. ____ I feel like I am on the verge of a total collapse.
16. ____ I feel that I am losing control of my life.
17. ____ I feel that I am near a breaking point.
18. ____ I feel wound up like a coiled spring.
19. ____ I feel that I can't keep up with all the demands on me.
20. ____ I feel very much behind in my work.
21. ____ I feel tense and angry with those around me.
22. ____ I feel I must race from one task to the next.
23. ____ I feel that I just can't keep up with everything.
24. ____ I feel as tight as a drum.
25. ____ I feel very much on edge.

5, 8, 11, 13.

FIGURE 8.3

Source: Reprinted with permission of Walmyr Publishing Co. Copyright © 1992 by Walter W. Hudson and Neil Abell.

CLINICAL ANXIETY SCALE (CAS)

Name: _____ Today's Date: _____

This questionnaire is designed to measure how much anxiety you are currently feeling. It is not a test, so there are no right or wrong answers. Answer each item as carefully and as accurately as you can by

1 Rarely or none of the time
2 A little of the time
3 Some of the time
4 A good part of the time
5 Most or all of the time

1. ____ I feel calm.
2. ____ I feel tense.
3. ____ I feel suddenly scared for no reason.
4. ____ I feel nervous.
5. ____ I use tranquilizers or antidepressants to cope with my anxiety.
6. ____ I feel confident about the future.
7. ____ I am free from senseless or unpleasant thoughts.
8. ____ I feel afraid to go out of my house alone.
9. ____ I feel relaxed and in control of myself.
10. ____ I have spells of terror or panic.
11. ____ I feel afraid in open spaces or in the streets.
12. ____ I feel afraid I will faint in public.
13. ____ I am comfortable traveling on buses, subways or trains.
14. ____ I feel nervousness or shakiness inside.
15. ____ I feel comfortable in crowds, such as shopping or at a movie.
16. ____ I feel comfortable when I am left alone.
17. ____ I feel afraid without good reason.
18. ____ Due to my fears, I unreasonably avoid certain animals, objects or situations.
19. ____ I get upset easily or feel panicky unexpectedly.
20. ____ My hands, arms or legs shake or tremble.
21. ____ Due to my fears, I avoid social situations, whenever possible.
22. ____ I experience sudden attacks of panic which catch me by surprise.
23. ____ I feel generally anxious.
24. ____ I am bothered by dizzy spells.
25. ____ Due to my fears, I avoid being alone, whenever possible.

1, 6, 7, 9, 13, 15, 16.

FIGURE 8.4

Source: Reprinted with permission of Walmyr Publishing Co. Copyright © 1992 by Walmyr Publishing Co.

INDEX OF PARENTAL ATTITUDES (IPA)

Name: _____ Today's Date: _____

Child's Name: _____

This questionnaire is designed to measure the degree of contentment you have in your relationship with your child. It is not a test, so there are no right or wrong answers. Answer each item as carefully and as accurately as you can by placing a number beside each one as follows.

1 = None of the time
2 = Very rarely
3 = A little of the time
4 = Some of the time
5 = A good part of the time
6 = Most of the time
7 = All of the time

1. ____ My child gets on my nerves.
2. ____ I get along well with my child.
3. ____ I feel that I can really trust my child.
4. ____ I dislike my child.
5. ____ My child is well behaved.
6. ____ My child is too demanding.
7. ____ I wish I did not have this child.
8. ____ I really enjoy my child.
9. ____ I have a hard time controlling my child.
10. ____ My child interferes with my activities.
11. ____ I resent my child.
12. ____ I think my child is terrific.
13. ____ I hate my child.
14. ____ I am very patient with my child.
15. ____ I really like my child.
16. ____ I like being with my child.
17. ____ I feel like I do not love my child.
18. ____ My child is irritating.
19. ____ I feel very angry toward my child.
20. ____ I feel violent toward my child.
21. ____ I feel very proud of my child.
22. ____ I wish my child was more like others I know.
23. ____ I just do not understand my child.
24. ____ My child is a real joy to me.
25. ____ I feel ashamed of my child.

2, 3, 5, 8, 12, 14, 15, 16, 21, 24.

FIGURE 8.5

Source: Reprinted with permission of Walmyr Publishing Co. Copyright © 1993 by Walter W. Hudson.

CHILD'S ATTITUDE TOWARD MOTHER (CAM)

Name: _____ Today's Date: _____

This questionnaire is designed to measure the degree of contentment you have in your relationship with your mother. It is not a test, so there are no right or wrong answers. Answer each item as carefully and as accurately as you can by placing a number beside each one as follows.

1 = None of the time
2 = Very rarely
3 = A little of the time
4 = Some of the time
5 = A good part of the time
6 = Most of the time
7 = All of the time

1. _____ My mother gets on my nerves.
2. _____ I get along well with my mother.
3. _____ I feel that I can really trust my mother.
4. _____ I dislike my mother.
5. _____ My mother's behavior embarrasses me.
6. _____ My mother is too demanding.
7. _____ I wish I had a different mother.
8. _____ I really enjoy my mother.
9. _____ My mother puts too many limits on me.
10. _____ My mother interferes with my activities.
11. _____ I resent my mother.
12. _____ I think my mother is terrific.
13. _____ I hate my mother.
14. _____ My mother is very patient with me.
15. _____ I really like my mother.
16. _____ I like being with my mother.
17. _____ I feel like I do not love my mother.
18. _____ My mother is very irritating.
19. _____ I feel very angry toward my mother.
20. _____ I feel violent toward my mother.
21. _____ I feel proud of my mother.
22. _____ I wish my mother was more like others I know.
23. _____ My mother does not understand me.
24. _____ I can really depend on my mother.
25. _____ I feel ashamed of my mother.

2, 3, 8, 12, 14, 15, 16, 21, 24.

FIGURE 8.6

Source: Reprinted with permission of Walmyr Publishing Co. Copyright © 1993 by Walter W. Hudson.

CHILD'S ATTITUDE TOWARD FATHER (CAF)

Name: _____ Today's Date: _____

This questionnaire is designed to measure the degree of contentment you have in your relationship with your father. It is not a test, so there are no right or wrong answers. Answer each item as carefully and as accurately as you can by placing a number beside each one as follows.

1 = None of the time
2 = Very rarely
3 = A little of the time
4 = Some of the time
5 = A good part of the time
6 = Most of the time
7 = All of the time

1. ____ My father gets on my nerves.
2. ____ I get along well with my father.
3. ____ I feel that I can really trust my father.
4. ____ I dislike my father.
5. ____ My father's behavior embarrasses me.
6. ____ My father is too demanding.
7. ____ I wish I had a different father.
8. ____ I really enjoy my father.
9. ____ My father puts too many limits on me.
10. ____ My father interferes with my activities.
11. ____ I resent my father.
12. ____ I think my father is terrific.
13. ____ I hate my father.
14. ____ My father is very patient with me.
15. ____ I really like my father.
16. ____ I like being with my father.
17. ____ I feel like I do not love my father.
18. ____ My father is very irritating.
19. ____ I feel very angry toward my father.
20. ____ I feel violent toward my father.
21. ____ I feel proud of my father.
22. ____ I wish my father was more like others I know.
23. ____ My father does not understand me.
24. ____ I can really depend on my father.
25. ____ I feel ashamed of my father.

2, 3, 8, 12, 14, 15, 16, 21, 24.

FIGURE 8.7

Source: Reprinted with permission of Walmyr Publishing Co. Copyright © 1993 by Walter W. Hudson.

INDEX OF BROTHER RELATIONS (IBR)

Name: _____ Today's Date: _____

Brother's Name: _____

This questionnaire is designed to measure the way you feel about your brother. It is not a test so there are no right or wrong answers. Answer each item as carefully and as accurately as you can by placing a number beside each one as follows.

> 1 = None of the time
> 2 = Very rarely
> 3 = A little of the time
> 4 = Some of the time
> 5 = A good part of the time
> 6 = Most of the time
> 7 = All of the time

1. ____ I get along very well with my brother.
2. ____ My brother acts like he doesn't care about me.
3. ____ My brother treats me badly.
4. ____ My brother really seems to respect me.
5. ____ I can really trust my brother.
6. ____ My brother seems to dislike me.
7. ____ My brother really understands me.
8. ____ My brother seems to like me very much.
9. ____ My brother and I get along well together.
10. ____ I hate my brother.
11. ____ My brother seems to like having me around.
12. ____ I really like my brother.
13. ____ I really feel that I am disliked by my brother.
14. ____ I wish I had a different brother.
15. ____ My brother is very nice to me.
16. ____ My brother seems to respect me.
17. ____ My brother thinks I am important to him.
18. ____ My brother is a real source of pleasure to me.
19. ____ My brother doesn't seem to even notice me.
20. ____ I wish my brother was dead.
21. ____ My brother regards my ideas and opinions very highly.
22. ____ My brother is a real "jerk".
23. ____ I can't stand to be around my brother.
24. ____ My brother seems to look down on me.
25. ____ I enjoy being with my brother.

1, 4, 5, 7, 8, 9, 11, 12, 15, 16, 17, 18, 21, 25.

FIGURE 8.8

Source: Reprinted with permission of Walmyr Publishing Co. Copyright © 1993 by Walter W. Hudson.

INDEX OF SISTER RELATIONS (ISR)

Name: _____   Today's Date: _____

Sister's Name: _____

This questionnaire is designed to measure the way you feel about your sister. It is not a test so there are no right or wrong answers. Answer each item as carefully and as accurately as you can by placing a number beside each one as follows.

1 = None of the time
2 = Very rarely
3 = A little of the time
4 = Some of the time
5 = A good part of the time
6 = Most of the time
7 = All of the time

1. ____ I get along very well with my sister.
2. ____ My sister acts like she doesn't care about me.
3. ____ My sister treats me badly.
4. ____ My sister really seems to respect me.
5. ____ I can really trust my sister.
6. ____ My sister seems to dislike me.
7. ____ My sister really understands me.
8. ____ My sister seems to like me very much.
9. ____ My sister and I get along well together.
10. ____ I hate my sister.
11. ____ My sister seems to like having me around.
12. ____ I really like my sister.
13. ____ I really feel that I am disliked by my sister.
14. ____ I wish I had a different sister.
15. ____ My sister is very nice to me.
16. ____ My sister seems to respect me.
17. ____ My sister thinks I am important to her.
18. ____ My sister is a real source of pleasure to me.
19. ____ My sister doesn't seem to even notice me.
20. ____ I wish my sister was dead.
21. ____ My sister regards my ideas and opinions very highly.
22. ____ My sister is a real "jerk".
23. ____ I can't stand to be around my sister.
24. ____ My sister seems to look down on me.
25. ____ I enjoy being with my sister.

1, 4, 5, 7, 8, 9, 11, 12, 15, 16, 17, 18, 21, 25.

FIGURE 8.9

Source: Reprinted with permission of Walmyr Publishing Co. Copyright © 1993 by Walter W. Hudson.

INDEX OF FAMILY RELATIONS (IFR)

Name: _____   Today's Date: _____

This questionnaire is designed to measure the way you feel about your family as a whole. It is not a test, so there are no right or wrong answers. Answer each item as carefully and as accurately as you can by placing a number beside each one as follows.

    1 = None of the time
    2 = Very rarely
    3 = A little of the time
    4 = Some of the time
    5 = A good part of the time
    6 = Most of the time
    7 = All of the time

1. ____ The members of my family really care about each other.
2. ____ I think my family is terrific.
3. ____ My family gets on my nerves.
4. ____ I really enjoy my family.
5. ____ I can really depend on my family.
6. ____ I really do not care to be around my family.
7. ____ I wish I was not part of this family.
8. ____ I get along well with my family.
9. ____ Members of my family argue too much.
10. ____ There is no sense of closeness in my family.
11. ____ I feel like a stranger in my family.
12. ____ My family does not understand me.
13. ____ There is too much hatred in my family.
14. ____ Members of my family are really good to one another.
15. ____ My family is well respected by those who know us.
16. ____ There seems to be a lot of friction in my family.
17. ____ There is a lot of love in my family.
18. ____ Member of my family get along well together.
19. ____ Life in my family is generally unpleasant.
20. ____ My family is a great joy to me.
21. ____ I feel proud of my family.
22. ____ Other families seem to get along better than ours.
23. ____ My family is a real source of comfort to me.
24. ____ I feel left out of my family.
25. ____ My family is an unhappy one.

1, 2, 4, 5, 8, 14, 15, 17, 18, 20, 21, 23.

FIGURE 8.10

Source: Reprinted with permission of Walmyr Publishing Co. Copyright © 1993 by Walter W. Hudson.

Handbook of Research Design and Social Measurement. Miller includes a variety of instruments that are designed to measure community attitudes, organizational tension, organizational structure, group cohesiveness, and dozens of other issues. He also includes a section on social indicators. Instruments such as these, many of which may be copyrighted and must be either purchased or used with permission of the copyright holders, can be used to assess larger system change in ways similar to those used with individuals, families, and other, more clinical interventions.

Graphics and Statistics

Instruction on using social statistics and the graphs into which they are often translated is beyond the scope of this book. However, there are many research methods texts in social work and other fields, as well as social statistics books for social workers, sociologists, psychologists, and others, that provide detailed information. It is important to note, however, that evaluation of practice, particularly single-subject design evaluations, often make use of statistical measures and graphic portrayals of the statistical analyses that are conducted. A knowledge of statistics and graphic presentation is important to the use of the single-subject design methodologies. Those who have not been educated on statistics, including graphic presentation, will want to consider consulting appropriate literature or enrolling in pertinent courses to develop competence in the subject.

One of the features of using single-subject design is to depict the services on graphs and charts. A trend line, following the general approach of time series statistics and designs, is often used so social workers and others can readily determine the degree of progress or decline in a client's work on problems. Some of the trend charts developed by Tripodi (1994) depict the ways in which that approach is used. A chart shows the baseline and the intervention phases, as well as the ways a client handles each phase on the standardized or self-anchored instrument used in the services provided.

A variety of special statistics may be used in association with single-subject designs. Tripodi (1994) emphasizes the "C" statistic, which can, with the individual measurement entered into the formula for the statistic, indicate whether a client's changes are statistically significant. The statistic measures the baseline and interventions and indicates the degree to which there is a trend in the time series followed in the services provided to the client. Those interested in applying that statistic to their single-subject work may want to consult Tripodi's book to learn more specifically how to use the statistic for assessing single-subject design change.

SINGWIN Software

Another tool for developing graphic presentations about single-subject designs is in the software program included with Bloom et al. (1999). The software is called SINGWIN, and it was developed for the book by Charles Auerbach, David

Schnall, and Heidi Heft Laporte. The book provides detailed instructions on using the software, which requires that the baseline and intervention data be entered into a spreadsheet that shows each of the baseline and intervention measures. It also includes some sample cases on which the software user may practice.

After the data are entered, the SINGWIN program offers a number of alternatives for analyzing them. It divides the data into the baseline and intervention phases, as entered by the operator. It can show the "celeration" line. The celeration line illustrates the computation of the "C" statistic, which indicates whether or not a change from the baseline to the treatment phase reflects a statistically significant change. Other graphs and statistics that can be shown include:

1. T-test
2. Autocorrelation
3. Gelfand
4. 2 SD (standard deviation) bands
5. Descriptives (descriptive statistics)
6. Chi Square
7. Proportion/Frequency
8. Regression
9. Effect Size
10. Transform Data

The program also can construct the following graphs:

1. Line Chart
2. Over Lay Chart
3. Bar Graph
4. Band Graphs Sheward Charts (2 SD and Interquartile Range)
5. Moving Average Line
6. Celeration Line
7. Difference Line
8. Regression Plots
9. Scatter Plots

There are also suboperations within several of these choices. Using the software is relatively simple and is explained well in Bloom et al. (1999). The SINGWIN software—which may be augmented in a new edition of the book soon—is a useful means for better understanding one's single-subject case.

Assessment Scales

In addition to the use of instruments and specific statistics with single-subject designs, there are also many assessment scales used in social work and other kinds of human practice. These are designed to establish preliminary understanding of clients, to plan treatment, and, at a later date, to reassess the client to determine the degree, if any, of progress that has been made. For example, the Child and Adolescent Functional Assessment Scale is a 12-page instrument that can be administered by a clinician to evaluate the functioning of a young client. It can be secured from CAFAS, 2140 Old Earhart Road, Ann Arbor, Michigan 48105, telephone (734) 769-9725, or fax (734) 769-1434. CAFAS also produces interview manuals and training manuals to facilitate the use of these instruments. There are many more such instruments and devices for evaluating clients and charting their care that are available through books, journals, and the Internet.

Conclusion

More and more, social workers, like other human services professionals, are turning to structured evaluation instruments in their own areas of responsibility as a means to better understand their clients and chart their progress. Some of the principles and concepts, as well as some of the sample instruments, in this chapter outline the ways in which single-subject designs are used in the assessment and treatment of clients. At the individual or treatment levels, these ideas are of utmost importance to social workers entering practice soon. Such approaches are likely to be central to the organization and practice of social work in the future.

Questions for Further Study

1. In your own words, describe the ways in which you might use one or more of the Hudson Scales shown in this chapter.

2. What are some of the things a social worker might want to consider in determining how many intervention sessions are appropriate for a client—especially in the baseline phase?

3. How might single-subject methods be used in tracing the development of an organization or agency staff? Do similar principles apply to those followed in using the method with individuals and families?

4. What are some of the reasons that statistics and graphic presentation of statistics are important in single-subject design efforts?

References

Bloom, M. (1999). Single-system evaluation. In I. Shaw & J. Lishman, *Evaluation and social work practice* (pp. 198–218). Thousand Oaks, CA: Sage.

Bloom, M., Fischer, J., & Orme, J. (1999). *Evaluating practice: Guidelines for the accountable professional* (3rd ed.). Boston: Allyn & Bacon.

Blythe, B. J., & Briar, S. (1985). Direct practice effectiveness. In A. Minahan, R. M. Becerra, S. Briar, C. J. Coulton, L. H. Ginsberg, J. G. Hopps, J. F. Longres, R. J. Patti, W. J. Reid, T. Tripodi,

S. K. Khinduka, J. M. Atkins, & K. R. Greenhall (eds.), *Encyclopedia of social work* (18th ed., pp. 399–407). Silver Spring, MD: NASW Press.

Corcoran, K., & Fischer, J. (1999a). *Measures for clinical practice: A sourcebook: Vol. 1. Couples, families, and children* (3rd ed.). New York: Free Press.

Corcoran, K., & Fischer, J. (1999b). *Measures for clinical practice: A sourcebook: Vol. 2. Adults* (3rd ed.). New York: Free Press.

Fischer, J. (1973, January). Is casework effective? A review. *Social Work, 18*(1), 5–20.

Gabor, P. A., Unrau, Y. A., & Grinnell, R. M., Jr. (1998). *Evaluation for social workers: A quality improvement approach for the social services* (2nd ed.). Boston: Allyn & Bacon.

Irwin, T. D., & Beck, A. T. (1972). *Depression: Causes and treatment.* Philadelphia: University of Pennsylvania Press.

Miller, D. C. (1991). *Handbook of research design and social measurement* (5th ed.). Newbury Park, CA: Sage.

Reid, W. J., & Zettergren, P. (1999). A perspective on empirical practice. In I. Shaw & J. Lishman, *Evaluation and social work practice* (pp. 41–62). Thousand Oaks, CA: Sage.

Royse, D., & Thyer, B. A. (1996). *Program evaluation: An introduction* (2nd ed.). Chicago: Nelson-Hall.

Tripodi, T. (1994). *A primer on single-subject design for clinical social workers.* Washington, DC: NASW Press.

Nurius, P. L., & Hudson, W. W. (1993). *Human services: Practice, evaluation, and computers: A practical guide for today and tomorrow.* Pacific Grove, CA: Brooks-Cole.

9

Needs Assessments and Satisfaction Studies

Among the evaluation approaches used by social workers are assessments of need, which determine whether to embark upon or enhance specific programs, and satisfaction studies, which determine how well recipients of services react to them. Both are common forms of evaluation. They are used not only in human services work but also in business. A needs assessment is comparable to a business marketing plan, which helps determine whether there is a market for a particular product or service. Measures of satisfaction are used by almost all businesses. At times, they are used to immediately identify serious problem areas of their business or problematic employees. When they are compiled and analyzed as more complete studies of customer satisfaction, they are interpreted for statistical significance and to determine the range of reactions to the services or products provided.

Needs Assessment

In many circumstances, new programs or services are not organized or delivered until the need for a program or service is established. An organization may want to have confidence that a service will be used before it expends the energy and money necessary to launch it. Funding agencies also follow a requirement for needs assessment. Before grants or contracts can be provided for new programs and services, funders often require the presentation of a reliable and comprehensive needs assessment.

Marlow (1998) refers to needs assessments as one of the types of applied research that generalist social workers encounter in their practice. She says such assessments, along with program evaluations and practice evaluations (all three of which are subjects of this book), tie in with the purposes of generalist social work that were originally enunciated by Betty Baer and Ron Federico in 1978, when they wrote a book that became the basis for generalist social work practice: enhancing the problem solving and developmental capacities of people, promoting humane and effective social services system operations that serve people, and linking people with resources, services, and opportunities. Generalist social work is the basis for master of social work programs and accredited bachelor of social work programs throughout the United States under the accreditation standards of the Commission on Accreditation of the Council on Social Work Education.

Of course, needs assessments, like any other planning device, may be misleading if appropriate methodologies are not used. The author recalls an experience in the early days of his work as a community social worker in Oklahoma. An organization board thought it might be useful to sponsor a winter school-vacation program for children. It also hoped to provide a summer day camp for children while they were out of school. A needs assessment for the winter program elicited a relatively large number of written responses indicating that such a program was undesirable and unnecessary, so no program was offered. When it came time for the summer day camp, the organization simply announced that it would take place. Fees, schedules, and program activities were announced. Sufficient numbers enrolled, and the summer program began its operations on schedule. The summer day camp continues to operate into the new century.

The need for both programs probably was not assessed correctly. Many of those who completed a survey about the winter program had no children or were negative about the agency operating children's services of any kind at any time. Although no formal needs assessment was conducted for the summer program, the author spent a good bit of time informally interviewing parents whose children were involved in other programs. It was clear that the summer day camp would have sufficient enrollment to operate.

It is likely that planning for both programs would have benefited from more-sophisticated needs assessment activities, such as those described here. For example, focus group sessions with potential enrollees and their parents might have yielded more-accurate results. Of course, the concept of focus groups, which are discussed later in this chapter, was not yet developed during this episode. However, today's social worker, dealing with a similar set of circumstances, might conduct such groups—not only to determine the specific need and possible enrollment, but also to involve families in defining and helping plan the program for either summer or winter activities.

The literature of social services and social work evaluation includes extensive information on needs assessments. It is a standard subject in virtually all of the texts that deal with program evaluation.

One of the subtle difficulties of carrying out needs assessments is the importance of separating needs from wants or desires. In some ways, needs may be viewed as wants that are imposed on a community. Outsiders or noncommunity members may assume that a community needs something that it may or may not really want, which probably eliminates it as a need. For example, outside experts may determine that a community needs a youth services center and youth recreation. However, community members may believe that there are adequate youth recreation services available, although some are informal and not listed in any official directory of the community's programs. Community leadership may be unwilling (or even unable) to raise funds to meet a need whose existence is only poorly defined. However, they may locate another need that has high priority with community residents. For example, better traffic control through traffic lights or police patrols may have high community priority, even though experts do not view that as a significant problem.

Most writers advocate that key community people be aggressively solicited to participate in a project, even if they are not wealthy enough to purchase space for a potential new program's operations. Much of community organization and planning experience suggests that needs be carefully and operationally defined so real needs, rather than peripheral assertions pressed by articulate or powerful people, will be carefully examined.

In many needs assessment situations, community members are asked to express their attitudes toward specific social problems, community changes, or possible program developments. Questionnaires are useful in assessing community needs. Henerson, Morris, and Fitz-Gibbon (1987) provide some excellent examples of questionnaires as well as instruments for following up with those who do not return mailed questionnaires. They also provide examples of instruments that can be effectively used with young children, such as ones that instruct the children to mark faces that range from happy to sad in a kind of pictorial Likert scale.

One of the difficulties in conducting studies of satisfaction is that these are studies of attitudes. Attitudes are an especially difficult kind of factor to pin down and study operationally. Practically, behavior can be studied, but it is exceptionally difficult to relate behavior to attitudes. As Henerson et al. (1987) note, it is not possible to measure attitudes directly and, therefore, researchers must operate on inferences. And, they point out, attitudes change rapidly. However, evaluations generally focus on the attitudes of groups of people, not a specific individual. Therefore, the kind of precision that is necessary in assessing intervention results, as discussed in Chapter 8, may not be as important in measuring attitudes toward a community's needs or a program.

The following sections describe some of the suggestions evaluation experts offer for programs that attempt to assess and establish the need for human services programs.

Purposes of Needs Assessments

Gabor, Unrau, and Grinnell (1998) specify the purpose or goals of needs assessments as:

> The main purpose of all needs assessments is to determine the nature, scope, and locale of a social problem (if one exists) *and* to identify a feasible, useful, and relevant solution(s) to the problem(s). In a nutshell, the ultimate goal of all needs assessments is to improve the human condition by identifying a social problem(s) and proposing a solution(s) to the problem(s). (p. 41)

These authors also identify four uses of needs assessments: educating people about social needs, justifying the initial need for a program, budgeting and planning, and providing marketing information for future needs (Gabor et al., 1998). Although the assumption is often made that needs assessments are solely used to justify new programs, they also provide information to help carry out other uses, such as helping the public, funders, and board members understand more about social needs and their extent, developing budgets and carrying out other planning activities, and organizing information that can be used to market a specific service.

Royse and Thyer (1996, p. 23) offer reasons for conducting needs assessments:

1. To determine if an intervention exists in a community
2. To determine if there are enough clients with a particular problem to justify creating a new program
3. To determine if existing interventions are known or recognized by potential clients
4. To determine what barriers prevent clients from accessing existing services
5. To document the existence of an ongoing/exacerbating social problem

It is critical to know with some precision exactly how potential clients and a community react to a specific program or service. Key informants, one of the kinds of subjects used in needs assessments, should be knowledgeable and involved in the issue under discussion. They may be agency staff or board members who are well versed in the kinds of work the agency performs. They should also be well informed about community resources.

Many times, clients and community leaders may not fully understand the intricacies of a newly developing program. For example, one of the growing approaches to serving families who have children with disabilities is the parent-to-parent program. In such programs, parents who have children with disabilities are matched with families who have children with similar disabilities. The help they are able to give each other is often more useful than the assistance of professionals such as social workers or teachers because parents are exposed to the realities of obtaining services—which people and which organizations can truly assist, how a case can be made for services, and many other pieces of information and advice that can best be obtained from someone who has experienced the problem and the service system. However, family members and professionals may not completely understand what a parent-to-parent program is and, therefore, may indicate there is no need for one. A valid needs assessment, under some circumstances, may require education so potential clients and community people have the knowledge to make judgments about need.

Marlow (1998) offers some practice wisdom on the subject of needs assessments. She says that many times needs assessments do not seem necessary because the need for services appears to be obvious. She points out, however, that one's conclusions are simply one's subjective opinion. There also are many other elements in addition to simply assuming need associated with a precise needs assessment.

Professor Marlow (1998, pp. 75–76) suggests a variety of designs for assessing need. To determine the best design, she poses a series of questions:

1. Whose need is being assessed?
2. Who will have input into the design of the needs assessment?
3. When will the needs assessment be carried out?
4. What type of understanding of the need is required?
5. What level of description is useful?

Answers to such questions will help guide the construction of a needs assessment. Marlow is quite clear about the fact that a number of different kinds of needs assessment designs can be implemented. She discusses such varieties as panel studies, trend studies, cross-sectional studies, and participatory studies. Different kinds of studies rely on different kinds of data sources, some of which are discussed next. In addition, different studies demand different approaches—for example, focus groups, individual interviews, mail surveys, and community forums.

Marlow (1998) is wise in pointing out the need to specify whose needs are being addressed. Frequently in social work there is an assumption that the immediate client or client system is the target of a service. However, that is not always the case, especially in areas of concern such as drug abuse and crime and delinquency. There is a great deal of difference between defining the need for an enforcement project that would make illegal drugs less available and a needs assessment dealing with the services provided to young drug offenders. The two obviously call for significantly different programs and interventions, as well as quite different resources.

Focus Groups and Public Forums

Focus groups are often a useful tool for conducting needs assessments. Although one of their primary uses is in marketing (when manufacturers ask potential customers to identify the strengths and weaknesses of a new product), they are also useful in many other contexts. Attorneys often use them to assess their arguments before a trial. Political candidates may also use focus groups to evaluate their campaign materials and platforms. Quite sophisticated instruments are available for focus groups in which participants turn a dial on a handheld electronic unit. The higher they turn the dial, the more satisfied they are with the product or the argument. Of course, focus groups are used somewhat differently in human services needs assessment—assessments are not nearly so specific as whether someone is willing to purchase a product or to vote for a defendant in a trial.

According to Balch and Mertens (1999), "Focus groups are particularly well suited to identify and describe in depth issues that are not well known or understood by the researchers" (p. 267). Generally, focus groups are discussions guided by an interviewer that have small numbers (6 to 12) of participants. Probing, clarifying terms, and helping participants build on each other's contributions are all part of focus group operations. As these authors suggest, focus groups are often useful in cross-cultural situations or where needs for specific problems are being identified. The Balch and Mertens article discusses the use of focus groups to explore the experiences of deaf and hard of hearing people with the courts. They found the method to be quite useful with their interviewees, who they divided into five groups based on their preferred modes of communication as well as their educational levels. The groups, which were in different cities, ranged from highly educated deaf adults who read and wrote English and who primarily communicated by using American Sign Language to adults who relied on oral communications such as lip reading and speech. One person who was deaf and blind and required interpreters participated in a group, as well as some participants who used Mexican Sign Language.

Another outstanding source for learning about the use of focus groups in needs assessment and other activities is Krueger (1994).

The use of community or public forums is another technique for assessing need and obtaining public reactions to projected programs. An announcement is made that a public meeting will be held on a subject, and those who attend usually are highly concerned about the issue. Public forums are often used when land zoning decisions are slated for action. The public may support or oppose such actions at public forums at which decision-makers are likely to be present. The author has written of one such decision, dealing with the possible construction of a manufacturing plant in his neighborhood that might use toxic substances (Ginsberg, 1996).

Public meetings are also used in many states for discussion of a Social Services Block Grant. Public input is required as part of the process for receiving funds. A state's plan for expending those funds becomes the subject of an open meeting.

Community forum participants do not necessarily vote on the issues under discussion, although they may in order to convey a sense of their opinions. The agency whose programs are under discussion is obligated to consider the comments and suggestions and to demonstrate that they have been studied and perhaps implemented.

Those who use the community forum approach find that it is important to use a variety of methods for assessing the ideas of a total group—not simply the few most articulate attendees. At times, community meetings may become highly tendentious and emotional. Maintaining decorum, neutralizing highly negative assaults between participants, and making certain that all ideas are expressed and heard are priorities. Failing to follow such procedures can lead to a distorted perception of the forum's conclusions and the attitudes of the participants.

Data Sources for Needs Assessments

A variety of sources of information can be used in carrying out a needs assessment. Direct contact with community people is not the only source. Effective needs assessments also address existing sources of data in reaching conclusions about human requirements. Information available in the reports of the U.S. Bureau of the Census are important in any needs assessment exercise or project. As Rossi, Freeman, and Lipsey (1999) suggest, Current Population Surveys and the most current census data are valuable sources of information on many elements necessary for effective needs assessment. The data are available in libraries and directly from the Bureau of the Census, often in print form or on CD-ROMs. Census data also can be obtained on the Internet.

Rossi et al. (1999) also point to the use of social indicators for assessing need, including U.S. Department of Justice annual statistics on household crime victimization. Those data provide some insight into a serious social problem. Planners and needs assessment specialists may assume that the indicators are at least roughly applicable to their own communities and can, therefore, be used as indicators of local need, even though the data are collected nationally. Some examples of social and program outcomes indicators are also found in Chapter 12.

Agency records are also a useful source of information. A drug and alcohol treatment agency can provide information that approximates the level of need for such services in a community. Data showing the length of waiting lists for services can also document the need for additional resources in an area of concern. School personnel, law enforcement officials, clergy, health and mental health specialists, and many other groups can offer valid information about the extent and nature of human need in their community.

Sometimes, as Rossi et al. (1999) suggest, an assessment of the community's knowledge about a problem can establish a need for an educational or public information program. The authors add that targets can be identified in effective needs assessments that will help guide program efforts to the proper communities or institutions.

Satisfaction Studies

A growing phenomenon in the human services, adapted in some ways from businesses that serve the public, is the satisfaction study. Corporations and other organizations constantly conduct satisfaction studies as a means of evaluating themselves, their services, and their personnel. Typical is the instrument called *Air-Talk*, which is distributed throughout Atlanta, Georgia's massive airport, Hartsfield Atlanta International Airport. It is a brief, 8½ × 11 inch coated paper document that is tri-folded. On the outside is a business reply permit and an address so that those who complete it may return the document easily and at no cost.

The survey instrument provides open space for stating concerns or compliments. Then there are six scales for the traveler to complete with the range of responses being "much better" to "much worse" compared to other airports. The six items are airport facilities, food service, customer service in retail shops, parking, and ground transportation. A collection of responses can give the airport a good idea of traveler reactions to their facilities and services.

Some other satisfaction studies most Americans are familiar with are the questionnaires in restaurants, hotels, and in national automobile manufacturing concerns. The backs of restaurant checks or separate surveys often ask customers to evaluate the quality of service, the food, the courtesy of the staff, and the cleanliness of the facility, as well as other elements. Burger King, for example, provides customers with a simple form that asks for a rating of each restaurant's appearance and cleanliness, the food quality, and the speed and courtesy of the service. Customers can rank these as excellent, good, or poor. They are also asked to state the day of the week, time, and date of the visit. Customers have the option of including their name, address, and telephone number. Hotels often place similar instruments in rooms to ask guests to evaluate elements of the hotel's resources, including the restaurants, bars, rooms, public rooms, front desk services, and other services. Guests are asked to mail or drop off the survey form inside the hotel. Some also ask that especially helpful staff be identified so they can be rewarded for their efforts. The follow-up from the hotels and restaurants varies. Some offer free meals or rooms in response to the help the customer has provided. A few hotel top management staff send letters to respondents, thanking them for their help.

Most of these efforts may not be identified as evaluation research. Instead, they are used to spot immediate problems so action can be taken. A discourteous service staff member, a hotel room whose plumbing or television is broken, or failures of the maintenance or housekeeping people must be identified quickly and addressed so the problems do not recur.

Food companies also use satisfaction studies. Candy bar manufacturers and purveyors of canned goods may have a toll-free telephone number on their packages so customers can identify any problems that might exist. A code on the product tells the company when and where the product was manufactured. Sometimes a company sends coupons for free products in thanks for feedback.

For manufacturers and others who deal with the public, the responses to such quality questions are invaluable as a management tool. Failing to correct such problems immediately can be costly to a company. However, these examples may not be formal program evaluations. The information is essentially ad hoc and not necessarily helpful in a comprehensive evaluation of a product or a company's consumer relations. In contrast, an aggregation of the evaluations and a statistical analysis of them can provide the company with a picture of how well it is performing in terms of its client reactions.

Social agencies and other human services providers also make extensive use of satisfaction studies for approximately the same reasons as businesses—to address and eliminate immediate problems and to make long-term, comprehensive assessments of the satisfaction of those they serve.

Skewed Reactions

One of the difficulties of all satisfaction studies is that the results often appear to be skewed. Although it may be that the results are honest portrayals of reactions to services, one may be suspicious of the validity of the sample and responses that are often more positive than should be expected.

On one hand in satisfaction studies, the most critical and intolerant of customers or clients may respond. Do people who are simply neutral about their hotel rooms fill out the surveys? Perhaps not. Only the most disappointed or angry may respond. The same may be true for restaurants. In the social services, the same kinds of phenomena may apply.

On the other hand, as Royse and Thyer (1996) show, "In practically every instance, the majority of respondents indicate satisfaction with services received" (p. 94). They note that in a survey of hospitalized patients, 86 percent were either very satisfied or somewhat satisfied. When they assessed their physicians, 95 percent were either very or somewhat satisfied. The authors suggest this is a worldwide phenomenon and that most recipients of health and social services are satisfied with what they received. There even is no difference of any consequence between voluntary and involuntary recipients. However, there may be a significant difference between those who respond and those who do not respond to such surveys.

Some believe that qualitative, open-ended, responses are better than the closed-ended instruments because they help customers or clients respond to their surroundings in ways that may not be covered in a satisfaction form. Long, open-ended responses may be of special help in assessing a program.

A difficulty with satisfaction study instruments is that they are not always validated or scientifically constructed. They simply ask respondents to tell an organization what they think of selected aspects of a program and what their experiences have been. This may be sufficient for an organization's evaluation activities, even though it cannot necessarily make a claim that it has collected a reliable, comprehensive picture of its clients' attitudes.

Royse and Thyer (1996) found that the works of Robert Hammond (1975) are helpful in designing survey instruments. Hammond, in a model for satisfaction that he developed, first identified a program population that includes not only clients but also staff and agency administration. A program also is part of an environment, Hammond says, and that environment includes the methods used by the organization, the goals or intentions of the organization, and the organizational resources. With this information, evaluators construct instruments that collect opinions about the program and the organization's performance. These elements can be augmented or simplified so that evaluators are able to conduct a relatively simple or fairly complex satisfaction instrument. Hammond's writing is about community education programs, but the same principles of design can be applied to social work and social services satisfaction instruments.

It is important to understand that satisfaction studies are often critical in an organization. For academic personnel, the teacher evaluation instrument is one of the most important elements in a professorial career. Salaries are set, in part, because of results of teaching evaluations. Promotions through the ranks are determined, at least in part, by the results of those evaluations. Although students often complete them in brief periods of time and only rarely write qualitative comments, evaluations are seriously considered and have major consequences for the teacher who is evaluated. Rarely are these documents scientific, validated instruments. Nevertheless, deans, presidents, and promotion committees study them carefully and make basic career decisions about faculty members based on the results.

Examples of Satisfaction Instruments

Figures 9.1 through 9.7 show a series of satisfaction instruments originally published in Tripodi (1994) that can be used as examples. They are not scientifically validated, but they provide feedback for the management of human services organizations that use them. Some follow-up on clinical interventions.

FIGURE 9.1 *Client Questionnaire to Monitor Clinical Social Worker's Implementation of Posthospital Planning*

1. Were insurance and discharge forms filled out by the social worker?
   Yes ___ No ___ Don't know ___
2. Did the social worker discuss medication with you?
   Yes ___ No ___ Don't know ___
   With your family?
   Yes ___ No ___ Don't know ___
3. Did the social worker discuss what your living arrangements with your family will be after you leave the hospital?
   Yes ___ No ___ Don't know ___
4. Did the social worker discuss different community living arrangements for you?
   Yes ___ No ___ Don't know ___
5. Did the social worker talk with your family?
   Yes ___ No ___ Don't know ___
6. Did the social worker refer you to another social worker in the community?
   Yes ___ No ___ Don't know ___
7. Did the social worker discuss employment with you?
   Yes ___ No ___ Don't know ___
8. Did the social worker discuss education with you?
   Yes ___ No ___ Don't know ___
9. Did the social worker make an appointment to see you after you leave the hospital?
   Yes ___ No ___ Don't know ___

FIGURE 9.2   *Follow-Up Questionnaire*

Since you stopped receiving help from the social worker:

Have you received help from other resources or persons?
    Yes ___ No _✓_
       If yes, please explain _____
Have you had any recurrences of the major problem for which you received help?
    Yes ___ No _✓_
       If yes, please explain _____
Have you changed any of your daily habits?
    Yes ___ No _✓_
       If yes, please explain _____
Have there been any changes in your living circumstances?
    Yes ___ No _✓_
       If yes, please explain _____
Have you been ill?
    Yes ___ No _✓_
       If yes, please explain _____
Have any of your family members been sick?
    Yes ___ No _✓_
       If yes, please explain _____
Have there been any changes in your personal relationship with family and friends?
    Yes _✓_ No ___
       If yes, please explain *I am dating women more often.* _____
Have any other major problems occurred?
    Yes ___ No _✓_
       If yes, please explain _____
Have there been any unexpected positive or negative changes resulting from the services you received from the social worker?
    Yes _✓_ No ___
       If yes, please explain *I have felt more energetic.* _____

FIGURE 9.3 *Follow-Up Questionnaire for Tom and His Relationship with Jerry*

Does Jerry try to pick fights with you?
    Yes ___ No ___
        If yes, indicate how often he does this:
        Once a week ___ Two to three times per week ___
        Four to five times per week ___
        Six to seven times per week ___
Do you try to pick fights with Jerry?
    Yes ___ No ___
        If yes, indicate how often you do this:
        Once a week ___ Two to three times per week ___
        Four to five times per week ___
        Six to seven times per week ___
Have you argued with Jerry in the past week?
    Yes ___ No ___
        If yes, indicate about how many arguments you have had:
        One ___ Two to five ___ Six to eight ___
        Nine or more ___
To what extent do you believe you are responsible for the arguments and fights
with Jerry?
    Not at all responsible ___ Somewhat responsible ___
    Completely responsible ___
To what extent do you believe Jerry is responsible for arguments and fights with you?
    Not at all responsible ___ Somewhat responsible ___
    Completely responsible ___
Do you believe your father:
    Likes you and Jerry about the same ___ Favors you ___
    Favors Jerry ___
Do you believe your mother:
    Likes you and Jerry about the same ___ Favors you ___
    Favors Jerry ___
Do you like or dislike Jerry?
    Dislike ___ Like ___ Neither like nor dislike ___
Does Jerry like or dislike you?
    Dislike ___ Like ___ Neither like nor dislike ___
In the past week, have Jerry and you gone places together to have a good time (such as
the movies, a baseball game, a tennis match, sailing)?
    Yes ___ No ___
        If yes, indicate how many times ___
Please describe the nature of your relationship with Jerry _____
Has your relationship with Jerry changed since you have had contacts with the social
worker?
    Yes ___ No ___
        If yes, please explain _____
How could the relationship between you and Jerry be improved? _____

FIGURE 9.4 *Follow-Up Questionnaire about the Intervention and the Clinical Social Worker*

To what extent has the social worker been sensitive to your needs as expressed in interviews?

Very sensitive ___ Moderately sensitive ___
Neither sensitive or insensitive ___
Moderately insensitive ___ Very insensitive ___

Did the social worker meet with you on time for your appointments?

All of the time ___ Most of the time ___
Some of the time ___ Not at all ___

Did the social worker review progress with you?

Yes ___ No ___

If yes, how often?
Every session ___ Every other session ___
Every third session ___
At least every fourth session ___

Did the social worker provide you with graphic information about your progress?

Yes ___ No ___

Did the social worker explain how to make self-ratings of anxiety?

Yes ___ No ___

Did the social worker explain how to use the standardized instrument for measuring depression?

Yes ___ No ___

Did the social worker help you identify the problem(s) you worked on?

Yes ___ No ___

If yes, please describe the problem(s) _____

Did the social worker provide you with good advice that you could use on everyday practical problems?

Yes ___ No ___

Did the social worker help you to understand when and why you become anxious?

Yes ___ No ___

Did the social worker use role-playing of interpersonal situations in your sessions?

Yes ___ No ___

Were you comfortable discussing your personal problems with the social worker?

Yes ___ No ___

If no, what could the social worker have done to make you more comfortable?

_____

Did the social worker give you homework assignments after each session?

Yes ___ No ___

If yes, to what extent were these assignments helpful?
Very helpful ___ Helpful ___
Moderately helpful ___ Not at all helpful ___

Was the social worker helpful to you?

Yes ___ No ___

Please describe _____

Source: A Primer on Single-Subject Design for Clinical Social Workers, by T. Tripodi, 1994, Washington, DC: NASW Press. Copyright © 1994 by National Association of Social Workers, Inc. Reprinted with permission of NASW Press.

FIGURE 9.5 *Follow-Up Questionnaire for Client: Assertive Behaviors*

Have you failed to be assertive in interpersonal situations in which you should have been assertive?
    Yes ___ No _✓_
        If yes, please explain _____

Have other problems occurred for you since you finished your work with the social worker?
    Yes ___ No _✓_
        If yes, please explain _____

Do you understand why you should be assertive in certain situations?
    Yes _✓_ No ___
        If yes, did you acquire this understanding in your work with the social worker?
        Yes _✓_ No ___
        If no, how should the social worker have helped you acquire this understanding?
_____

Did you discuss with the social worker interpersonal situations in which you should be assertive?
    Yes _✓_ No ___
        If no, should you have discussed these situations with the social worker?
        Yes ___ No ___

Have you made progress in being assertive since your first contact with the social worker?
    Yes _✓_ No ___
        If yes, please explain *I have understood my reluctance to be assertive, and I have overcome my hesitation to be assertive by practicing with the social worker.*

Have you received professional help from other persons since you finished your work with the social worker?
    Yes ___ No _✓_
        If yes, please explain _____

Have you felt a need to continue to work with the social worker on assertiveness or on other problems?
    Yes ___ No _✓_
        If yes, please explain _____

Have any events occurred recently that facilitated your assertiveness?
    Yes ___ No _✓_
        If yes, please explain _____

Have any events occurred recently that prevented you from being assertive?
    Yes ___ No _✓_
        If yes, please explain _____

Have you reported the daily number of times you were assertive in a consistent manner?
    Yes _✓_ No ___
        If no, please explain _____

Did the social worker help you to become more assertive?
    Yes _✓_ No ___
        If no, how could the social worker have helped? _____

Source: A Primer on Single-Subject Design for Clinical Social Workers, by T. Tripodi, 1994, Washington, DC: NASW Press. Copyright © 1994 by National Association of Social Workers, Inc. Reprinted with permission of NASW Press.

FIGURE 9.6   *Follow-Up Questionnaire for Client: Excessive Coffee Consumption*

Have you been drinking more than two cups of coffee per day?
    Yes ✓ No ___
       If yes, please explain *I've been upset.*

Have other problems occurred for you since you finished your work with the social worker?
    Yes ✓ No ___
       If yes, please explain *My wife was diagnosed as having cancer, and she's very tired during the day.*

Do you understand why you should not drink more than two cups of coffee per day?
    Yes ✓ No ___
       If no, should the social worker try to help you understand?
          Yes ___ No ___

Have you made progress in drinking less coffee since your first contact with the social worker?
    Yes ✓ No ___
       Please explain *At first there was progress when I was able to go on excursions with my wife. But then I drank a lot more after I learned about her illness.*

Have you received professional help from other persons since you finished your work with the social worker?
    Yes ___ No ✓
       If yes, please explain _____

Have you felt a need to continue to work with the social worker on reducing your coffee consumption or on other problems?
    Yes ✓ No ___
       If yes, please explain *I need to control my coffee drinking when I get upset.*

Have any events occurred recently that facilitated your reduction in coffee consumption?
    Yes ___ No ✓
       If yes, please explain _____

Have any events occurred recently that prevented you from reducing your coffee consumption?
    Yes ✓ No ___
       If yes, please explain *My wife is ill, diagnosed as having cancer.*

Have you reported the daily number of cups of coffee consumed in a consistent manner?
    Yes ✓ No ___
       If no, please explain _____

Have you been able to substitute decaf for regular coffee?
    Yes ___ No ✓
       If no, please explain *It doesn't taste as good as regular coffee.*

Have you had frequent stomachaches in the past two weeks?
    Yes ✓ No ___

Have you had any other illnesses in the past two weeks?
    Yes ✓ No ___
       If yes, please explain *I've had headaches and feelings of nausea.*

Did the social worker help you to drink fewer cups of coffee?
    Yes ✓ No ___
       If no, how could the social worker have helped?
        She helped by having my wife and I go on excursions, but I wasn't prepared for illness. I need to be able to deal with my wife's illness as well as my coffee drinking.

Source: A Primer on Single-Subject Design for Clinical Social Workers, by T. Tripodi, 1994, Washington, DC: NASW Press. Copyright © 1994 by National Association of Social Workers, Inc. Reprinted with permission of NASW Press.

FIGURE 9.7 *Follow-Up Questionnaire for Jack: Reduction of Negative Remarks to His Father*

Have you made unwarranted negative remarks to your father?

    Yes _✓_ No ___

        If yes, please explain _I have made a few negative comments, but they were not as negative as before._

Have other problems occurred for you since you finished your individual work with the social worker?

    Yes ___ No _✓_

        If yes, please explain _____

Do you understand what leads you to make negative remarks to your father?

    Yes _✓_ No ___

        If yes, did you acquire this understanding in your work with the social worker?

        Yes _✓_ No ___

        If no, how should the social worker have helped you acquire this understanding? _____

Did you discuss with the social worker interpersonal situations in which you should reduce your negative remarks to your father?

    Yes _✓_ No ___

        If no, should you have discussed these situations with the social worker? _____

Have you made progress in reducing unwarranted negative remarks to your father since your first contact with the social worker?

    Yes _✓_ No ___

        Please explain _I've decreased the number of negative remarks to my father._

Have any events occurred recently that facilitated a reduction in unwarranted negative remarks to your father?

    Yes _✓_ No ___

        If yes, please explain _My father has spent more time with me in recreational activities._

Have any events occurred recently that prevented you from reducing unwarranted negative remarks to your father?

    Yes ___ No _✓_

        If yes, please explain _____

Did the social worker help you to reduce the daily number of negative remarks to your father?

    Yes _✓_ No ___

        If no, how could the social worker have helped? _____

Source: A Primer on Single-Subject Design for Clinical Social Workers, by T. Tripodi, 1994, Washington, DC: NASW Press. Copyright © 1994 by National Association of Social Workers, Inc. Reprinted with permission of NASW Press.

Conclusion

Two of the most widely used evaluation devices are described in this chapter. Needs assessments are often a requirement for the creation of new human services programs or for the expansion of social programs. They are used in a variety of ways in the human services but also in business and industry, especially when there is a new product to evaluate or a new service to provide.

Satisfaction studies are another device used in business and industry as well as the human services to assess customer or client reactions to a product or service provided.

Both needs assessments and satisfaction studies play significant roles in social work and human services programs. Whether a program will be offered and the nature of that program are strongly influenced by the results of a needs assessment. Similarly, nothing can pose a more serious problem for social work staff members than a report from a client or group of clients that they are dissatisfied with their services. However, it is also true that strong statements of satisfaction can be a positive factor in a social work career. In any case, social workers need to have careful understandings of both kinds of evaluations. They are long-term and immediate factors in social work careers.

Questions for Further Study

1. Describe three sources of data that can be useful in carrying out a needs assessment. Discuss the advantages and disadvantages of each.

2. The chapter suggests that those interviewed often need education and information before they can answer the questions of a needs assessment. Discuss at least two circumstances in which such education and information may be necessary and explain why they are necessary.

3. Most service-providing agencies are concerned about the degree of satisfaction of those they assist, whether they pay or not. Describe three reasons why agencies are concerned about client satisfaction.

4. Visit a restaurant and determine whether it provides a customer satisfaction instrument. If it does not, ask the manager why it does not use such an instrument with its customers. If it does, describe the instrument and discuss its strengths and weaknesses.

References

Balch, G. I., & Mertens, D. M. (1999, Spring–Summer). Focus group design and group dynamics: Lessons from deaf and hard of hearing participants. *The American Journal of Evaluation*, 265–277.

Gabor, P. A., Unrau, Y. A., & Grinnell, R. M., Jr. (1998). *Evaluation for social workers: A quality improvement approach for the social services* (2nd ed.). Boston: Allyn & Bacon.

Ginsberg, L. (1996, Winter). A personal experience in 1990s community organization: Back to the future. *Reflections*, 6–11.

Hammond, R. L. (1975, March/April). Establishing priorities for information and design specifications for evaluating community education programs. *Community Education Journal.*

Henerson, M. E., Morris, L. L., & Fitz-Gibbon, C. T. (1987). *How to measure attitudes.* Thousand Oaks, CA: Sage.

Krueger, R. A. (1994). *Focus groups: A practical guide for applied research* (2nd ed.). Newbury Park, CA: Sage.

Marlow, C. (1998). *Research methods for generalist social work.* Pacific Grove, CA: Brooks-Cole.

Rossi, P. H., Freeman, H. E., & Lipsey, M. W. (1999). *Evaluation: A systematic approach* (6th ed.). Thousand Oaks, CA: Sage.

Royse, D., & Thyer, B. A. (1996). *Program evaluation: An introduction* (2nd ed.). Chicago: Nelson-Hall.

Tripodi, T. (1994). *Single-subject design for clinical social workers.* Washington, DC: NASW Press.

Part IV

Research Methods and Evaluation Concepts

The final part of the text includes information about experimental methods in carrying out evaluations and some other current approaches to social work evaluation. It also includes examples of evaluations in the human services to help readers connect some of the more theoretical concepts with real experiences in evaluation. In some ways, this section applies many of the concepts discussed in the earlier chapters to the actual practice of evaluation in social work.

Three of the chapters, which discuss special topics in research were written by authors with expertise in their subject matter.

Chapter 10 covers the basics of research methodology, and it may be a review for those who have studied social research methods. Dr. Michelle Mohr Carney, a faculty member in the College of Social Work at the University of South Carolina, summarizes some of the basics and offers case examples. This material is offered in many evaluation texts as the major ways in which evaluations should be conducted—as one form of experimental methodology or another. Dr. Carney does not, of course, take the position that the methods in her chapter are the most desirable for evaluations but simply offers information on the basics of the approaches.

A supplement to Dr. Carney's content is Dr. Larry Nackerud's Chapter 13, which suggests that for many evaluations, classical experimental methods cannot be effectively applied. Dr. Nackerud, an associate professor at the University of Georgia School of Social Work, offers alternatives, some of which he and his colleagues used in the complicated evaluation of welfare reform in Georgia. The interview guide used in that evaluation is Appendix 2 of this text. He makes interesting and original points, most of which are new to the social work evaluation literature.

In Chapter 11, Dr. Abraham Wandersman, a psychologist at the University of South Carolina, discusses fundamentals of research, offers guidelines for some kinds of evaluation, and provides concrete examples of evaluation projects. Dr. Wandersman is the coeditor of a text on "empowerment evaluation," an idea that is particularly applicable to social work.

Chapter 12 focuses on the outcomes approach to evaluation and the use of indicators in program evaluation. Much of the content comes from the approach used by the United Way of America, which is currently highly important to many social agencies that use the approach in evaluating their work and in making requests to their local United Ways.

Chapter 14 is a summary of many program evaluations, based on excellent work by top evaluation organizations such as the Urban Institute and the Manpower Demonstration Research Corporation. It also provides some examples of Leon Ginsberg's experiences—not all of them happy—with evaluation in social work.

10

Experimental Research Designs in Evaluation

Michelle Mohr Carney

College of Social Work
University of South Carolina

Why program evaluations? The profession of social work certainly does not lend itself to easy evaluation. Subjects are living, breathing entities connected to seemingly endless systems of human organizations and communities. Yet, it is the fact that the subjects are humans that makes evaluation so vital to the profession. Clients deserve to get the best services available, and the only way to assure this is to evaluate the programs that are providing those services. If providing effective programs is not enough to provide motivation to conduct program evaluation, the changing funding scene should offer more incentive. Most funding agencies, including United Ways (as discussed in Chapter 12), require agencies to evaluate their programs and services. They want to be sure that the money they are spending supports quality programming.

Program evaluation should be viewed as a mechanism to not only evaluate services but also to identify problems in programming and to strengthen the program based upon the newfound knowledge. Program evaluation is not a one-time look at program effectiveness; it is an ongoing process of evaluation and feedback to the program to provide the strongest, most effective services to clients.

Evaluation in applied settings is challenging at best. It is tempting to utilize anecdotal accounts of program effectiveness rather than attempting to create a system of evaluation that is rigorous enough to show causation. However, strive for the strongest design possible and avoid saying "this program works," without any evidence to support that notion.

Program evaluation is a formal, systematic process of examining program effectiveness. Its aim is to gather information and to provide new knowledge about the program to change or strengthen the final product. This chapter builds on the research foundation students gain through introductory courses. It provides the information necessary for students to advance beyond knowledge of research methodology to real application of those methods in social work evaluation. Many of the terms used in this chapter will be familiar to students from their introductory research course. However, as a review, Table 10.1 (designed by the author) provides a summary of key terminology as defined by Rubin and Babbie (1997, pg. G1–G9).

TABLE 10.1 *Key Terminology*

Key Term	Definition
Control Group	In experimental research, a group of participants to whom no intervention is provided and who should resemble the treatment group in all other aspects. The comparison of the two groups upon conclusion of the evaluation points to the effectiveness of the intervention.
Dependent Variable	The variable that is assumed to depend on or be caused by another (called the independent) variable.
External Validity	Refers to the extent to which the findings of a study can be generalized to settings and populations beyond the study conditions.
Generalizability	The ability of a research finding to be inferred to other groups in addition to the group specifically observed.
Independent Variable	A variable whose values are presumed to cause an effect or to determine the dependent variable.
Internal Validity	The degree to which an effect observed in an experiment, or as the result of an intervention, was actually produced by the intervention and not due to other factors.
Interrater Reliability	The extent of consistency among different observers in their judgments, as reflected in the percentage of agreement or degree of correlation in their independent ratings.
Representativeness	That quality of a sample of having the same distribution of characteristics as the population from which it was selected. By implication, descriptions and explanations derived from an analysis of the sample may be assumed to represent similar ones in the population.
Validity	A descriptive term used of a measure that accurately reflects the concept that it is intended to measure.
Variables	Logical groupings of characteristics of persons or things.

Source: Adapted from *Research Methods for Social Work*, by A. Rubin and E. Babbie, 1997, Pacific Grove, CA: Brooks-Cole.

The Evaluation Continuum

A program is evaluated against its objectives. It is very important in program evaluation to have clear program goals and objectives before attempting to evaluate a program's effectiveness. Then one decides the type of information to be gained from the evaluation and chooses a research design that will reach that intended end.

One straightforward and excellent resource for designing program evaluations is Fitz-Gibbon and Morris (1987). In their book, they identify a whole range of designs (many of them mentioned in this chapter) and discuss the pros and cons of using each. They provide guidance on when to use which kind of design, which design is geared towards the program being evaluated, and the ways in which data are collected and available.

Evaluation research designs range from exploratory to control (experimental) along a continuum of increasingly more rigorous methodologies, as shown in Figure 10.1.

Exploratory Designs. Exploratory designs (also known as pre-experimental research designs) are the least rigorous and therefore do not provide conclusive data about program effectiveness. These designs are useful when the intention is to become familiar with a phenomenon or to gather preliminary information about the relationship between the intervention and the outcome. Evaluators often choose to conduct exploratory research to identify variables for further study. The information gained through exploration may then be used to develop a hypothesis and conduct further investigation. Exploratory designs fall to the left of the research continuum, at the least restrictive end. If the program outcomes appear to be positive, that change cannot be attributed to the intervention alone when an exploratory design is utilized. These designs have no elements of control and therefore do not address alternative explanations that may be influencing the outcome. Examples of exploratory designs include: the one-shot case study, the cross-sectional survey design, and the longitudinal case study design. These designs are discussed in detail later.

Descriptive Designs. Exploratory designs gather information about potential variables that can then be used in descriptive research. Descriptive designs (pre-experimental and quasi-experimental research designs) are useful when the intention of a study is to gain an accurate description of program activities. These

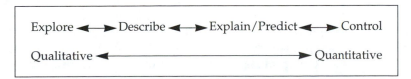

FIGURE 10.1 *The Evaluation Continuum*

designs can be used to gain a better understanding of variables as they naturally occur, without manipulation. Descriptive designs examine association or correlation between a program and its outcomes, but they do not control for the effects of alternative explanations. Examples of descriptive designs include: the one group pretest–posttest design, the static group comparison design, and the time series design. These designs are also discussed in detail later.

Explanatory Designs.   Explanatory designs are more rigorous than exploratory and descriptive designs. Whereas the two previously discussed designs seek understanding of a problem through exploring and describing potential factors, these designs enable the evaluator to identify problem causation and to infer the influence of the intervention on the alleviation of the problem. They do not offer the element of control found in experimental designs, but they are useful in investigating important relationships between variables. Explanatory designs are quite useful in program evaluation. The rigid demands of the experimental designs are absent, but the evaluator can make statements about the influence of the program on program participants or about the relationship between services received and changes in participant behavior. These designs seek to establish a causal relationship between the independent variable (the program intervention) and the dependent variable (the intended change in participant behavior). Alternative explanations are a concern with these designs and must be controlled for or ruled out.

Experimental Designs.   Experimental designs are the most rigorous of the research designs and offer high levels of control for threats to internal validity. They are explanatory designs, and therefore test hypotheses about the causal relationship between variables, but in experimental designs the evaluator is able to manipulate and isolate the independent variable or intervention. These types of designs are very difficult, but not impossible, to implement in real world settings. Because of their demanding requirements, they are often not chosen as designs in program evaluation. The essential components of experimental designs according to Rubin and Babbie (1997) are: "(1) randomly assigning individuals to experimental and control groups, (2) introducing the independent variable (which typically is a program or intervention method) to the experimental group while withholding it from the control group, and (3) comparing the amount of experimental and control group change on the dependent variable" (pp. 285–286). The following case example (Figure 10.2) illustrates an experimental design used in evaluating the effectiveness of a program designed to reduce juvenile recidivism.

The design used for the Figure 10.2 example was the pretest–posttest control group design. Figure 10.3 depicts the design of the study.

Experimental research designs are discussed in detail later. These designs fall to the extreme right of the research continuum (Figure 10.4), offering the most certainty with regard to causal statements about the relationship between the independent and dependent variables.

Case Example: An Evaluation of Wraparound Services

The problem of juvenile crime has received increasing attention in recent years. Compounding the growing crime problem is the high rate of recidivism among delinquent youths. What to do with these youths is emerging as a vital issue for the 1990s, and there is little agreement about what is the most effective action to follow.

From 1993 to 1996, a study was conducted to address the challenge of serving juvenile delinquent youths in the community by involving the family, community, school, church, and significant individuals in each youth's life. Exploring the use of wraparound services, this study sought to determine the program's impact on further juvenile court contacts and the level of subsequent offenses for juvenile offenders. Study participants were randomly selected from the population of youths who entered either of the two juvenile court sites and the Children's Services site. They were randomly assigned to either a treatment (intervention) or control (conventional services) group. The study investigated whether youths who received wraparound services were less likely to commit subsequent delinquent acts and whether offense levels were comparable to those who received conventional services. The number of prior offenses for one year before entry into the program was used as the first measure, and the total number of subsequent offenses upon concluding the program was used as the second measure. Families of both the treatment (intervention) and control (conventional services) groups were followed during an eighteen-month period.

FIGURE 10.2   *Case Example*

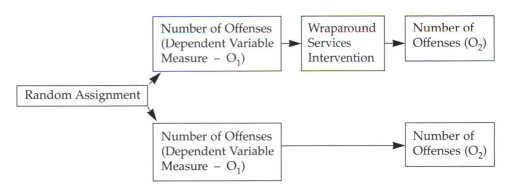

FIGURE 10.3   *Experimental Research Design Applied to Program Evaluation*

FIGURE 10.4   *The Research Continuum*

Elements of a Strong Program Evaluation

Ideally, a program evaluator would like to be able to say whether an intervention "caused" the improved condition of the program participants. However, as discussed previously, this requires a research design that offers control over extraneous variables and potential threats to internal validity. Both explanatory and experimental research designs provide enough rigors to investigate causal relationships. Whenever possible, designs that fall into these groupings should be employed. A strong program evaluation, as well as a strong research design, utilizes a large enough sample to ensure power and a control or comparison group gained either through random assignment or matched pairs.

When conducting program evaluations, the size of the sample is often determined for the researcher, whether it is the number of program participants or the number of individuals that the agency can serve with current staff. However, the size of the sample is related to the precision of findings and to the power of statistical analyses. Readers should refer to Cohen (1988) for a full discussion of effect size from the perspective of statistical power analysis.

Randomization and Matching

One of the essential components of experimental design research is that the treatment (intervention) group and the control (comparison) group be comparable. This is necessary to determine if an intervention produced results that would not have happened in its absence. The groups should be similar on basic demographic variables as well as on variables that are related to the evaluation study in order to detect change. One way to do this is through randomization, or random assignment of the participants to either a treatment or control group. Using the previous case example, randomization produced two youth groups that were similar with regard to the dependent variable number of offenses as well as a myriad of other important variables. The random assignment was used to give each youth who met the criteria of the program an equal probability of being assigned to either the intervention or comparison group. Although randomization produces equivalent groups, "randomization does not eliminate or help identify variability due to extraneous variables; it is designed to eliminate bias by spreading variability due to extraneous variables equally across groups being studied" (Pedhazur & Schmelkin, 1991, p. 222).

Creating comparable groups can also be accomplished through matching, or creating matched pairs. Using the case example, if the evaluator chose to match the groups based on the number of previous offenses, with offenses ranging from five to fifteen, what would be the process? First, they would rank the youths by their number of offenses. They would then randomly assign the youth with the highest number of offenses to either the intervention (treatment) or comparison (control) group. In this case, a toss of a coin suggested that the youth with the highest number of offenses be randomly assigned to the intervention group and the youth with the next highest level of offenses go to the comparison group. At the next step, the process was reversed. The youth with the next highest level of offense went to the comparison group, with the next youth being assigned to the intervention group. The process continued until all youths were assigned to a group. The average number of offenses should be comparable between the matched pairs. In fact, the difference was only 0.2. Figure 10.5 illustrates this process.

This process is more deliberate than randomization and can be done with or without random assignment; however, matching without random assignment does not control for all possible biases with regard to who gets assigned to which group (Rubin & Babbie, 1997). The objective in matching is similar to that of randomization: to achieve two groups that are equivalent. However, in matching it is the overall average description of the two groups that must be the same. Rubin and Babbie suggest that there are two important reasons to consider randomization over matching. First, the evaluator may not be aware of all the variables important to the study. Without knowledge of every relevant variable, the groups are likely to be unequal. Second, many statistical processes include a basic assumption that the subjects are randomly assigned. Choosing to match rather than randomly assign could create problems in the analysis.

Alternative Explanations

Alternative explanations are those things other than a program that may influence a participant's outcome. The study design chosen—pre-experimental, quasi-experimental, or experimental—largely determines the degree to which an evaluator can control for alternative explanations. Pre-experimental and quasi-experimental designs offer the least control over alternative explanations, making it difficult if not impossible for an evaluator to say with certainty that a change in a program participant's behavior was the direct result of the program or intervention. The possibility

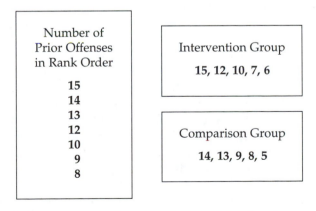

FIGURE 10.5 *Matching on Number of Prior Offenses*

of another influence exists. Experimental designs provide the most control over alternative explanations, but they are difficult to carry out in real world settings and are often costly. In controlling for alternative explanations or increasing internal validity, a more rigorous research design provides for more certainty that a program participant's outcomes are a result only of the program intervention.

Threats to Internal Validity

In any program evaluation, one goal of the evaluator is to determine the program's influence, or its ability to have an impact on program participants. In the previous example, an evaluator would hope to assert that those youths who received wraparound services would commit fewer subsequent crimes than those who received conventional court and children's services programming. In other words, the evaluator would want to be able to attribute the change in the program participants to the program intervention and not to something else. To offer this, the study must have a high degree of internal validity. When internal validity is high, control for alternative hypotheses is also high. A study with a high degree of internal validity allows a program evaluator to make stronger conclusions about the program intervention. The change in the participants can be attributed to the intervention and not to other potentially intervening variables such as age, gender, or previous criminal behavior. To attribute change in participant behavior to the program instead of other factors that could have a potential influence, internal validity threats must be considered. Figure 10.6 highlights those threats to internal validity that are generally acknowledged. Readers should refer to Campbell and Stanley (1963) for a detailed discussion of factors that jeopardize internal and external validity, as well as the basic logic behind the research designs discussed in this chapter.

History.   History's threat to internal validity refers to specific events that occur between the first and second measurements of program outcomes. In the juvenile crime case, the reduction in subsequent criminal behavior was used as a measure of program effectiveness. The desired outcome was that the type of program intervention employed—wraparound services—would reduce subsequent offenses for those youths who received the intervention. However, what if a new law were passed in the state in which the study was conducted that was designed to crack down on crime? In the past, a youth could have faced a judge an average of twelve times before being sentenced to a juvenile correction facility; now that number would drop to three. The new process would be widely publicized in hopes that youths would get the message that juvenile crime was not going to be tolerated. Could a reduction in subsequent criminal behavior be attributed solely to the program intervention? The type of study design utilized would, in part, determine that. Without a control or comparison group, it would be difficult to determine what influence this larger system change might have on the program participants. The change in the way youth crime was punished—not wraparound

Threats to Internal Validity

1. *History*—specific events that occur between the first and second measurement of the program outcomes.
2. *Maturation*—changes in program participants (physical, mental, status) that result from the passage of time and not the program intervention.
3. *Testing*—the effect of taking one test on the score of a second test (also known as sensitization).
4. *Instrumentation Error*—involves both the instrument used to measure and the observer doing the measurement. If an instrument has not been adequately standardized or tested for reliability, the information gained from the use of that instrument is invalid. If the evaluator uses a standardized, valid instrument but fails to implement strict data collection procedures or to adequately train data collectors, the information gained may be inconsistent or invalid.
5. *Statistical Regression*—the tendency of program participants at either extreme on the first measure to move toward an average score on the second measure.
6. *Selection Bias*—the program intervention and comparison groups are not known to be equal.
7. *Experimental Mortality*—when program participants drop out before the program is complete.
8. *Reactive Effects*—participants may be motivated to work hard at succeeding or they may feel demoralized by being studied. In either situation, the change in the participants' behavior could be attributed to reactive effects instead of the intervention program.
9. *Statistical Conclusion Validity*—problems with the data produce invalid conclusions.

FIGURE 10.6 *Threats to Internal Validity*

Source: Adapted from *Experimental and Quasi-Experimental Designs for Research,* by D. T. Campbell and J. C. Stanley, 1963, Boston: Houghton Mifflin.

services—might have impacted the youths' criminal behavior. This validity threat could be controlled through the use of a pretest–posttest control group design or by keeping a log book or journal to gather information about potential history threats.

Maturation.   Maturation as a threat to internal validity refers to changes in program participants (physical, mental, status) that result from the passage of time and not the program intervention. In the example, the program participants are ages 9 to 18. The evaluation took place over a three-year period. A youth who entered the program at 9 because of unruly behavior, might simply outgrow the behavior as he or she grew older. Maturation threats also include changes in individuals related to the evaluation itself, such as people who grow more or less bored, tired, anxious, or motivated. This threat can be controlled through the use of randomization with a control or comparison group—because any effects should be equally apparent in both groups—and by minimizing the length of the study.

Testing.   The use of a pretest may result in problems with internal validity. Program participants who take a pretest may score better on the posttest because they remember the questions asked or because they get a general sense of the content covered. Conversely, scores may decrease on the posttest for participants who are anxious about test taking or who get careless in answering because they rely on their knowledge of the pretest and do not carefully respond. This testing threat to internal validity is known as sensitization. This threat can be controlled in two ways: (1) by using randomization with the control group (because the threat should occur equally in the control or comparison group and the program intervention group) and (2) not giving a pretest.

Instrumentation Error.   Instrumentation threats to internal validity involve both the instrument used to measure and the observer doing the measurement. If an instrument has not been adequately standardized or tested for reliability, the information gained from the use of that instrument may be invalid. Similarly, if an instrument has been found valid to measure one behavior but it is being used to measure change in a different behavior, it cannot be considered valid for the new usage. For example, if an instrument has been found valid to measure aggression and the instrument is used—unchanged—to measure assertion, the result would be an invalid measure of assertion. Additionally, if a different measure were used at posttest than at pretest, any score change might be a function of the change in instrument and not attributed to the intervention. In all cases, the threat lies in the instrument itself.

If on the other hand, an evaluator uses a standardized, valid instrument but fails to implement strict data collection procedures or to adequately train data collectors, the information gained also may be inconsistent or invalid. With the juvenile delinquent youths, assume an observer is charged with using a valid instrument to measure subsequent delinquent behavior—with delinquent behavior defined as any contact with the juvenile court or children's services systems. If the observer starts out collecting information about all subsequent contacts but soon forms the opinion that those youth who are entering the system with unruly behaviors are not really acting criminally, a change will occur in the data collection system if the observer does not count those behaviors in the observations. The observer may also choose to observe differently based on gender or may become bored with the process of observing. The instrument is not flawed, but the collection of the information is incomplete. The instrumentation threat happens when the change in the program participants' behavior is attributed to a faulty instrument or flawed observation and not to the program intervention. This threat can be controlled by using instruments with high validity and reliability and by establishing intra- and interrater reliability, by determining that raters of equal ability rate phenomena in the same ways.

Parenthetically, a useful and condensed guide for analyzing data developed in an evaluation is Fitz-Gibbon and Morris's *How to Analyze Data* (1987). The book gives a simple and clear review of basic statistics and statistical tests. It also provides examples of a variety of graphic displays of data, which are often useful in evaluation reports. It is a useful alternative to some of the more complex books on statistical analysis and should be a helpful guide to an evaluator carrying out an evaluation program that involves quantitative information.

Statistical Regression.   Often in program evaluation there are participants who tend to be at the extreme ends of behaviors. From the earlier example, one piece of information used to gauge program effectiveness was prior offenses compared with subsequent offenses. The number of prior youth offenses ranged from one to thirty. Statistical regression refers to the tendency of program participants at either extreme to move toward an average number. Those with extremely high numbers of previous offenses would be likely to commit fewer subsequent offenses, naturally. They would move toward an average number of offenses. The same would be true for those at the other extreme. They would also move toward an average number of subsequent offenses. In each case, it is possible that the youth at either extreme regress to the mean, or move toward an average number of subsequent offenses. The measure then is not of program effectiveness but of statistical regression. This threat can be controlled by randomly assigning from the same pool of participants. For example, pool all of the extreme cases, then randomly assign participants to comparison and intervention groups. The threat should then occur equally in both groups.

Selection Bias.   When the program intervention and comparison groups are not equal, selection bias can occur. This often happens when random assignment is not possible or the evaluation is done with preexisting groups. Without random assignment, it is not possible to ascertain the comparability of the intervention and comparison groups. This threat can be controlled through randomization.

Experimental Mortality.   When program participants drop out before a program is complete, it is referred to as experimental mortality. This threat to internal validity is particularly a problem in programs that last a long time, or for programs that involve long follow-up periods. The loss of a few participants is not unusual, but it becomes a problem in an evaluation when many participants leave because it cannot be assumed that those who drop out were no different than those who remain in the program. There may be similarities between those who leave that would bias the evaluation. To control this threat, Campbell and Stanley (1963) suggest using all program intervention and comparison/control participants who complete both the pretest and posttest, including those in the program intervention group who failed to get the intervention. Another way to counter this threat is to locate participants who drop out and test them, too.

Reactive Effects.   Program participants' view of their involvement in the evaluation process can create a threat to internal validity. Participants may be motivated to work hard at succeeding, or they may feel demoralized by being studied. In either situation, the change in the participants' behavior could be attributed to reactive effects and not the intervention program. For example, the juvenile study included an eighteen-month follow-up period. Suppose that during this time the evaluator called only the program families every other month to conduct a brief interview. Those families called would often remark that they looked forward to the call even though the interview was always the same. The families that considered the interview call a "special" check-in might have done better. The change, however, might be attributed to their positive feelings about being involved in the study and their subsequent desire to work harder, rather than to the program intervention. Treating the intervention and comparison groups equally can control this threat. If a program intervention group is called for eighteen months, the comparison group should be called for that length of time.

Statistical Conclusion Validity.   Problems with data produce invalid conclusions. This happens when there is low statistical power, either because of a small sample size or an alpha result that is set too low, or the assumptions of the statistical test are violated. This threat to internal validity is a problem in program evaluations in which studies are constrained by the number of program participants and seek to make statements about the relationship between the intervention and the outcomes under circumstances that are not rigorous enough to prove causation.

It is also imperative that alternative hypotheses be eliminated in order to make valid statements about the relationship between a program intervention and the participants' outcomes. The best way to do that is to control them. One way is through the research design. Experimental designs eliminate alternative hypotheses through random selection and random assignment. Whenever possible, evaluators should choose the most rigorous design. If the design does not provide the level of control desired, evaluators should look for other ways to eliminate alternative hypotheses. Table 10.2 summarizes key threats to internal validity and suggested methods of control.

External Validity

External validity refers to the extent to which the findings of an evaluation study can be generalized to a larger population. Suppose that a study has been conducted utilizing an experimental research design. What is already known? The evaluator can conclude that a control group was used, that individuals were randomly assigned to either a treatment or control group, and that the independent variable was offered to only one group. It is also known that the study controlled

TABLE 10.2 *Methods to Increase Internal Validity*

Threats to Internal Validity	Method of Control
History	use pretest–posttest control group design or keep a logbook or journal to gather information about potential history threats
Maturation	randomize with a control or comparison group
Testing	randomize with the control group; do not give a pretest
Instrumentation Error	use instruments with high validity and reliability, and establish intra- and interrater reliability
Statistical Regression	randomly assign from the same pool of participants
Selection Bias	randomize
Experimental Mortality	use all program intervention and comparison/control participants who complete both the pretest and posttest, including those in the program intervention group who failed to get the intervention; seek participants who drop out
Reactive Effects	treat the intervention and comparison groups equally
Statistical Conclusion Validity	use large sample sizes and correct statistical tests

for all threats to internal validity, and therefore, causal inferences can be made. It should be noted that although internal validity is necessary for external validity, it is not, alone, sufficient. However, clearly, when threats to internal validity abound, it makes little sense to attempt to generalize the findings (Pedhazur & Schmelkin, 1991).

Suppose an evaluator finds that a particular intervention works to reduce juvenile delinquency for the youths in the intervention group when compared with those in the control group. Can it be assumed that the intervention will work for all juvenile delinquent youths? In other words, can the findings be generalized to the larger population? Generalizability depends on whether a study's population is representative of the larger population. The group of juvenile delinquent youths in the evaluation study would have to represent the general characteristics of all juvenile delinquent youths. The ability of a sample to represent a population determines the level of external validity, along with problems with interaction. "When it is concluded that treatments, or independent variables, interact with attributes of the people being studied or the settings, generalizations are limited accordingly" (Pedhazur & Schmelkin, 1991, p. 230).

Other potential threats to external validity include reactive effects (or the novelty of being included in a research study), pretest and posttest sensitization, and bias on behalf of those doing the evaluation. It is difficult, if not impossible, to compile an exhaustive list of threats to external validity. Many threats to external validity depend on the type of study being conducted and the type of generalizations the evaluator wishes to make (Pedhazur & Schmelkin, 1992). It should be noted though that "certain methods of case sampling and the use of large samples can increase the likelihood that a research finding will have good external validity" (Yegidis, Weinbach, & Morrison-Rodriguez, 1999, p. 121).

Research Designs

Research is the process of gathering information to create new knowledge. It is driven by a problem, and it involves an analysis of the relationship between the problem and its cause. It is the role of the evaluator to determine what kind of knowledge is being sought. Is there very little known about the particular problem and its causes? If so, the evaluator would be interested in conducting exploratory research. Is there a great deal known about the problem? Then the evaluator may seek to make causal inferences about variables and their relationships to the problem. In this case, the evaluator would want to conduct explanatory research. Evaluators must first decide what type of information or knowledge they wish to gain, then the research design becomes the map.

Research designs provide the process for carrying out an evaluation. As discussed previously, research designs range from exploratory to experimental, producing information that ranges from anecdotal to causal. The research design determines what threats to internal and external validity will arise, and in many cases what type of analysis can be conducted. Following is a discussion of the most widely utilized research designs. The standard notations in Figure 10.7, originally defined by Campbell and Stanley (1963), are used to discuss each design. The in-

---

X = Independent variable (presumed cause, intervention treatment)
O = Observation (Measurement, Test)
$_{1,2}$ etc. = Measurement sequencing that follows O
R = Random Assignment

A temporal sequence is indicated from left to right.
Symbols in the same row are for the same group.
When the symbols are stacked above one another, it implies simultaneous occurrence.

FIGURE 10.7   *Standard Notations for Discussing Research Designs*

dividual figures showing the various research designs are also adapted from the scholarship of Campbell and Stanley.

Threats to internal and external validity are a major concern when conducting research. They can significantly influence findings as well as generalizability. For pre-experimental and quasi-experimental designs, internal validity is low and threats to internal validity are high. Experimental designs provide more control over internal validity threats, but few designs control for all threats. Table 10.3 summarizes each design and its corresponding threats to internal validity. The reader should consult Campbell and Stanley (1963) for a full discussion of these threats.

Pre-Experimental Designs

These designs provide very little control and are plagued by multiple threats to internal validity. These designs cannot provide the evaluator with relationship or causal information, but they are very useful for gathering information to be used for further investigation.

One-Shot Case Study.   The one-shot case study is the most simplistic research design (Figure 10.8). There is an intervention (X), followed by a measurement (O) for one group. There is no information about the group before the intervention and no other group against which to compare those who received the intervention. For example, assume an evaluator is interested in increasing teens' knowledge about pregnancy prevention through a series of afterschool programs. At the end of the programming, the evaluator gives each teen present a questionnaire to measure knowledge about pregnancy prevention. The evaluator will be able to make some statements about the group's knowledge of prevention techniques, but it will not be clear whether the teens already possessed the knowledge or learned it from the program. These designs, although simple, offer little more than general information.

Cross-Sectional Survey Design.   The cross-sectional survey design (Figure 10.9) is unique because it does not have an independent variable or intervention (X). It is very exploratory in nature, used primarily to gain information about a specific topic or problem area. This design is widely used in needs assessments and to survey groups of individuals about a particular issue. For example, if the director of social work field work in an educational institution were interested in determining students' needs with regard to their field experience, this design would be useful to gain that information on a large scale. The director would create a brief questionnaire and administer it to all of the social work students in the field. The responses to the questionnaire would be the single point of measurement.

Longitudinal Case Study Design.   The longitudinal case study design (Figure 10.10) is the one-group posttest-only design with repeated posttest measures. Participants receive an intervention (X) and are then measured repeatedly ($O_1, O_2,$

TABLE 10.3   *Design Threats to Internal Validity*

Research Design	Internal Threat
Pre-Experimental Designs	
One-Shot Case Study X O	History, Maturation, Selection, Mortality
One-Group Pretest–Posttest Design O_1 X O_2	History, Maturation, Testing, Instrumentation, Statistical Regression
Static Group Comparison X O_1 O_1	Selection, Mortality
Cross-Sectional Survey Design O	History, Maturation, Selection, Mortality
Longitudinal Case Study Design X O_1 O_2 O_3	History, Maturation, Selection, Mortality
Quasi-Experimental Designs	
Nonequivalent Control Group Design O_1 X O_2 O_1 O_2	Statistical Regression
Time Series Design O_1 O_2 O_3 O_4 X O_5 O_6 O_7 O_8	History, Instrumentation
Experimental Designs	
Pretest–Posttest Control Group R O_1 X O_2 O_1 O_2	Controls for all threats
Solomon Four-Group Design R O_1 X O_2 R O_1 O_2 R X O_2 R O_2	Controls for all threats
Posttest-Only Control Group Design R X O_1 R O_1	Controls for all threats

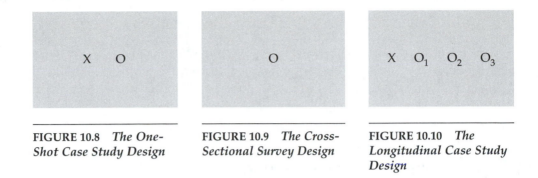

FIGURE 10.8 *The One-Shot Case Study Design*

FIGURE 10.9 *The Cross-Sectional Survey Design*

FIGURE 10.10 *The Longitudinal Case Study Design*

O_3). Using a variation of the case example, suppose a group of juvenile delinquent youths receive wraparound services (X), and the evaluator is interested in whether subsequent criminal behavior will escalate with increasing time between the intervention and the measurement period. The evaluator may count subsequent offenses at six months (O_1), twelve months (O_2), and eighteen months (O_3) to measure additional criminal behavior over a longer period of time. The information gained could be helpful when identifying potential programming for delinquent youths.

One-Group Pretest–Posttest Design. The one-group pretest–posttest design (Figure 10.11) can be used to determine the influence of an intervention or independent variable on the dependent variable for one group. This design utilizes a measurement before the intervention and a measurement after the intervention. There is no control or comparison group, and, therefore, no control for alternative explanations. Any change between measures cannot be attributed to the intervention alone. Suppose a social worker wants to increase pregnancy prevention knowledge among high school ninth-grade students. To do this, the students might begin a series of afterschool sessions that follow a prevention curriculum. The social worker collects information about the participants' level of knowledge with a pretest before beginning the sessions. At the conclusion of the sessions, the social worker gives a posttest and concludes that the participants' knowledge has increased significantly. Can the social worker assume that it was the afterschool sessions that increased the participants' knowledge? Not with this research design, because there are no controls for alternative explanations. Pregnancy prevention might have been the topic in health class that semester, or there might have been some other source from which participants gained their information.

Static Group Comparison. The static group comparison design (Figure 10.12) is similar to the posttest-only design with the addition of a comparison group. The groups are not randomly assigned, and therefore cannot be considered equal, but an evaluator can identify a group that is comparable to the study group on basic

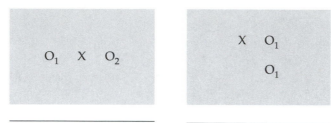

FIGURE 10.11   *The One-Group Pretest–Posttest Design*

FIGURE 10.12   *The Static Group Comparison Design*

demographic variables and other variables important to the evaluation. For example, take again the evaluator who is interested in increasing teens' knowledge about pregnancy prevention through a series of afterschool programs. In the posttest-only design, after concluding the sessions the evaluator gives each teen present a questionnaire to measure knowledge about pregnancy prevention. The evaluator is able to make some statements about the group's knowledge of prevention techniques, but it is not certain if the teens already possessed the knowledge or if they learned it from the program. With the addition of a comparison group, which is not from the same population and is not necessarily comparable with the intervention group, the evaluator will be able to compare the program participants' level of knowledge with similar students. This comparison provides the evaluator with additional information, but this design still lacks internal validity. There is no evidence that the groups are equivalent, and there is little control for alternative explanations of the results of the experiment.

Quasi-Experimental Designs

Quasi-experimental designs are somewhat stronger designs than pre-experimental designs, but they still suffer shortcomings. Campbell and Stanley (1963) suggest that these designs should only be used when the use of a more rigid design is not possible. This caution stems from the fact that quasi-experimental designs do not employ random assignment; therefore, the conclusions gained from their use and recommendations should be stated appropriately. However, in program evaluation it is often difficult, if not impossible, to achieve random assignment, and it can be inappropriate or unethical to withhold treatment from clients. Rather than avoiding evaluation, programs should use a quasi-experimental research design. These designs have less internal validity, but they "still provide a moderate amount of support for causal inferences" (Rubin & Babbie, 1997, p. 292).

Nonequivalent Control Group Design.   The nonequivalent control group design (Figure 10.13) elaborates on the one-group pretest–posttest design with the

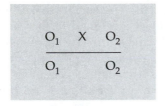

FIGURE 10.13 *The Nonequivalent Control Group Design*

addition of a comparison group. An initial measurement is taken for both groups, one group receives an intervention, and a second measurement is obtained for both groups. Using the pregnancy prevention program, an evaluator would be able to measure knowledge of prevention techniques before and after the intervention for the program group and compare those findings to a group of similar students who did not receive the prevention program. The same problems with a comparison exist for this design as for the static group comparison design. The difference here is that with the information gained at the pretest it may be possible to ascertain the comparability of the two groups. If the two groups are found to be equivalent, then this design controls most threats to internal validity.

Time Series Design. In the time series design (Figure 10.14), there is one group that receives multiple measurements before the intervention (treatment) and multiple measurements after the intervention. This design is useful for establishing a pattern of behavior via multiple measurements before the intervention. By establishing a pattern of behavior over time, any change after the intervention can be compared with the previous behavior. Suppose a social worker is working with children to increase the amount of time they remain focused during a class session. The social worker can choose to count the number of times

$$O_1 \quad O_2 \quad O_3 \quad O_4 \quad X \quad O_5 \quad O_6 \quad O_7 \quad O_8$$

FIGURE 10.14 *The Time Series Design*

the children get up as a measure of losing focus. The social worker will record this number for one week. Then an intervention designed to increase the children's ability to focus on classroom activities will be introduced. When the social worker determines that the intervention has been sufficiently implemented, the worker will begin a series of post-intervention measures. Time series designs allow for comparisons between the average pretest measure and the average posttest measure, as well as between post measures, to ascertain change over time (Yegidis et al., 1999).

This method is comparable to single-subject designs for evaluating one's own practice, as discussed in Chapter 8.

True Experimental Designs

True experimental designs fall to the extreme right of the evaluation continuum, providing the strongest design with high levels of control for internal validity. The essential components of experimental designs, according to Rubin and Babbie (1997), as mentioned earlier, include random assignment to experimental and control groups; introducing the independent variable, a program or intervention method to the experimental group while withholding it from the control group; and comparing the amount of change on the dependent variable.

Pretest–Posttest Control Group.   This design is often referred to as the classical experimental design (Figure 10.15). Individuals are randomly assigned to either an intervention (treatment) or control group. One group receives the intervention, and the other group receives no treatment. Randomization ensures comparability between the two groups. A first measure of the dependent variable is taken for each group before the implementation of the intervention to one of the groups. A second measure is then obtained for both groups. This design is used most frequently for assessing change from the first measurement to the second measurement as a result of the intervention. Suppose that all ninth-grade students in the pregnancy example are pooled together and then randomly assigned to either a group that receives the pregnancy prevention curriculum or to a control group. The evaluator has pretest and posttest information for all ninth graders and

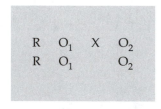

FIGURE 10.15   *The Pretest–Posttest Control Group*

can, therefore, compare the change in knowledge from the pretest to the posttest and across groups. The evaluator is able to ascertain whether the afterschool sessions have increased students' knowledge by comparing the measurement information gained from the two groups. Although this design has generally strong internal validity, the testing threat poses a concern.

Solomon Four-Group Design.   The Solomon four-group design (Figure 10.16) combines the pretest–posttest control group design and the posttest-only control group design. There are four randomly assigned groups: two intervention (treatment) and two control groups. Using the pregnancy prevention program, this design would produce the same scenario as in the classical experimental design, but instead of two groups of youths there would be four. Only two groups would receive the pretest. Comparisons could then be made between pretests and posttests, and groups who did and did not receive the pretest. Changes in prevention-technique knowledge in the intervention groups could be attributed to the afterschool sessions if the findings were similar for both the treatment groups (with and without pretest). This design eliminates the testing threat to internal validity present in the previous design, and although it requires twice as many participants to carry out, it controls for all threats to internal validity.

Posttest-Only Control Group Design.   In this design (Figure 10.17), one group receives the intervention, and the other group receives no intervention. The group that receives no services serves as the control group against which the intervention group will be compared to determined intervention benefit. Suppose that all of the ninth-grade students are pooled and randomly assigned to either an intervention or a control group. Instead of gathering a pretest measure, the intervention is offered to one group, and upon conclusion, both groups are tested (measured). Knowledge of prevention techniques can be compared across groups. Because the groups are randomly assigned, they can be considered equivalent. Any influence from extraneous variables should be seen equally in both groups. Changes in prevention-technique knowledge in the intervention group can be attributed to the afterschool sessions. The major threats to internal validity are controlled by the inclusion of a control group.

$$
\begin{array}{llll}
R & O_1 & X & O_2\text{—Treatment Group} \\
R & O_1 &   & O_2\text{—Control Group} \\
R &   & X & O_2\text{—Treatment Group} \\
R &   &   & O_2\text{—Control Group}
\end{array}
$$

FIGURE 10.16 *The Solomon Four-Group Design*

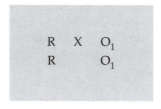

FIGURE 10.17 *The Posttest-Only Control Group Design*

Conclusion

This chapter begins with a discussion of evaluation research along a continuum that ranges from exploratory to experimental. It was suggested that, whenever possible, the most rigorous research be conducted. The process of obtaining equivalent groups has been discussed through randomization and matched pairs, as well as the influences of alternative explanations and how to control them. The chapter includes a table and figure highlighting threats to internal validity and suggested methods for controlling those threats. The most widely utilized research designs are discussed along the research continuum, from pre-experimental to experimental. Potential threats associated with each design are also discussed.

Questions for Further Study

1. Describe a situation, other than the text examples, in which a true experimental design might be useful in evaluating a program.

2. What does the author mean by "maturation" as a threat to the internal validity of a study?

3. In what ways, in your opinion, does experimental research differ from accreditation and licensing as a means for evaluating social programs?

4. How might the "time series" design mentioned in this chapter be similar to and different than the use of the same design in Chapter 8, Single-Subject Designs?

References

Campbell, D. T., & Stanley, J. C. (1963). *Experimental and quasi-experimental designs for research.* Boston: Houghton Mifflin.

Cohen, J. (1988). *Statistical power analysis for the behavioral sciences* (2nd ed.). Hillsdale, NJ: Erlbaum.

Fitz-Gibbon, C. T., & Morris, L. L. (1987). *How to design a program evaluation.* Thousand Oaks, CA: Sage.

Morris, L. L., Fitz-Gibbon, C. T., & Freeman, M. E. (1987). *How to communicate evaulation findings.* Newbury Park, CA: Sage.

Pedhazur, E. J., & Schmelkin, L. (1991). *Measurement, design, and data analysis: An integrated approach.* Hillsdale, NJ: Erlbaum.

Rubin, A., & Babbie, E. (1997). *Research methods for social work* (3rd ed.). Pacific Grove, CA: Brooks-Cole.

Yegidis, B., Weinbach, R., & Morrison-Rodriquez, B. (1999). *Research methods for social workers.* Boston: Allyn & Bacon.

11

Program Development, Evaluation, and Accountability

Abraham Wandersman
University of South Carolina

It Sounded Like a Good Idea,
But Is It Really Working?

Each year billions of dollars in tax money, charitable contributions, and philanthropic foundation dollars are spent to do good things in communities. Is that money making a difference? Picture oneself as a board member of a foundation who has to make funding decisions about community programs. The board gets many more requests for funding than they could possibly fund. It makes sense to ask grantees, "How can we know if your program, supported by our grant money, actually accomplishes its goals?"

Schorr (1997) describes several types of answers to this question often given by nonprofit organizations and government agencies.

Trust and Values. "Trust us. What we do is so valuable, so complex, so hard to document, so hard to judge, and we are so well intentioned that the public should support us without demanding evidence of effectiveness. Don't let the bean coun-

Source: This chapter is adapted from a chapter in J. H. Dalton, M. J. Elias, J. A. Linney, and A. Wandersman, 2000, *Community Psychology: Linking Individuals and Communities,* 1st edition, by Wadsworth Publishing Company. Copyright © 2000 by Wadsworth Publishing Company. Reprinted with permission of Wadsworth, a division of Thomson Learning. Fax 800-730-2215.

ters who know the cost of everything and the value of nothing obstruct our valiant efforts to get the world's work done" (Schorr, 1997, p. 116).

Potential problem with this answer: We don't know the process of how the program works, and we don't know whether there are any results.

Process and Outputs.   "Our agency sees 200 eligible clients yearly in the 20 parent education programs we offer with our two licensed staff who are funded by your grant." Probably the most typical answer, with detailed documentation of programs or services provided and resources expended.

Potential problem: In the past, parent education classes have been funded in the optimistic expectation that they would somehow reduce the incidence of child abuse. However, a few classroom sessions have never been shown to change parenting practices among parents at greatest risk of child abuse (Schorr, 1997, pp. 119–120). Similarly hopeful but undocumented expectations underlie many community programs.

Results-Based Accountability.   Using program evaluation, we can show that a specific program made a difference and achieved its intended effects, as desired by its stakeholders. We can also modify it to become even more effective.

Potential problems: Agency staff often are not trained to do evaluation. Also, what happens if the evaluation shows that the program does not have the intended results?

Government, nonprofit and private sectors are being challenged to show results (e.g., U.S. General Accounting Office, 1990; United Way of America, 1996). At first, this can be a frightening prospect. Here are some common complaints and fears about program evaluation (compiled by the Northwest Regional Educational Laboratory, 1999):

> Evaluation can create anxiety among program staff.
>
> Staff may be unsure how to conduct evaluation.
>
> Evaluation can interfere with program activities, or compete with services for scarce resources.
>
> Evaluation results can be misused and misinterpreted, especially by program opponents.

Yet program evaluation does not have to be frightening. Results-based accountability requires us to understand program evaluation and how programs can be improved to achieve their goals. When done well, it can strengthen a program's quality as well as its ability to resist critics.

What Are the Key Points of This Chapter?

This chapter addresses program accountability by describing both program evaluation and program development. Program evaluation refers to the collection of evidence to judge the effectiveness of community programs or other community interventions: deciding whether their "good ideas really work." Program development refers to the planning and implementing of a program: determining its purposes and setting goals, carrying out the program, improving it for the future. The major theme is that well-designed, user-friendly evaluation generates feedback and ideas for promoting high-quality program development, through continuous program improvement.

To do this, the chapter first describes the logic of program evaluation and the importance of program theory. Next it describes a four-step model for evaluating community programs (the *Prevention Plus III* approach) that involves identifying program goals and outcomes, evaluating program process, and evaluating attainment of desired program outcomes and wider impacts. The author applies this perspective to community programs, especially mentoring programs that bring together adult mentors and students, and emphasizes how useful evaluation can be for continuous feedback and improvement of programs.

Evaluation feedback for modifying an existing program can be extended to address the planning of a new program as well. That is the approach of *Comprehensive Quality Programming*, which uses nine accountability questions and corresponding strategies to incorporate a continuous improvement approach into all phases of program development. The author applies this approach to two mentoring programs, one existing and one new, and concludes by discussing how program development and evaluation can be intertwined.

The Logic of Program Evaluation

Project D.A.R.E. (Drug Abuse Resistance Education) has been the most popular school-based drug-use prevention program in the United States, but there is limited evidence of its effectiveness. For instance, results from a longitudinal evaluation of the program in 36 schools in Illinois provide only limited evidence for D.A.R.E.'s impact on student's drug use immediately following the intervention, and no evidence of impact on drug use one or two years after receiving D.A.R.E. instruction. In addition, D.A.R.E. programs had only limited positive effects on psychological variables (e.g., self-esteem) and no effect on social skills variables (e.g., peer pressure resistance skills) (Enett et al., 1994).

How can one explain this lack of measurable outcomes in a popular intervention? Unfortunately, the cited study focused on outcomes for students who received D.A.R.E. and a comparison group which did not. Due to that outcome focus, the study was not able to explain why the expected outcomes did not occur. There are at least two reasons why programs don't work: theory failure and implementation failure. *Theory failure* concerns program theory: the rationale for why a particular intervention is considered appropriate for a particular problem with a specific target population. Program theory also helps choose appropriate measurements or methods to study the effects of the program. *Implementation failure* concerns quality of program implementation. Suppose there is an excellent program that has been demonstrated elsewhere to work with the target population, but the implementation in one location may be weak due to a lack of resources, inexperienced personnel, insufficient training, or other reasons.

Since the 1960s, the field of program evaluation has developed concepts and methods for examining program theory and implementation based on the methods of the social sciences (see Patton, 1997; Rossi, Freeman, & Lipsey, 1999; Worthen, Sanders, & Fitzpatrick, 1997). Theory and implementation are often studied using process and outcome evaluations. This chapter uses many of the basic concepts of the program evaluation field. However, it relies heavily on approaches which make program evaluation user-friendly in order to make it accessible to a wider audience.

Professional evaluators are trained to think causally. They recognize that an intervention or prevention activity is based on an underlying program theory or model of the causal factors contributing to the problem to be prevented. This model may be clearly stated by the prevention program's developers, or the program may only be based on implicit assumptions. Effects are not likely to occur if:

The underlying assumptions of program theory are incorrect,

The program, even if implemented well, doesn't affect the variables specified by program theory, or

The activity or program is not implemented adequately.

For social scientists, this type of thinking becomes so automatic that it is easy to forget it is not universal. Agency staff often need a "critical friend" to help them identify their underlying assumptions about their program theory, goals, and implementation.

For instance, a common community prevention activity is sponsoring a Red Ribbon Awareness Campaign. A local group wants to effect a reduction in alcohol, tobacco, and other drug use by mobilizing citizens to display red ribbons. Why would wearing a red ribbon lead to reductions in such use? For example, the logic may be that a red ribbon stimulates awareness of the hazards of alcohol use, which then either reduces one's own consumption of alcohol or at least stimulates asking a sober friend to drive. Questioning the connections between the display of red ribbons and the ultimate outcome of reduction of drunk driving requires critical thinking about cause and effect. It is important for school and community practitioners to use causal thinking and, as much as possible, to develop a causal model for a community program. That model then can indicate questions for evaluation of program process and outcome, which will help demonstrate program effectiveness.

The United Way, foundations, and other agencies have adopted and promoted the use of logic models for assessment (e.g., United Way of America, 1996; also see Chapter 12). The logic model is also used to help assess several grant programs of the U.S. Federal Center for Substance Abuse Prevention. The principal purpose of a logic model is to show, on one piece of paper: the logical connections between the conditions that contribute to the need for a program in a community, the activities aimed at addressing these conditions, and the outcomes and impacts expected to result from the activities (Julian, Jones, & Dey, 1995; McEwan & Bigelow, 1997).

The logic model is a graphic representation of the program. Figure 11.1 illustrates this format. Its top row consists of four circles, representing program conditions, activities, outcomes, and impacts. For a specific program, the logic model would have multiple examples in each circle, representing multiple conditions, activities, outcomes, and impacts. The circles are linked together with lines that show the expected logical relationships among them, based on the program theory. These relationships among circles also show the sequence of intended events that occur as a result of program activities.

In the first circle, conditions include risk processes, community problems, or organizational difficulties that the program seeks to address. The second circle includes the activities that address each condition; one or more activities can aim at solving each of the conditions. The third circle contains the immediate outcomes that result from the activity (e.g., changes in knowledge or attitudes of program participants, or changes in an organization or community) and intermediate outcomes (e.g., individual behavioral changes, or changes in regulations, legislation, or relationships among community organizations). The fourth circle concerns the eventual impacts of the program on the community at large. For example, impacts in alcohol, tobacco, and other drugs have to do with lowering alcohol and other drug abuse in the community and related consequences of lowered substance use, such as lower crime and better health.

Row 2 of Figure 11.1 illustrates the steps in program development and their relationships to the logic model. A program developer assesses the need for a program (often with community surveys or interviews), plans a program to address

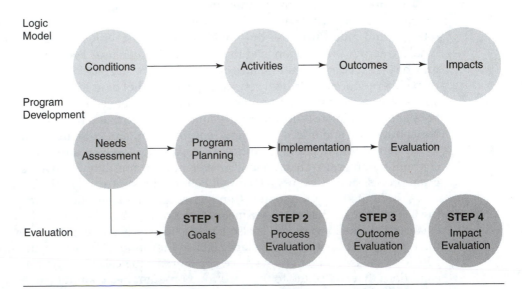

FIGURE 11.1 *Four-Step Program Evaluation*

the need, implements the program, and evaluates whether the program has been successful. Row 3 of Figure 11.1 shows how program evaluation relates to the logic model and to program development. That is the focus of the next section.

A Four-Step Model of Program Evaluation

Linney and Wandersman (1991) sought to design materials that would stimulate analytical thinking about the ways in which prevention programs might affect outcomes, realistic thinking about the effect of any one preventive effort, and careful planning for implementation. Their volume, *Prevention Plus III*, was developed to teach people at the local level the basics about evaluation and how to conduct elementary evaluations of their own programs. The book boils program evaluation down to four basic steps (goals and desired outcomes, process evaluation, outcome evaluation, and impact evaluation) that relate to the logic model (see Figure 11.1, Row 3).

Step 1: Identifying Goals and Desired Outcomes

Starting with goals sets the project's sights. Goals represent what a project is striving for (e.g., children who have positive social relationships and are well educated so that they will be productive members of society). Goals tend to be ambitious and set a framework for outcomes. Outcomes are more specific and represent what the project is accountable for. Goals can be general; outcomes must be specific and measurable (Schorr, 1997).

If a community program has prevention/promotion aims, goals and outcomes concern problems to be prevented or competencies and health outcomes to be promoted. Alternatively, if a community initiative addresses a wider community issue or problem, the changes it seeks to create indicate its goals and outcomes.

In Step 1, program developers describe:

The primary goals of the program. (e.g., increasing parent involvement in the schools or reducing drug use).

Target group(s) of the program. Who does it try to reach (e.g., teachers, children of a specific age, parents, general public)? Target groups can be described by demographic characteristics (e.g., age, sex, race, socioeconomic status), developmental transitions (e.g., entering middle school, divorce, bereavement), risk processes (e.g., low grades, multiple conduct incidents in school), locality, or other criteria.

What outcomes are desired? Examples include increases in attitudes rejecting smoking or decreases in school absences. Well-formulated outcomes are: clearly defined and specific, realistic and attainable, and measurable.

Figure 11.2 illustrates the four-step evaluation method with worksheets adapted from *Prevention Plus III* (Linney & Wandersman, 1991). Step 1 in that figure

FIGURE 11.2   *Selecting Goals and Outcomes*

Step 1: Identify Goals and Desired Outcomes

    A. Make a list of the primary goals of the program.
        Ask yourself: "What were we trying to accomplish?"
        1.
        2.
        3.

    B. What groups did you want to involve?
        Ask yourself: "Whom were we trying to reach?"
        For each group, how many persons did you want to involve?
        1.
        2.
        3.

    C. What outcomes did you desire?
        Ask yourself: "As a result of this program, how would we like participants to
        change? What would they learn? What attitudes, feelings or behaviors would
        be different?"
        1.
        2.
        3.

Step 2: Process Evaluation

    A. What activities were implemented?
        Ask yourself: "What did we actually do to implement this program?" Form a
        chronology of events.

        Date   *Description of Activity*

        For each activity above, indicate the following:

Activity length (hrs.)	*Percentage of time goal*	*Activity attendance*	*Percentage of attendance goal*

        Total duration of all activities (in hours) =
        Total attendance at all activities =
        Other services delivered:_____

    B. What can you learn from this experience?
        What topics or activities were planned but not delivered? What happened that
        these were not accomplished?

FIGURE 11.2   *Continued*

Activity	*Problem*

Who was missing that you had hoped to have participate in the program?

What explanations can you give for any discrepancy between the planned and actual participation?

What feedback can be used to improve the program in the future?

Step 3: Outcome Evaluation

Desired Outcome	*Measure*
1.	1.
2.	2.
3.	3.

Step 4: Impact Evaluation

Desired Impact	*Measure*
1.	1.
2.	2.
3.	3.

Source: Adapted from *Prevention Plus III: Assessing Alcohol and Other Drug Prevention Programs at the School and Community Levels: A Four-Step Guide to Useful Program Assessment,* by J. A. Linney and A. Wandersman, 1991, Rockville, MD: U.S. Department of Health and Human Services, Office of Substance Abuse Prevention.

shows the questions that program planners need to ask themselves to specify program goals, target groups, and desired outcomes.

Step 2: Process Evaluation

In Step 2, the activities designed to reach the desired outcome are described. They answer the question, "What did the program actually do?"

Purposes of Process Evaluation.   Process evaluation has several purposes. First, monitoring program activities helps organize program efforts. It helps ensure that all parts of the program are conducted as planned. It also helps the program use resources where they are needed; for example, not spending most of its money on only one activity or target group. Further, it provides information to help manage the program and modify activities, leading to midcourse corrections that enhance the project's outcomes.

Second, information in a process evaluation provides accountability that the program is conducting the activities it promised to do. This can be furnished to administration, funding sources, boards of directors, or other stakeholders.

Third, after a later evaluation of outcomes and impacts, the process evaluation can provide information about why the program worked or did not work. By providing information on what was done and who was reached, program planners can identify reasons for achieving outcomes or not achieving them. Process evaluation information also can provide information for future improvements and for sharing practical tips with others planning similar programs.

Fourth, process evaluation can help decide whether or not one is ready to assess the effects of the program. For example, if a program has been in existence for only a short time and has implemented only the first activity of a seven-activity program, then it is premature to assess program outcomes.

Fifth, sometimes conditions change and what was planned isn't what actually happens. Process evaluation helps keep track of such changes. Answering process evaluation questions before, during, and after the planned activities documents what actually happened.

Conducting a Process Evaluation.   A process evaluation centers on two related questions: What were the intended and actual activities of the program? After it was implemented, what did program planners and staff learn from their experiences?

Regarding activities, process evaluation asks: *Who* was supposed to do *what* with *whom* and *when* was it to be done? (See Figure 11.2.)

Who refers to the staff who deliver the services. How many staff? What kinds of qualifications and training do they need?

What refers to what the staff are asked to do (e.g., hold classes, show movies, model behavior).

Whom refers to the target groups for each activity.

When refers to the time and setting of the activity (e.g., during school assemblies, after school).

The more clearly the questions are answered, the more useful the process evaluation will be. (See Figure 11.2, Step 2 for specific questions.) All of the information gathered in the process evaluation can be used to improve (or discard) the activity in the future (see Part B of Step 2, Figure 11.2).

Step 3: Outcome Evaluation

Outcome evaluation assesses the immediate effects of a program. The "bottom line" of program evaluation concerns these immediate effects (Figure 11.2, Step 3) and ultimate program impacts (Step 4). (Note that the field of program evaluation uses the terms outcomes and impacts as they are described in this chapter. The field of public health reverses these terms and uses the term outcomes to mean long-term indicators and impacts to mean short-term indicators.)

Outcome evaluation as the term is used in program evaluation and community psychology is concerned with measuring the short-term or immediate effects of a program on its participants or recipients. It attempts to determine the direct effects of the program, such as the degree to which a drug-use prevention program increased knowledge of drugs and the perceived risk of using drugs.

Basically, Step 3 looks at the desired outcomes defined in Step 1 and seeks evidence regarding the extent to which those outcomes were achieved (see Figure 11.2, Step 3). Evidence of program outcomes for a drug-abuse prevention program could include increased awareness of drug dangers or improved scores on a measure of social skills for resisting pressure to use drugs. Planning how to collect this data or evidence is best begun along with planning program goals and outcomes.

Outcome Measures. These should be closely linked to goals, but more specific. There are several potential ways to measure outcomes.

Self-report questionnaires are commonly used to measure outcomes. They must be chosen with care; instrument reliability and validity should be considered. The test–retest reliability of a measure is a particular concern if it is to be given before and after an intervention. Construct validity, the extent to which a questionnaire measures what it claims to measure, also is an important concern. Does a particular measure of problem-solving skills actually measure those skills? Predictive validity is also a concern. Does a measure of attitudes about drug use predict actual drug use one year later? Program developers and evaluators need to consider these questions in light of their program theory. What measures of what constructs will best reflect the true outcomes of the program? A measure of self-esteem useful for adults may not work well for adolescents, or for drug-related outcomes.

Self-report questionnaires are not the only means of collecting outcome data. For some purposes, it is useful to obtain information from other sources about a participant, such as ratings of a child by a parent or ratings of students by teachers. Persons completing questionnaires who are not reporting on themselves are termed *key informants*. Behavior observation ratings may be useful, although they are often cumbersome to collect.

Step 4: Impact Evaluation

Impact evaluation is concerned with the ultimate effects desired by a program. In alcohol and other drug prevention programs, the ultimate effects might include: reduction in overall drug use (prevalence), reduction in rate of new students starting drug use (incidence), decreases in drunk-driving arrests, and decreases in school disciplinary actions for drug or alcohol offenses. (See Figure 11.2, Step 4.)

Outcomes (Step 3) are immediate or short-term results of a program, whereas impacts (Step 4) are ultimate or longer-term effects of the program. Sound program theory and planning of goals and outcomes helps delineate what are expected outcomes and impacts.

Archival data, based on records collected for other purposes, help assess impacts. Examples include medical records, juvenile court or police records, or school grades and attendance records. Questionnaires may also be useful for measuring impact. For instance, evidence related to incidence and prevalence of drug use may be obtained from questionnaires.

Summary Illustration of the Four-Step Evaluation Model

Suppose a coalition in the community implemented a prevention program to reduce adolescents' use of alcohol, tobacco and other drugs. The four-step *Prevention Plus III* evaluation model would be applied as follows. Figure 11.3 presents each step using adaptations of *Prevention Plus III* forms (Linney & Wandersman, 1991).

Step 1: Identifying Goals.   This step involves specifying program goals, objectives, and target groups. The overall program goals are to reduce overall drug use and drug-related arrests, accidents, and illnesses among youth (and eventually, adults). Two specific program objectives are to increase citizen knowledge of drug-related issues and their commitment to action on those issues. Additional objectives are to increase adolescents' skills in resisting pressure from peers and media to use drugs and to decrease local sales of tobacco to minors. Specific target groups include citizens at large, parents of adolescents, students in grades 7–9, and local stores that sell tobacco products (see Step 1 of Figure 11.3).

Step 2: Process Evaluation.   The program is to be implemented in several ways. A media campaign and public meetings will be conducted to raise public awareness of drug-related issues. School classes (grades 7–9), including exercises and dramatic skits, and school assemblies will be conducted on drug-related issues, including skills for resisting drug use. A parent training course will focus on communications skills with adolescents. A behavioral intervention for testing stores' willingness to sell tobacco products to minors, and reinforcing their refusals to sell, will be implemented (see Biglan et al., 1996). To conduct the process evaluation, the following will be recorded: the number of meetings, classes, assemblies, and training workshops planned and actually held; the staff time spent on each; and attendance at each session. The time and persons involved in training of student testers and implementation of the behavioral intervention for testing stores will also be recorded (see Part A of Step 2, Figure 11.3). After each program component is implemented, the process evaluation also will include a discussion of what program staff and planners learned from the experience (see Part B of Step 2, Figure 11.3).

Step 3: Outcome Evaluation.   Before and after public meetings, and in surveys of community members conducted before and after the media campaign, a questionnaire will assess changes in citizens' knowledge of drug abuse issues, and the number of volunteers for coalition activities. A questionnaire measuring parenting

FIGURE 11.3   *Defining Goals and Outcomes*

Step 1: Identify Goals and Desired Outcomes

    A. Make a list of the primary goals of the program.
    Ask yourself: "What were we trying to accomplish?"

        1. Decrease adolescent use of alcohol, tobacco, and other drugs
        2. Decrease rates of accidents, illness, and other drug-related conditions, and drug-related arrests

    B. What groups did you want to involve?
    Ask yourself: "Whom were we trying to reach?"
    For each group, how many persons did you want to involve?

        1. Local citizens (all residents of locality)
        2. Parents in training course (20 families in first year)
        3. Adolescents in grades 7–9 in school (500 in first year)
        4. Local stores selling tobacco (25 stores)

    C. What outcomes did you desire?
    Ask yourself: "As a result of this program, how would we like participants to change? What would they learn? What attitudes, feelings, or behaviors would be different?"

        1. Increase citizen knowledge of drug-related issues and problems
        2. Increase citizen commitment to action on these issues
        3. Increase parent skills in communicating with children about drug use
        4. Increase teens' skills in resisting pressure to use drugs
        5. Decrease local sales of tobacco to minors

Step 2: Process Evaluation Worksheet

    A. What activities were implemented?
    Ask yourself: "What did we actually do to implement this program?" Form a chronology of events.

    Date   *Description of Activity*

        1. Public awareness campaign: TV, radio, newspapers (ads, letters, columns, brochures, interviews)
        2. Public meetings: schools, religious congregations, etc.
        3. Curriculum and materials in school health classes
        4. Dramatic skits in schools by student team
        5. Parent communication skills training (6 sessions)
        6. Intervention to test and reduce store willingness to sell tobacco to teens

(continued)

FIGURE 11.3   *Continued*

For each activity above, indicate the following:

Activity length (hrs.)	Percentage of time goal	Activity attendance	Percentage of attendance goal
1. 12 hours	100%	N/A	N/A
2. 46 hours	92%	250	50%
3. 100 hours	80%	400	80%
4. 10 hours	100%	400	80%
5. 12 hours	100%	18	90%
6. 50 hours	50%	25 store visits	25%

Total duration of all activities (in hours) = 305 hours
Total attendance at all activities = 1,068 persons
Other services delivered:_____

1. 100 total actions to increase community awareness, involving media campaigns (Activity 1)
2. Guest lectures in community college classes

B. What can you learn from this experience?
What topics or activities were planned but not delivered? What happened that these were not accomplished?

Activity	Problem
1. Tobacco sales testing not completed	Training, logistics took longer than planned

Who was missing that you had hoped to have participate in the program?
    Youth, parents from high-risk family and neighborhood environments
    Not enough business, civic, and religious leaders

What explanations can you give for any discrepancy between the planned and actual participation?
    Competing news events overshadowed some media campaigns
    Courses, materials for youth need to be more appealing

What feedback can be used to improve the program in the future?
    Improve "teen appeal" of course materials
    Skits were a hit, use that format more
    Identify potential student and community leaders, involve them
    Involve youth, parents from high-risk environments in planning

Step 3: Outcome Evaluation

Desired Outcome	Measure
1. Increased citizen knowledge of drug-abuse issues	Scores on survey of knowledge

FIGURE 11.3   *Continued*

Desired Outcome	Measure
2. Increased citizen commitment to action to prevent drug abuse	Number of volunteers for anti-drug activities
3. Increased parent communication skills with teens re: drug use	Self-report survey of parent skills parent skills before & after training sessions
4. Increased student resistance	Teacher ratings, student questionnaires on student resistance skills before & after training
5. Decreased sales of tobacco	Number of times clerks were willing to sell when teen assessment teams attempted purchases before & after behavioral intervention

Step 4: Impact Evaluation

Desired Impact	Measure
1. Decreased drug-related traffic accidents, arrests	Police records: number of drug-related accidents, arrests; before & after program
2. Decreased school disciplinary actions related to drug use	School records: number of drug-related disciplinary actions before & after program
3. Decreased incidence of drug-related conditions, accidents	Hospital records: number of drug-related emergency room visits; number of admissions for drug-related conditions before & after program

Source: Adapted from *Prevention Plus III: Assessing Alcohol and Other Drug Prevention Programs at the School and Community Levels: A Four-Step Guide to Useful Program Assessment,* by J. A. Linney and A. Wandersman, 1991, Rockville, MD: U.S. Department of Health and Human Services, Office of Substance Abuse Prevention.

skills for communicating with adolescents will be given before and after the parent training course, to measure changes in these areas among course participants. In the schools, questionnaires completed by students and teachers will measure students' gains in skills for resisting drug use (measured before and after class exercises, for instance). Student questionnaires could also be used to measure changes in attitudes and behavior regarding drug use. Finally, behavioral tests of store clerks' willingness or refusal to sell tobacco to minors will be conducted and recorded (see Step 3 in Figure 11.3).

Step 4: Impact Evaluation.   Long-term effects of the program could be measured, for example, by changes in drug-related school disciplinary actions, police arrest and accident records for youth, and hospital records of drug-related treatment (see Step 4 in Figure 11.3).

While the four-step program evaluation method in *Prevention Plus III* was initially developed for evaluation in the alcohol, tobacco and other drug abuse domain, it is adaptable to any program area, such as community-based mental health prevention programs (McElhaney, 1995) and juvenile justice prevention (Morrissey, 1998).

Examining Mentoring from a Program Evaluation Perspective

This section illustrates the program evaluation concepts by examining mentoring and describes the literature. Second, it presents a *Prevention Plus III* mentoring case study.

In 1997, President Bill Clinton, with the assistance of many others including General Colin Powell, launched a widely publicized volunteerism summit. A major goal of the summit was to establish many more mentoring relationships for high-risk youth (moving from 300,000 in 1997 to one million by the year 2000). Mentoring is viewed as a major strategy to help high-risk youth (Powell's new war, 1997).

The term *mentoring* comes from Greek mythology in which Mentor was a trusted friend of Odysseus and served as a guardian and tutor to Odysseus' son when Odysseus was away (Haskell, 1997). Mentoring relationships generally involve an older, more experienced person and a younger, less experienced person. The mentor helps develop the character and competence of the mentee or assists the mentee in reaching goals, while also displaying trust, confidence, and praise, modeling positive behavior and serving as an advocate for the mentee (Haensly & Parsons, 1993; Haskell, 1997; Slicker & Palmer, 1994). Yet consider the following summary of findings on mentoring programs:

The evidence from the 10 available evaluations consistently indicates that noncontingent, supportive mentoring relationships do not have desired effects on outcomes such as academic achievement, school attendance, dropout, various aspects of child behavior including misconduct, or employment. This lack of demonstrated effects has occurred whether mentors were paid or unpaid, and whether mentors were college undergraduates, community volunteers, members of the business community, or school personnel. However, when mentors used behavior management techniques in one small, short-term study, students' school attendance improved. This is consistent with the findings from studies of school behavior management. In another larger, longer term experimental evaluation by the same researchers, unspecified mentoring relationships significantly increased delinquency for youth with no prior offenses but significantly decreased recidivism for youth with prior offenses (Office of Juvenile Justice and Delinquency Prevention [OJJDP], 1995).

This summary of findings of mentoring programs creates a desire to want to know more about a specific program, since many programs did not have desired effects, but some did. Is it worth the necessary time, energy, and money to ensure that a mentoring program is having positive effects? An examination of mentoring programs in terms of stated goals, process, outcomes, and ultimate impacts is essential, if one is to understand why some mentoring programs fail while others flourish. A case in point is the Big Brothers/Big Sisters mentoring program. Almost as the OJJDP report cited previously was leaving the press, Public/Private Ventures (PPV) issued a report which concluded that the Big Brothers/Big Sisters mentoring program worked.[1]

The most notable results are the deterrent effects on the initiation of drug and alcohol use, and the overall positive effects on academic performance that the mentoring experience produced. Improvement in grade-point average among Little Brothers and Little Sisters, while small in percentage terms is still very encouraging, since nonacademic interventions are rarely capable of producing effects in grade performance (Sipe, 1996).

The PPV study of Big Brothers/Big Sisters followed 487 children with mentors in noncontingent mentoring relationships over a period of 18 months. Children in mentoring relationships were markedly less likely to use drugs or alcohol, engage in violence, or be truant from school. What can account for the contrast between the studies reviewed by OJJDP and those reported by PPV? There are several possibilities. Studies emphasized by OJJDP included programs which matched groups of children or adolescents to a single mentor. In fact, the negative effects attributed by OJJDP to mentoring were interpreted by the original researchers (Fo & O'Donnell, 1974) as stemming from negative peer influences from contact between students mentored in groups. This spreading of maladaptive behavior occurred between student group members and does not seem applicable to the pairing of individual student-mentor pairs (characteristic of Big Brothers/Big Sisters and similar programs). Another prominent difference between the PPV study and those reviewed by OJJDP is the length of time the mentoring relationships were studied. Few of the programs reviewed by OJJDP examined mentoring relationships beyond one year. Finally, the OJJDP review summarized program evaluations of mentoring programs for both adolescents and children, without distinguishing between them.

Both the Big Brothers/Big Sisters mentoring program and the programs reviewed by OJJDP began with similar goals and desired outcomes (prevention of

---

[1]This analysis of the differences between the OJJDP summary and the PPV summary was written by Kevin Everhart.

delinquency, promotion of mental health and achievement). They differed, however, in the manner in which processes and activities were logically linked to desired outcomes. Consider the differences between a mentoring relationship at six months and again at 18 months. Or consider the same adult mentoring a 17-year-old adolescent, versus an 11-year-old. One can see how two simple procedural variables (duration of mentoring relationship and age of child to be matched with a mentor) may have profound influence on the kinds of outcomes that may be expected. Thus, a program evaluation that carefully looks at process and outcomes is needed. An evaluation of a mentoring program which used the four-step method from *Prevention Plus III* as a guide is presented next.

Mentoring: **A Prevention Plus III** *Evaluation*

The C.O.P.E. mentoring program in a rural county in South Carolina paired "at-risk" middle school students with adult volunteer mentors who met with their mentees during school hours. The targeted students were identified as "at-risk" by teachers and other school staff based on characteristics such as social withdrawal, aggression, academic failure, or truancy. When the evaluators became involved in the project, it had already been in ongoing implementation for three years. The mentoring program is described in more detail in Wandersman et al. (1998) and Davino, Wandersman, and Goodman (1995).

The first step in the evaluation was to work with the school staff in the clarification of the mentoring program's goals and desired outcomes (Step 1 of the four-step method). The broad goal of the mentoring program was to improve mentees' quality of life in three domains: relationships, self-esteem, and school related problems. Next, this goal was developed into a more specific set of measurable outcomes for the program. Desired outcomes included: high satisfaction with the program and with the mentoring relationship among mentees and mentors; high scores on a mentee self-esteem measure; increased school grades; increased school attendance; and decreased school behavioral problems (see Figure 11.4, Step 1).

In order to assess the degree to which the program was successfully achieving its goals and desired outcomes, both process and outcome evaluation components were conducted. Several different stakeholders in the program were surveyed in an attempt to get their feedback about satisfaction with the current program and suggestions for improvement. These stakeholders included mentors, mentees, teachers, and school staff who ran the program. In addition, work sheets were completed to document important program components (e.g., mentor recruitment, support meetings, luncheons) as well as components which were desired by participants but which had not yet been included as part of the program (e.g., mentor orientation sessions, group outings with mentors and mentees).

Process evaluation results also showed that 53 percent of the mentees had contact with their mentor once a week or more, 23 percent met at least once a month but less than once a week, and 24 percent less than once a month. On an open-ended question asking for suggested improvements, mentees had several

FIGURE 11.4 *Selecting Goals and Outcomes*

Step 1: Identify Goals and Desired Outcomes

    A. Make a list of the primary goals of the program.
        Ask yourself: "What were we trying to accomplish?"
        1. Build satisfying and consistent mentoring relationships
        2. Improve mentee self-esteem
        3. Decrease school problems

    B. What groups did you want to involve?
        Ask yourself: "Whom were we trying to reach?"
        For each group, how many persons did you want to involve?

        At-risk middle school students: withdrawn, aggressive, academically failing, truant, pregnant, those with social problems
        As many as possible (100 currently)

    C. What outcomes did you desire?
        Ask yourself: "As a result of this program, how would we like participants to change? What would they learn? What attitudes, feelings, or behaviors would be different?"
        1. Have high satisfaction with program and mentor relationship
        2. Increased scores on self-esteem measures
        3. Increased grades and school attendance
        4. Decreased school behavior problems

Source: Adapted from *Prevention Plus III: Assessing Alcohol and Other Drug Prevention Programs at the School and Community Levels: A Four-Step Guide to Useful Program Assessment,* by J. A. Linney and A. Wanderman, 1991, Rockville, MD: U.S. Department of Health and Human Services, Office of Substance Abuse Prevention.

ideas. Overwhelmingly, their responses to this question concerned wanting to see their mentor more often. Some of the responses may have been driven by ulterior motives, such as "we should get out of class every day." However, for other students there seemed to be a real concern about not being able to count on the mentor to come often or at the scheduled time. An example of this was the suggestion that "there should be a rule that mentors have to come every week."

Results of the C.O.P.E. mentoring program were mixed. The stakeholder surveys showed consistently positive responses among participants in all groups. For example, the majority of mentees and mentors saw the program as "helpful" or "very helpful" to the students. Both groups also rated the quality of their relationships as "good" or "great," saw their relationship as "improving," and reported the fit between mentor and mentee as "good" or "great." However, comparisons between mentees and a comparison group (children on a waiting list for mentors) on self-esteem, grades, school attendance, and decreased school be-havior problems were not statistically significant.

Program participants felt good about the program, but measures of be-havioral changes showed no effect of mentoring. Some reasons for this lack of behavioral changes may be that the program was not long enough or intensive enough to affect outcomes such as grades and self-esteem, the mentors were not sufficiently trained, the program needed to be conducted for more hours per week or in a different way, or the measures chosen (e.g., self-esteem) were affected by too many factors other than mentoring effects. Whatever the reasons, results such as these suggested that program planners needed to step back and reexamine their goals and methods more closely. That is the topic of the next section.

Comprehensive Quality Programming: Nine Essential Strategies for Implementing Successful Programs

The outcome results of the C.O.P.E. mentoring program were disappointing. The measured outcomes of many treatment, prevention, and educational programs are often disappointing. Yet, as with C.O.P.E., many participants and observers of a community program may believe that a program has the kernel of a good idea that will be effective, if the program is improved. Traditionally, program evaluation has been concerned with whether a program already developed is working, and why. However, this approach does not study how to develop an effective program in the first place.

Continuous improvement of programs relies on the use of evaluation data to plan and implement program modifications. Many barriers prevent program planners and staff from using such feedback well. First, programs may use an out-side evaluator, a person with no stake in the success or failure of the program (thus presumably more objective). Such an approach sets up an "us versus them" rela-tionship that can limit the quality and usefulness of the evaluation findings. Yet program practitioners often believe that they do not have the time, resources, or expertise to conduct their own evaluation. Second, program evaluation usually provides evaluation feedback at the end of program implementation, without op-portunities for midcourse corrections. Program staff thus often view evaluation as an intrusive process that results in a "report card" of success or failure but no use-ful information for program improvement. A third, related barrier is the general perception of evaluation research and findings as too complex, theoretical, or not user-friendly.

To overcome these above barriers, there has been a growing discussion of new and evolving roles for evaluators that encourage the self-determination of program practitioners (e.g., Dugan, 1996; Fetterman, 1994, 1996; Fetterman, Kaf-tarian, & Wandersman, 1996; Linney & Wandersman, 1991; Stevenson, Mitchell, & Florin, 1996). This new approach to evaluation, termed *Empowerment Evaluation*, attempts to break down the barriers inherent in traditional evaluation methods in favor of those which reflect an empowerment and/or citizen participation perspective (Fetterman, 1996). Empowerment Evaluation is an evolving approach in which program planners and developers learn the basics of program evaluation so that they can more systematically plan and implement their programs and thereby increase the probability of obtaining desired outcomes. Empowerment evaluators collaborate with community members and program practitioners to determine program goals and implementation strategies, serve as facilitators or coaches but not as outside experts, provide technical assistance to teach community members and program staff to do self-evaluation, and stress the importance of using information from the evaluation in ongoing program improvement. In sum, Empowerment Evaluation helps program developers and staff to achieve their program goals by providing them with tools for assessing and improving the planning, implementation, and results of their programs.

Using the Empowerment Evaluation philosophy, Wandersman et al. (1998) presented eight specific strategies that can guide self-evaluation and continuous program improvement. Since then a ninth strategy has been added (Step 1 from *Prevention Plus III*). The implementation of a quality prevention or community program requires the use of these nine essential planning and evaluation steps, as well as a commitment to use information from each to enhance program functioning continuously. The nine strategies are collectively termed Comprehensive Quality Programming (CQP). CQP is a straightforward approach that demystifies the evaluation process and demonstrates to program practitioners the value of evaluation in implementing quality prevention programs. CQP addresses the widespread interest in accountability of programs, and it uses the four steps of *Prevention Plus III* as part of its process. It also describes accountability and how CQP can help practitioners demonstrate accountability. Then each of the nine strategies are defined. Specific planning and evaluation tools for each are discussed.

Basic Program Accountability Questions

When beginning a new program, or continuing an existing one, program practitioners can start thinking about program effectiveness and program improvement issues by answering these accountability questions. Answering these questions can serve as a beginning guide to successful planning, implementation, and evaluation of programs.

Why is the intervention or program needed?

What are the program's goals, target population, and desired outcomes?

How does the program use the scientific knowledge and "best practice" of what works?

How will this new program fit in with existing programs?

How will the program be carried out?

How well was the program carried out?

How well did the program work?

What can be done to improve the program the next time you do it?

If the program (or parts of the program) was effective, what is being done to continue (institutionalize) the program?

Linking the Accountability Questions to CQP Strategies

This section addresses the accountability questions by providing strategies for answering them. The accountability questions can often serve as a useful teaching device to demonstrate to program practitioners and funders the relevance and importance of evaluation. The questions are understandable and often spark an interest and appreciation for the link between solid evaluation and continued funding. Table 11.1 is a chart of the accountability questions and the relevant strategic planning or evaluation focus for answering them. Wandersman et al. (1998) describe the corresponding planning and evaluation tools needed to provide answers to the accountability questions.

Table 11.1 shows how CQP expands upon the four steps of *Prevention Plus III*. What Wandersman et al. (1998) realized was that *Prevention Plus III* (Strategies 2, 6,

TABLE 11.1 *Accountability Questions and Corresponding CQP Strategies*

Accountability Questions	CQP Strategies
1. Why is the program needed?	Needs, assets assessment
2. What are the program goals, target population, and desired outcomes?	Identifying goals and desired outcomes
3. How does your program use scientific knowledge and best practices?	Review research literature and best practices
4. How will this new program fit with existing programs?	Community feedback and planning
5. How will you carry out the program?	Planning, implementation
6. How well was the program carried out?	Process evaluation
7. How well did the program work?	Outcome, impact evaluation
8. What can you do to improve the program the next time?	Process, outcome, impact evaluation
9. If the program was effective, what is being done to institutionalize it?	Implementation Strategies

7, and 8 in Table 11.1) can help program developers perform their programs better, but it did not help them ask whether they were doing the "right" program. Thus, using only *Prevention Plus III* would be like tuning up an engine and making it run better so that the driver could drive at 65 mph instead of 30, but the car just might be going down the wrong road faster. Questions 1–4 in the CQP questions help the program developer choose the right program, and the later questions help the program developer improve the program and keep it going.

Question 1. Why Is an Intervention Needed? How does one know of the need for a program? Frequently programs are selected because they are popular or have been implemented at other local sites, rather than because they have been demonstrated to effectively prevent a specified problem in your setting. For example, Kaskutas, Morgan, and Vaeth (1992) described the experience of a guidance counselor who was working on a project as part of an interagency collaboration who "discovered after two months of planning a drug group [for] the senior high school kids in the project who were nonworking, that there were no senior high kids in the project who didn't have jobs!" (p. 179). Therefore, there was no need for the program.

In order to determine which types of programs are needed in a given community, school, or other agency, a planning strategy called a needs assessment is often used (Soriano, 1995; Witlein & Altschuld, 1995; also see Chapter 9). This assessment is designed to gather information about the issues most in need of improvement or intervention in a community or organization (e.g., youth violence, alcohol, and drug abuse). A good needs assessment also includes a resource assessment and identification of community and organizational strengths. Kretzmann and McKnight (1993) discuss the necessity of assessing a community's assets. This can lead to discovering community resources that can be used to develop programs that fit the culture of the community well. Assets may include individual talents, microsystems that can offer social support systems for persons involved in the program, or organizations that can provide funding, a meeting space, or a venue for public discussion of program goals. Assets assessment also provides a counterpoint to needs assessment. The identification of community problems involved in needs assessment is balanced by an assessment of community strengths. Assets assessment is consistent with the ideals of citizen participation and community empowerment.

Question 2. What Are the Goals, Target Population, and Desired Outcomes of the Program? After the need for a program has been determined, it is essential to specify the goals of the program, the specific target group(s) of the program, and the desired outcomes. This is Step 1 of the four-step evaluation method covered earlier.

Question 3. How Does the Program Use Scientific Knowledge and Best Practices of What Works? Once program personnel have decided that there is a need to address a specific program, how do they decide which program or intervention to use? For example, administrators of school and community programs are showered with glossy mailings advertising multimedia curriculum products for programs such as violence prevention, sex education, and substance abuse prevention. How does one decide which program to choose? This decision is frequently based on convenience or availability. Does one rely on the program used last year, regardless of success, or use the program that can be borrowed without cost from another source, or maybe use the program advertised at the last convention? It is important to keep in mind that although convenience and availability are important, they do not ensure program effectiveness.

A goal of prevention science is to provide two kinds of information. One is empirical (usually quantitative) findings about the effectiveness of programs in attaining identified goals. Another is (usually qualitative) information about *best practices*, the elements and methods of programs that work best for a particular type of problem within a particular type of population. These types of knowledge are useful in answering the question of what program to select. To be effective, programs need to be based on a theory of the target problem and be tied to current and relevant research (Buford & Davis, 1995; Goodman & Wandersman, 1994; Green & Lewis, 1986; Leviton, 1994; Weiss, 1995). Best practices knowledge helps not only in program selection but also in program planning and implementation.

Question 4. How Will This New Program Fit in With Existing Programs? Will this program enhance, interfere with, or be unrelated to other programs that are already offered? Will it be part of a comprehensive and coordinated package or simply a new program in a long list of programs?

When designing a new program, it is important to be sure that it fits well with the community's needs as well as the available services already in place (Elias, 1995). To reduce duplication, practitioners should be familiar with the programs already existing in their school or community. In order to prevent overlap of programs or the implementation of a program that does not fit with overall agency or community goals, a process called program mapping can be used.

Program mapping is an assessment of how well a proposed program's goals and methods will fit with the broader goals or motivating philosophy of the sponsoring organization. Programs can fit into an organization in three basic ways. They can have an "add-on" effect (one program adds to another), a "synergistic" effect (one program multiples the effect of another), or an "interference" effect (one program diminishes another).

Question 5. How Will the Program Be Carried Out?   What are the steps that program personnel will take to carry it out? During this planning stage, program developers must identify how they will implement the program. Outlining how a program will be implemented includes determining specific steps to carry out the program, identifying and training persons to carry out each of these steps, and developing a timeline or schedule for this plan. Program staff should specify what will happen during scheduled program activities and where these activities will take place. All of these components must be clearly defined in order to effectively plan and implement a program.

Question 6. How Well Was the Program Carried Out? Was the program actually implemented as planned? Was all of the program delivered? If not, which components were not delivered? What went right and what went wrong? Evaluating how a program was implemented is called process evaluation (Step 2 of the *Prevention Plus III* method discussed earlier).

Question 7. How Well Did the Program Work? Did the program have the desired effects and proposed outcomes? Were there any unanticipated consequences? Evaluating outcomes and impacts comprised Steps 3 and 4 of the *Prevention Plus III* method discussed earlier.

Question 8. What Can Be Done to Improve the Program for Next Time? Many programs are repeated. Given that no program is perfect, what can be done to improve the program's effectiveness and efficiency in the future? If the process and outcome of a program are well documented, the opportunity to learn from previous implementation efforts is enormous. Keeping track of program components that worked well ensures that such components will be included in the future. Assessing what program components did not work provides the opportunity for refinement and improvement. Lessons about what went well with a program and what areas can use improvement come from such informal sources as personal observations and verbal reports from participants and staff, or such formal sources as participant satisfaction measures and evaluations of the program process and outcome. However gathered, information for program improvement is obtained from the answers to Questions 1–7.

Program staff who are open to learning from the results of evaluation can continuously improve their programs. Instead of seeing evaluation as purely a documentation tool, it should be viewed as a feedback mechanism that can guide future planning and implementation.

Question 9. What Is Being Done to Institutionalize the Program? After service providers have gone through the time, energy, and money to develop a successful program, what will they do to see it continued? Unfortunately, this is an often neglected question in prevention programming. Even when programs have successful outcomes, they often are not continued, due to a lack of funding, staff turnover, or loss of momentum. Lerner's (1995) review of prevention programs for youth development concluded that there are numerous effective programs to prevent risks and problem behaviors, but unfortunately, these programs were rarely sustained over time.

Goodman and Steckler (1987) define institutionalization as developing community and organizational supports for health promotion and prevention programs so that they remain viable in the long term. They have identified factors related to successful institutionalization such as identifying resources and making program components accessible and user-friendly to host organization staff.

CQP never ends. Even for an effectively implemented, thoroughly institutionalized program, its staff start over again with Question 1.

Examples of CQP in Action

Two examples of using CQP to improve community programs are described next.

C.O.P.E.: Using the CQP Strategies in an Ongoing Program

CQP can be used to improve ongoing programs. Using the CQP strategies to continuously improve programs takes program evaluation beyond an accountability system that documents program effectiveness for funders, to a system of continuous program improvement, using evaluation data to refine and enhance programs (Fetterman, 1996; Mark & Pines, 1995; Morrissey & Wandersman, 1995). A common goal of both practitioners and researchers is to ensure that programs are useful and effective. CQP provides a rationale and a means to meet this goal.

How can information from the evaluation of the C.O.P.E. mentoring program (described earlier in this chapter) be used for program improvement through CQP? During the process evaluation, feedback highlighting areas in need of improvement was gathered. For example, some mentees reported that their mentor was inconsistent in making contact on a weekly basis. Mentors, on the other hand, reported problems with scheduling and a feeling of being overburdened and overwhelmed with their many work, family, and volunteer commitments. These are problems that need to be addressed.

The use of lessons learned to make midcourse corrections also indicated to program personnel some issues which had been overlooked when the original program plans were made. For example, both mentors and teachers expressed a desire to have more contact with each other and to work as a team in helping the mentee/student. However, no formal roles for teachers had been built into the program, and no formal process for connecting concerned mentors with their mentees' teachers had been established. Improvements in this area were implemented immediately since this information was obtained during ongoing process evaluation (Strategy 6 of CQP) instead of after the fact (Strategy 7 of CQP) as in traditional outcome evaluation.

Open-ended questions regarding suggestions for improvement also were valuable in that they allowed individuals with many different perspectives on the program to contribute valuable information to the process of making midcourse corrections. Mentors wanted more formal support and training in skills they needed to fulfill their role. Mentees wanted more formalized structures to maintain consistency of contact (rules), while teachers wanted contact with mentors as well as respect for the importance of academics and not missing class. These suggestions illuminated some current problems in the program as well as possible routes to correcting them.

Thus the process evaluation allowed program staff to document generally high levels of satisfaction among different groups of participants, look at problems in the implementation of their plans (e.g., maintaining weekly contact), assess additional groups to include (e.g., teachers), and solicit suggestions for program improvement from diverse groups. Based on the feedback, school officials hired someone to coordinate more activities for mentors and mentees, check in with mentors each month, and raise the mentor morale through such gestures as small gifts of appreciation. Mentors were even sent a roll of LifeSavers™ candy, with a note saying "You're a lifesaver."

TROOPERS: Using the CQP Strategies at the Start of a Program

C.O.P.E. began using CQP strategies several years after the program's inception. It is best to develop programs using CQP strategies at the start of a program. Following is a description of an attempt to use CQP strategies, with an empowerment evaluation philosophy, at the beginning of a different mentoring initiative, called TROOPERS, in an elementary school in rural South Carolina (Everhart, Haskell, Wandersman, Laughlin, & Sullivan, 1998). The evaluation team worked with the mentoring program staff at the beginning of the program and used CQP strategies throughout.[2]

When the evaluation team initially asked the first accountability question (Why is an intervention needed?), the community agencies with whom the evaluation team were consulting were somewhat vague in their response. They knew that they wanted a mentoring program, in large part because other communities within the state were receiving positive attention for mentoring initiatives. The coalition of agencies also recognized a deficit in their own approach to substance abuse prevention; other than D.A.R.E., there was an absence of prevention programs in the community targeting elementary school children.

The evaluation team conducted a series of meetings during which the needs of children within the community were discussed. Community stakeholders voiced concern that children and adolescents in the community were faced with an absence of positive role models. Concern for the moral development of children in the community was also expressed, in light of conduct problems, drug and alcohol abuse, and poor school achievement. The stakeholders were convinced of the need for a program to address these concerns. They were further convinced of the need for character education within the community as a means of addressing their concerns.

Should a more systematic needs assessment have been conducted? Although this option was suggested by the evaluation team, the coalition of agencies was under pressure to meet a deadline for program initiation imposed by their funding source and was operating within a time frame that did not permit completing a new needs assessment.

Having identified an area of need, the coalition of agencies was assisted in working through the second accountability question, "What are the goals, target population, and desired outcomes of the program?" This question defines the scope and mission of the program and provides the framework for evaluation. The

---

[2]The CQP description here was written by Kevin Everhart.

goal of the TROOPERS program, broadly defined, was to "build character," (i.e., to increase the social and academic competence of child participants). All children in the third grade in one elementary school were targeted for the intervention (see the third question), with a subset of children demonstrating greatest risk for social and academic problems being selected for the more comprehensive mentoring intervention. Desired outcomes regarding improved peer social skills, increased adaptive classroom behavior, improved self-esteem, and improved classroom social climate, were identified, as was methodology for measuring outcomes. These desired outcomes were linked to the desired impact of increased rates of high school completion, decreased crime and juvenile delinquency, and a decrease in the use of alcohol, tobacco, and other drugs.

In answering the third question—"How does your program use the scientific knowledge and best practices of what works?"—the evaluation team assisted the community coalition with selecting and establishing procedures and assessment strategies that had been "road tested" through previous efforts. To address character development, the evaluation team recommended an empirically validated classroom-based moral reasoning development program (Schuncke & Krogh, 1983). Complementary story books and videotapes were selected to reinforce this program, adding a skill development dimension focusing on social problem solving and conflict resolution skills. These would help third graders face critical transitions at school, including heavier academic demands and more complex peer relations.

Also, the selection of the third grade as a target for the program was based on considerations regarding cognitive and moral reasoning development during the latency stage and the salience of adult role models and positive adult attention in developing and solidifying attitudes. Thus, the team's model of the problem (academic demands, changes in peer relations, development of attitudes regarding moral behavior) was matched with approaches which could most readily harness the resources available to children at the targeted developmental level.

A model of the intervention was developed in which curriculum-guided mentorship, targeting third-grade children, was proposed to produce small but sustainable changes in children's attitudes and behavior. These changes may, over time, permit the development of higher-level coping strategies to counter risk factors for delinquency and substance abuse. Mentorship cannot alter all contextual risk factors in a child's life, of course, but it can provide important protective processes and nudge outcomes in positive directions.

The mentorship element was integrated into the developing program with the rationale that behavioral practice and modeling are central to promoting changes in moral conduct. Elements of the program (e.g., curriculum, materials, mentors, teachers) were combined into coordinated, synergistic initiatives. This addressed the fourth accountability question, "How will this new program link with existing programs?"

In addition, the intervention was designed to create changes at multiple levels: classroom environment and individual behavior. It addressed multiple targets:

a curriculum-only condition was designed as a prevention effort for all students, whereas a curriculum-plus-mentoring component was designed as a secondary prevention initiative for "at-risk" children. The former represents primary or universal prevention, while the latter represents secondary and selected prevention.

In answer to the fifth accountability question—"How will you carry out the program?"—a plan for program implementation was developed in accordance with a flexible time line. This plan included the "what" and "where" of program implementation. At the organizational level, planners developed a broad agenda for meeting program goals in the course of the school year. At the individual and microsystem levels, the roles and responsibilities of teachers, school personnel, mentors, stakeholders, and evaluators were delineated through comprehensive planning sessions. In addition, benchmarks for accountability were specified to ensure that teachers, mentors, and others adhered to plans and accomplished objectives. These benchmarks were integrated into a manual for service delivery, which provided clear instructions regarding responsibilities.

Careful attention to the what and where of carrying out the program provided the foundation for answering the sixth program accountability question, "How well was the program carried out?" Several mechanisms were instituted to promote the integrity of program implementation. Learning from the pitfalls of previous mentoring programs, which failed to promote close ties between volunteers and children, multiple safeguards were instituted to foster the development of a high-quality relationship and to remind mentors of their commitment. A feedback system was instituted in which mentors completed weekly logs documenting meetings with mentees and evaluated children's progress with regard to the character education curriculum. In addition to documenting time spent together, the log included questions related to relationship development and provided a mechanism for mentors to report problems or concerns. In addition, a checklist was designed to document the use of curriculum materials by teachers and to obtain their ratings of the materials' effectiveness and age-appropriateness. A paper trail of mentor logs and teacher ratings served two purposes. First, it promoted adherence to program design. Second, it permitted the team to examine the degree to which the specified course of action was followed faithfully.

Ultimately, careful groundwork in addressing the first six accountability questions left the team well positioned to assess outcomes and impacts (Question 7: "How well did the program work?"). Measurement instruments representing outcomes were selected for reliability and validity, and other survey items were developed according to unique attributes of the program and desired outcomes.

Outcome and impact evaluations after implementation of the program indicated that it attained many of its goals. Based upon teacher ratings, grades, and self-report data, the results of the evaluation indicated improvement in several aspects of children's classroom behavior and academic performance compared with a comparison school which did not have the program. Further gains were evident among "high risk" children matched with mentors. They evidenced significantly lower levels of acting-out behavior and higher levels of on-task behavior, resulting in improved spelling and reading grades. Mentored children also had increased levels of self-esteem. Not all desired outcomes were obtained; no changes in frustration tolerance were evident, for example, and math grades did not improve. Still, the results were impressive in that they suggest a relationship between successful program development and use of the accountability questions and the CQP essential strategies and tools.

The next CQP question is "What can be done to improve the program next time?" In the second year of the program, the team used first-year survey feedback from children, mentors, teachers, and parents to make adjustments and improvements in the program. These included developing improved mechanisms for communication between parents, mentors, and teachers. The team increased efforts to attend to children's perceptions of the mentoring relationship as it unfolded, while providing for early detection of unpromising relationships. Guided by the research report from Public/Private Ventures (Sipe, 1996; described earlier), the team included measurement of the types of strategies mentors use in developing relationships with mentees and how these strategies develop over time. Having failed to find effects of the program with regard to social climate perceptions in the first year, the team selected and amended another measure of potentially greater sensitivity. In response to criticisms regarding the amount of paperwork, measures (surveys, logs, and checklists) were screened to eliminate redundant or unnecessary information. The team developed a more systematic method of determining members of the secondary prevention (mentoring) target group. The team also developed a mechanism for parents to provide early feedback regarding concerns or questions about mentors.

Finally, the team addressed the ninth program accountability question, "What can be done to continue and institutionalize this effective program?" This question is perhaps the ultimate evaluation of the evaluation team itself, involving issues such as "Have we been effective mentors ourselves for teaching continuous program improvement? How successful have we been at using empowerment evaluation principles? How well integrated is the program within the network of community services provided?" Every area of the development and evaluation process in which the evaluation team played a leadership role now represented a potential risk point for continuing it. As the program entered the final year of the grant, stakeholders were negotiating ownership of the program, pursuing funding, and weighing the resources against possible gains. Staff were turning over, and the original program coordinator would soon be replaced by someone who would not know program history on a personal level. The task of the evaluation team was to modify existing structures and measures to accommodate change. For instance, this might mean eliminating sophisticated measures requiring specialized knowledge to interpret and replacing them with measures that could more readily be administered and utilized by existing school staff. Ultimately, this program could be streamlined for institutionalization by schools currently implementing it. For this to occur, it was essential that both process and outcome evaluation become integrated into the culture of participating schools.

Conclusion

Citizens, consumers, and practitioners should be able to elaborate and answer in detail the question: "It sounds like a good idea, but is it really working?"

Program evaluation is necessary to find out whether or not programs are working. As seen in this chapter, program evaluation concepts can be incorporated into program planning and program implementation. When this is done, the boundaries between program development and program evaluation are blurred for the sake of improving process and increasing the probability of successful results. Comprehensive Quality Programming is an example of this approach. While the CQP emphasis, so far, has been on the accountability of practitioners who receive money for prevention (or treatment or education), Wandersman (1999) notes that the accountability questions also apply to funders and researchers/evaluators. For example, when funders consider developing a new initiative, the questions of how do they know they need a new initiative, how will it use science and best practices, how does it fit with other initiatives, etcetera, should be asked and answered. For evaluators, the same questions would concern whether a new or intensified evaluation process is needed or justified, how well it fits with existing evaluation procedures, and how best practices for program evaluation will be used in planning this evaluation.

As society becomes more concerned about accountability and results for schools and for health and human services, evaluation can lead to fear and resistance or to openness, honesty, empowerment, and improvement. Evaluation and accountability need not be feared—if people work together for results.

1. Program success depends upon having a good theory of why something works and implementing it with quality.

2. Logic models link community needs or conditions with activities, outcomes, and impacts. Program development and program evaluation have similar components.

3. A four-step program evaluation model (from *Prevention Plus III*) boils program evaluation down to identifying goals and desired outcomes, process evaluation, outcome evaluation, and evaluation of impacts.

4. Effective programs are linked to accountability using comprehensive quality programming (CQP) strategies. CQP asks and answers nine accountability questions, which are listed in Table 11.1. These concern not only program evaluation but also development and institutionalization of effective programs.

References

Biglan, A., Ary, D., Koehn, V., Levings, D., Smith, S., Wright, Z., James, L., & Henderson, J. (1996). Mobilizing positive reinforcement in communities to reduce youth access to tobacco. *American Journal of Community Psychology, 24,* 625–638.

Buford, B., & Davis, B. (1995). *Shining stars: Prevention drug programs that work.* Louisville, KY: Southeast Regional Center for Drug-Free Schools and Communities.

Davino, K., Wandersman, A., & Goodman, R. M. (1995). *Cherokee County mentoring program evaluation interim report.* Unpublished manuscript, University of South Carolina.

Dugan, M. A. (1996). Participatory and empowerment evaluation: Lessons learned in training and technical assistance. In D. Fetterman, S. Kaftarian, & A. Wandersman (Eds.), *Empowerment evaluation: Knowledge and tools for self-assessment and accountability* (pp. 277–303). Thousand Oaks, CA: Sage.

Elias, M. J. (1995). Primary prevention as health and social competence promotion. *Journal of Primary Prevention, 16,* 5–24,

Enett, S., Rosenbaum, D., Flewelling, R., Bieler, G., Ringwalt, C., & Bailey, S. (1994). Long-term evaluation of drug abuse resistance education. *Addictive Behaviors, 19,* 113–125.

Everhart, K., Haskell, I., Wandersman, A., Laughlin, J., & Sullivan, P. T. (1998). *Integrating adult-child mentorship and character development to promote social and academic competence: A report on the TROOPERS Project.* Manuscript in preparation.

Fetterman, D. (1994). Steps of empowerment evaluation: From California to Cape Town. *Evaluation and Program Planning, 17,* 305–313.

Fetterman, D. (1996). Empowerment evaluation: An introduction to theory and practice. In D. Fetterman, S. Kaftarian, & A. Wandersman (Eds.), *Empowerment evaluation: Knowledge and tools for self-assessment and accountability* (pp. 3–46). Thousand Oaks, CA: Sage.

Fetterman, D., Kaftarian, S., & Wandersman, A. (Eds.). (1996). *Empowerment evaluation: Knowledge and tools for self-assessment and accountability.* Thousand Oaks, CA: Sage.

Fo, W. S., & O'Donnell, C. R. (1974). The Buddy System: Relationship and contingency conditions in a community intervention program for youth with nonprofessionals as behavior change agents. *Journal of Consulting and Clinical Psychology, 42,* 163–169.

Goodman, R. M., & Steckler, A. (1987). A model for the institutionalization of health promotion programs. *Family and Community Health, 11,* 63–78.

Goodman, R. M., & Wandersman, A. (1994). FORECAST: A formative approach to evaluating community coalitions and community-based initiatives. In S. Kaftarian & W. Hansen (Eds.), *Journal of Community Psychology Monograph Series,* Center for Substance Abuse Prevention Special Issue, 6–25.

Green, L., & Lewis, M. (1986). *Measurement and evaluation in health education and health promotion.* Palo Alto: Mayfield.

Haensly, P. A., & Parsons, J. L. (1993). Creative, intellectual, and psychosocial development through mentorship: Relationships and stages. *Youth and Society, 25,* 202–221.

Haskell, I. (1997). *The effectiveness of character education and mentoring: An evaluation of the Troopers school-based program.* Unpublished manuscript, University of South Carolina.

Julian, J. A., Jones, A., & Dey, D. (1995). Open systems evaluation and the logic model: Program planning and evaluation tools. *Evaluation and Program Planning, 18,* 333–341.

Kaskutas, L., Morgan, P., & Vaeth, P. (1992). Structural impediments in the development of community-based drug prevention programs for youth: Preliminary analysis from a qualitative formative evaluation study. *International Quarterly of Community Health Education, 12,* 169–182.

Kretzmann, J. P., & McKnight, J. L. (1993). *Building communities from the inside out: A path toward finding, and mobilizing a community's assets.* Chicago, IL: ACTA Publications.

Lerner, R. M. (1995). *America's youth in crisis: Challenges and options for programs and policies.* Thousand Oaks, CA: Sage.

Leviton, L. C. (1994). Program theory and evaluation theory in community-based programs. *Evaluation Practice, 15,* 89–92.

Linney, J. A., & Wandersman, A. (1991). *Prevention Plus III: Assessing alcohol and other drug prevention programs at the school and community level: A four-step guide to useful program assessment.* Rockville, MD: U.S. Department of Health and Human Services, Office for Substance Abuse Prevention.

Mark, M. M., & Pines, E. (1995). Implications of continuous quality improvement for program evaluation and evaluators. *Evaluation Practice*, 16, 131–139.

McElhaney, S. (1995). *Getting started: NMHA guide to establishing community-based prevention programs*. Alexandria, VA: National Mental Health Association.

McEwan, K. L., & Bigelow, D. A. (1997). Using a logic model to focus health services on population health goals. *Canadian Journal of Program Evaluation, 12*, 167–174.

Morrissey, E. (1998). *Evaluation of Camp Paupu Win*. Columbia, SC: South Carolina Department of Juvenile Justice.

Morrissey, E., & Wandersman, A. (1995). Total quality management in health care settings: A preliminary framework for successful implementation. In L. Ginsberg & P. Keys (Eds.), *New management in human services* (2nd ed., pp. 171–194). Washington, DC: NASW Press.

Northwest Regional Educational Laboratory (National Mentoring Center). (1999). *Making the case: Measuring the impact of your mentoring program* (p. 41). [Online] Available on World Wide Web: http://www.nwrel.org.

Office of Juvenile Justice and Delinquency Prevention. (1995). *Guide for implementing the comprehensive strategy for serious, violent, and chronic juvenile offenders*. Washington, DC: U.S. Department of Justice.

Patton, M. Q. (1997). *Utilization focused evaluation*. (3rd ed.). Thousand Oaks, CA: Sage.

Powell's new war. (1997, April 28). *Newsweek*, 28–37.

Rossi, P. H., Freeman, H. E., & Lipsey, M. (1999). *Evaluation: A systematic approach* (6th ed.). Newbury Park, CA: Sage.

Schorr, L. (1997). *Common purpose: Strengthening families and neighborhoods to rebuild America*. New York: Anchor Books.

Schuncke, G., & Krogh, S. (1983). *Helping children choose: Resources, strategies, and activities for teachers of young children*. Glenview, IL: Scott, Foresman & Company.

Sipe, C. L. (1996). *Mentoring: A synthesis of P/PV's research: 1988–1995*. Philadelphia, PA: Public/Private Ventures.

Slicker, E., & Palmer, D. (1994). Mentoring at-risk high school students: Evaluation of a school-based program. *School Counselor, 40*, 327–334.

Soriano, F. (1995). *Conducting needs assessments: A multidisciplinary approach*. Thousand Oaks, CA: Sage.

Stevenson, J., Mitchell, R. E., & Florin, P. (1996). Evaluation and self-direction in community prevention coalitions. In D. Fetterman, S. Kaftarian, & A. Wandersman (Eds.), *Empowerment evaluation: Knowledge and tools for self-assessment and accountability* (pp. 208–233). Thousand Oaks, CA: Sage.

United Way of America. (1996). *Measuring program outcomes: A practical approach: Effective practices and measuring impact*. Alexandria, VA: Author.

U.S. General Accounting Office. (1990). Drug education: School-based programs seen as useful but impact unknown [GAO/HRD-91-27]. Washington, DC: Author.

Wandersman, A. (1999). *Community interventions and effective prevention: Bringing evaluators/researchers, funders and practitioners together to promote accountability*. Manuscript in preparation.

Wandersman, A., Morrissey, E., Davino, K., Seybolt, D., Crusto, C., Nation, M., Goodman, R., & Imm, P. (1998). Comprehensive quality programming and accountability: Eight essential strategies for implementing successful prevention programs. *Journal of Primary Prevention*, 19, 3–30.

Weiss, C. H. (1995). Nothing as practical as good theory: Exploring theory-based evaluation for comprehensive community initiatives for children and families. In J. P. Connell, A. Kubisch, L. Schorr, & C. H. Weiss (Eds.), *New approaches to evaluating community initiatives: Concepts, methods, and contexts* (pp. 65–92). Washington, DC: Aspen Institute.

Witlein, B., & Altschuld, J. (1995). *Planning and conducting needs assessments*. Thousand Oaks, CA: Sage.

Worthen, B., Sanders, J., & Fitzpatrick, J. (1997). *Program evaluation: Alternative approaches and practical guidelines* (2nd ed.). White Plains, NY: Longman.

Recommended Readings _____

Fetterman, D., Kaftarian, S., & Wandersman, A. (Eds.). (1996). *Empowerment evaluation: Knowledge and tools for self-assessment and accountability.* Thousand Oaks, CA: Sage.

Linney, J. A., & Wandersman, A. (1996). Empowering community groups with evaluation skills: The Prevention Plus III Model. In D. Fetterman, S. Kaftarian, & A. Wandersman (Eds.), *Empowerment evaluation: Knowledge and tools for self-assessment and accountability* (pp. 259–276). Thousand Oaks, CA: Sage.

Patton, M. Q. (1997). *Utilization-focused evaluation* (3rd ed.). Thousand Oaks, CA: Sage.

Rossi, P. H., Freeman, H. E., & Lipsey, M. (1999). *Evaluation: A systematic approach* (6th ed.). Newbury Park, CA: Sage.

W. K. Kellogg Foundation. (1998). *Kellogg evaluation handbook.* Battle Creek, MI: Author.

Worthen, B. R., Sanders, J. R., & Fitzpatrick, J. L. (1997). *Program evaluation: Alternative approaches and practical guidelines* (2nd ed.). White Plains, NY: Longman.

Recommended Websites _____

www.eval.org

The American Evaluation Association website has listings and links for a variety of program evaluations resources and networks. Their topical interest groups list information and resources for two topics especially relevant to this chapter: collaborative, participatory, and empowerment evaluation, and program theory in evaluation. Other interest groups include health programs, alcohol and drug abuse and mental health, crime and justice, minority issues, feminist issues, international and cross-cultural evaluation, qualitative issues, and quantitative methods.

www.stanford.edu/~davidf/empowermentevaluation.html

The website for empowerment evaluation approaches based on the Fetterman, Kaftarian, and Wandersman volume listed in Recommended Readings and discussed in the chapter.

http://ctb.lsi.ukans.edu

This community tool kit has helpful suggestions for program development and program evaluation.

www.frca.org

The Family Resource Coalition of America at this website has published two assessment guides for programs related to family issues: "How are We Doing? A Program Self-Assessment Toolkit for the Family Support Field" and "Know Your Community: A Step-by-Step Guide to Community Needs and Resource Assessment" (suggested by Richard Jenkins).

12

Outcome Measures and Indicators

This chapter deals with a number of procedures and indicators used to evaluate social programs in the United States. It is especially focused on the United Way of America's use of outcome measures with the agencies it helps finance. Of course, United Way of America does not directly fund services. However, it supports and coordinates the efforts of local United Way organizations, which provide the direct support to local social services.

In most agencies and under most circumstances in which assessment and evaluation tools are used, there are management information systems available. These are computerized data sources that collect and organize information on a program's clientele, costs, services provided, and other factors. These become data for the agency's management. In addition, however, they become the basic material for the application of assessment and evaluation tools.

Assessment and Evaluation Tools

Many organizations use specific evaluation tools to assess their functioning. Some of the tools are developed by evaluation and academic organizations, often with financing from government and foundations. The tools and systems are disseminated to organizations that might use them to develop their programs and to evaluate their functioning. Organizations use one or several of these kinds of tools in their ongoing assessment and evaluation of their programs. Mental health services have been especially interested in these kinds of concrete and specific outcomes measurement instruments. During the second half of the twentieth century, mental health changed more than almost any other of the human services. First, there was an emphasis on deinstitutionalization, in which public hospital mental patients were discharged on the assumption that they would be better and more economically served in community programs. However, there is a constant concern that the community resources either do not exist or do not reach discharged patients—some of whom do not follow up with community care. Another factor that has complicated mental health services has been the advent of "managed care," through health maintenance organizations and health insurance companies. These structures determine whether to authorize payment for services, based on the documentation of the extent and nature of a patient's condition. This has also complicated the ability of mental health services to provide care to patients. Therefore, monitoring their ability to provide services and their efficiency and effectiveness is a critical issue in the mental health field.

Indicators are also used in the United Way outcomes measurement program, which is discussed later in this chapter. For the United Way of America, indicators are simply statistics or other quantifiable earmarks that can help a program determine the extent to which it has moved toward achieving its outcomes. Of course, it is necessary to specify indicators as evidence of the achievement of outcomes.

One example of an indicator program is *Toolkit*, (Kamis-Gould & Hadley, undated), which was developed for mental health organizations to help them assess their plans and their performances. It was financed under a grant from the federal Substance Abuse and Mental Health Services Administration, Center for Mental Health Services, by the Evaluation Center at the University of Pennsylvania Department of Psychiatry. The purpose of *Toolkit* is to provide evaluators with instruments and methods that have been tested that can be used to evaluate plans and operations. The kit adds a "report card," which is an assessment tool that can be used in conjunction with an evaluation. It was financed and developed because the more-general healthcare performance indicators rarely have specific measures for mental health services, especially now that they are operating in a new environment of managed care.

Measurement devices such as this provide data on which decisions can be made and focus on the most important concerns of mental health programs. The indicators are designed to be able to address large issues and concerns, but also to deal with and document more-precise performance data, such as the nature of clients, the services that are provided, and similar detailed information. The performance indicators are designed to efficiently measure the most critical elements of the system being evaluated.

The instrument outlines the many tasks and roles that are currently discharged in mental health by one level of service organization or another:

Regulations
Safety net
Policy development
Rate setting
Service contracting

Service financing
Financial risk
Research and evaluation
Quality assurance/utilization review
Authorization
Payment
Data processing
Claims processing
Interagency coordination
Reporting
Direct services

The document also deals with such critical issues as rural mental health, the differences between public and private mental health services, and the differences between managed care in public and private environments.

Further, the system proposes an evaluation model that deals with a mental health service's responsiveness, efficiency, and effectiveness. Each of those three dimensions is further broken into detailed measures of specific components of a program's functioning. *Toolkit* provides formulas and other guidelines for assessing all of those dimensions. For example, it offers measures to determine the adequacy of the size of a staff and a program's budget, as well as the degree of referrals an organization receives from community agencies. However, it also gives guidelines for assessing an organization's outreach to the larger community, the adequacy of its supply of various services such as hospitalization, and the satisfaction of clients with the services provided.

In addition to its suggested indicators and methods, *Toolkit* concludes with examples of performance indicator plans from several states that have used them.

Mental Health Outcomes Newsletters

In the mental health field, two newsletters published by Manisses Communications Group specialize in providing information on evaluation of mental health programs. One is called *Outcomes and Accountability Alert,* and the other is *Behavioral Health Outcomes.* An article from the March 1999 issue of *Outcomes and Accountability Alert* (Altshuler & Rush, 1999) describes a $6.5 million project in Texas to determine what the appropriate treatments are for schizophrenia, bipolar disorder, and major depressive disorder. Funding comes from a variety of private foundations and state and federal government agencies. About 1,200 patients will be followed for a year to compare costs and the effectiveness of treatment following usual procedures and following algorithms that are built into computer programs. The algorithms will help physicians gauge the intensity of the patient's problems and the impact of using various pharmaceuticals as well as other treatment. The evaluation will be conducted at multiple sites in Texas medical schools and mental health centers.

An article in *Behavioral Health Outcomes* (Goldstein, 1998) describes the work of a task force in Ohio that was developing an innovative mental health outcomes evaluation system, which Ohio officials hoped would be significantly different than previous evaluation schemes. Managed care had not yet come to Ohio, but the state wanted to be ready when it arrived. They wanted a system that would evaluate the quality of services available to clients rather than simply choosing them on the basis of cost.

The same issue of *Behavioral Health Outcomes* (October 1998) reports on a variety of evaluations of treatments: findings that lower incomes are associated with a higher mortality risk, that antidepressant therapy reduces medical costs for patients with some health conditions, and that cognitive-behavioral therapy is effective in treating bulimia.

The Georgia PERMES System

Georgia uses the Performance Measurement and Evaluation System (PERMES) to collect data that will assist in improving the performance and accountability of the state's mental health, mental retardation, and substance abuse systems and programs. All three of those programs are combined under the Georgia Department of Human Resources.

A grant from the federal Center for Mental Health Services helped Georgia begin the development of the system in 1997. The state evaluators identified 19 indicators that were based on the preferences of consumers, national research standards, and the priorities of the state's 13 mental health, mental retardation, and substance abuse boards. The 19 are broken into five categories with the sources specified, as in Table 12.1.

It is noteworthy that the PERMES approach primarily uses surveys of consumers with some reliance on the agency information systems and standardized instruments appropriate for specific groups of clients. Their surveys and data yielded a detailed report for the 1999–2000 program year that provided information on the outcomes for each of these indicators.

Management Indicators and Audits

An example of an indicator system used in teaching social workers to be managers is provided by Thomas Packard (2000). Packard, who is on the faculty of the San Diego State University School of Social Work, offers to send his management audit instrument to those who write and request it. Although he calls the system an audit, it probably falls more clearly under the indicator rubric, as defined in this text and as distinguished from financial and performance audits, which are described elsewhere.

Students in the management course described in Packard's article are responsible for conducting management audits in cooperation with the students' practicum instructor. Each audit assesses an agency on a series of 89 criteria that deal with the organization's effectiveness. The 89 are grouped into 12 categories,

TABLE 12.1 *Mental Health, Mental Retardation, and Substance Abuse Indicators*

System-Wide Indicators

- Availability of Services
- Accessibility of Services
- Satisfaction with Services
  (All three of these are based on responses to a
  consumer survey.)

Adult Mental Health Indicators

- Housing Choice (consumer survey)
- Employment (consumer survey)
- Consumer Functioning/Symptoms (based on the BASIS-32
  Clinical Assessment instrument results)
- Hospital Utilization (based on the agency information system)

Child and Adolescent Mental Health Indicators

- Family Supports (consumer survey)
- Consumer Involvement in Service Planning (consumer survey)
- Consumer Functioning/Symptoms (based on the CAFAS Clinical
  Assessment Instrument)
- Out of Home Placement (based on the agency
  information system)

Mental Retardation Indicators

- Housing Choice (consumer survey)
- Employment (consumer survey)
- Community Integration (consumer survey)
- Least Restrictive Residential Environment (from the agency
  information system)

Substance Abuse Indicators

- Sustained Recovery (from the agency information system)
- Employment (consumer survey)
- Consumer Functioning/Symptoms (Addiction Severity Index
  Assessment instrument)
- Treatment Usage/Penetration Rate (from the agency information
  system)

Source: 1999–2000 Performance Profile, MHMRSA Statewide Survey, by Georgia Department of Human Resources, Division of Mental Health, Mental Retardation, and Substance Abuse, 2000, Atlanta, GA: Author.

which include: "planning, management of the environment, client relations, program design and service delivery technology, structure, management information systems, budgeting and financial management, staffing and human resources, leadership, organizational culture and change, program evaluation, and quality of working life" (Packard, 2000, p. 44).

The management audits conducted by all the students are compiled. Distinctions are made between governmental and not-for-profit organizations. The management audits are used to help the organizations improve their functioning. In addition, agencies are helped as they develop change plans based on the assessments. Through the process, agencies develop and improve, and students learn to evaluate agencies and become more competent in the management of social agencies.

Cost-Benefit Analysis

Another measure of outcomes is the cost versus the benefit obtained because of the program or service provided. Posavac and Carey (1997) provide detailed information on making such comparisons and also identify a variety of costs that must be considered in the cost-benefit equation. Costs may be:

1. Variable or fixed, incremental or sunk (sunk costs are those that have already been paid)
2. Recurring or nonrecurring
3. Hidden or obvious
4. Direct or indirect (indirect are those that support the organization and make it possible to provide the services, such as the cost of maintaining the facilities, general support staff, parking lots)
5. Opportunity costs (those associated with selecting one program over another alternative because choosing one eliminates the possibility of also carrying out the other)

The benefits part of the equation is the complicated evaluation of programs, as discussed earlier in this chapter and in many other chapters of this text. How well the program carries out its objectives and how much they are worth relative to their costs is the kind of judgment that cost-benefit analysis engenders.

The United Way Outcomes Measurement Approach

In the 1990s, the United Way of America developed a plan for helping local United Ways become oriented to the results or outcomes of their activities. They published a book (United Way of America, 1996) that provides a step-by-step model for an organization to use in defining its outcomes. Concerns persisted for many years that voluntary agencies, the largest funders of which are local branches of the United Way, focused on what they did rather than on their programs' results. To overcome that concern, the United Way leadership from around the nation embarked on a project to help agencies think through not only their activities but also the results or outcomes of those activities. This philosophy and approach are somewhat similar to trends in other parts of American life and approaches found in other chapters of this text. The outcomes approach is similar to budget arrangements used in government and industry, such as zero-based budgeting, in which agencies seeking funds for a new fiscal year must justify every dollar—rather than simply calling for incremental increases over the previous year's allocation. It is also similar in some ways to the quality control and quality assurance approach in organizations, in which the effort is to effectively produce a product (or service) with the fewest possible errors. The outcomes approach is also comparable to single-subject design, in which it is not enough to meet with and counsel clients. One must also measure progress and demonstrate that clients are improving or have overcome the problems they initially presented. Counseling sessions completed may be the outputs, but the outcome has to be improved mental health and social functioning.

Decision makers in local United Ways as well as the leadership of their voluntary member agencies were trained and periodically retrained in the outcomes approach developed by the coordinating and service body for all United Ways, the United Way of America.

The system they developed is applicable not only to voluntary agencies that are affiliated with United Way but also as an evaluation system for virtually any human services program, public or private. The system deals with the long-known tendency of agencies and their employees to focus on their activities without always paying attention to the reasons for those activities or their ultimate results. Their book, *Measuring Program Outcomes: A Practical Approach* (United Way of America, 1996) says that most human service organizations do not always follow up on what happens to their participants after they are no longer involved with an agency. The book is written for program managers and executive directors. (United Way has allowed this author to use the ideas and some of the illustrations for this book, as well.)

For reasons that are obvious but that are specified in their work, outcomes—those results for participants down the road—are important to agencies. They formally define outcomes as "benefits or changes for individuals or populations during or after participating in program activities. . . . Outcomes may relate to behavior, skills, knowledge, attitudes, values, condition, or other attributes. They are what participants know, think, or can do; or how they behave; or what their condition is, that is different following the program" (United Way of America, 1996, p. 18).

The United Way of America does not equate outcomes with indicators, another subject of this chapter. Indicators, they believe, are specific data items that are used to determine how well a program is reaching its outcomes or targets, which are the program's sought-after level of achievement.

Figure 12.1 summarizes the Program Output Model promoted to its affiliates by the United Way of America. Note that it consists of four parts:

Inputs—the resources provided to or consumed by the program. These inputs are both financial and human resources. They are also the community or agency client needs. The agency works on the problems of, for example, people who have problems with alcohol, or the homeless, or children who are identified as needing structured and positive leisure activities.

Activities—what an agency does—its program. This is the subject matter of what some call a "formative" evaluation and what others call a "process" evaluation. What an agency does has no necessary connection with what it achieves for those it serves. Therefore, although it is necessary to know what the activities are, it is not sufficient to cite them as evidence that an agency has achieved what it sets out to achieve.

Outputs—the products of the activities. The numbers that have participated, the number of sessions that have been held, and the like are outputs. However, they do not necessarily achieve results. People with alcohol problems may attend daily meetings of Alcoholics Anonymous—and drink after they leave. Many young people may attend sessions on the pitfalls of teenage pregnancy—and engage in sex after the sessions.

Outcomes—the desired result. An agency seeks to change its clientele or community in specific ways. These are the desired final results of the agency's inputs, activities, and outputs.

The purpose of measuring outcomes, the United Way proponents say, is to help determine whether "programs really make a difference in the lives of people" (United Way of America, 1996, p. 4).

The Steps to Outcome Measurement

Figure 12.2 shows the eight steps (as a pyramid) that are followed in realizing the program's outcomes. Under the system, the program defines the outcomes it wants to measure, although it may have more than it ultimately assesses. Then the program identifies specific indicators, such as improved test scores in an educational program or permanent housing in a program that aims to reduce homelessness. A data collection plan is established and tested in the fifth step. Then the findings are analyzed and reported. The program follows its analysis and critique of its earlier work by improving the system. Finally, it uses the outcomes to provide direction for staff and to identify and implement staff and volunteer training needs. The outcomes are used in the development and justification of budgets and requests for external funding. The program helps board members focus on agency outcomes and program successes. Successful achievement of outcomes can also help an organization raise more money, build community support, and identify others with whom it may collaborate.

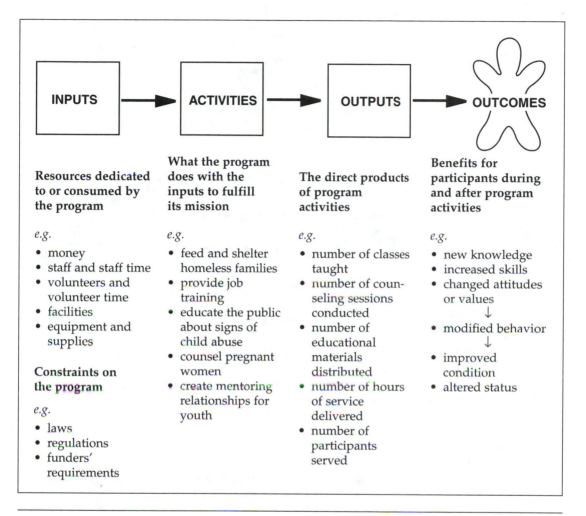

FIGURE 12.1   *Summary of Program Outcome Model*

Source: Reprinted from *Measuring Program Outcomes: A Practical Approach,* 1996, Alexandria, VA: United Way of America. Used by permission of United Way of America.

Traditional Models versus the Outcomes Approach

Figures 12.3 and 12.4 portray the evolution of the traditional model of services into the outcomes model. As Figure 12.3 shows, programs have traditionally stopped with their outputs in evaluating their efforts. (It should be noted that another of the inputs is a series of restraints that limit the ability of a program to do whatever it chooses. It cannot accept funds in any way it wants, nor can it carry

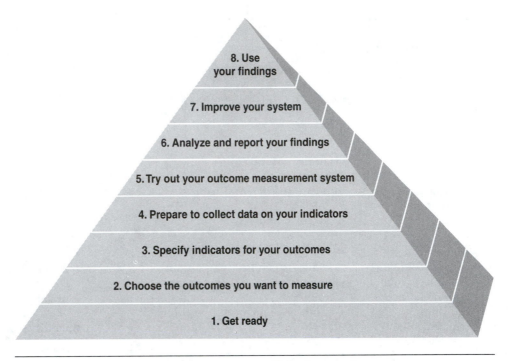

FIGURE 12.2   *Measuring Program Outcomes: Eight Steps to Success*

Source: Reprinted from *Measuring Program Outcomes: A Practical Approach,* 1996, Alexandria, VA: United Way of America. Used by permission of United Way of America.

out activities that violate the law. The constraints such as laws, regulations, and requirements for receiving funding—some of which are conditions specified by an agency's United Way—are significant agency inputs).

Figure 12.3 also shows that outputs are not necessarily measurable, long-term changes in agency clientele. The outputs are perhaps significant, but they do not necessarily imply long-term, permanent change.

Figure 12.4 presents the outcomes model and contrasts it with outputs. As the figure notes, the output of a neighborhood cleanup can be meetings, cleanup days, and heavy community involvement. However, an appropriate outcome is the improved safety and pride of the community that engaged in the cleanup.

Distinguishing Outcomes

Figure 12.5 shows some examples of what are and are not outcomes. Participant satisfaction is not an outcome. People may be satisfied with the service they re-

Most of us are familiar with the basic program model shown below. It has three major components: program inputs (resources), activities (services), and outputs (products).

- **Inputs** include resources dedicated to or consumed by the program. Examples are money, staff and staff time, volunteers and volunteer time, facilities, equipment, and supplies. For example, inputs for a parent education class include the hours of staff time spent designing and delivering the program.

  Inputs also include constraints on the program, such as laws, regulations, and requirements for receipt of funding.

- **Activities** are what the program does with the inputs to fulfill its mission. Activities include the strategies, techniques, and types of treatment that comprise the program's service methodology. For instance, sheltering and feeding homeless families are program activities, as are training and counseling homeless adults to help them prepare for and find jobs.

- **Outputs** are the direct products of program activities and usually are measured in terms of the volume of work accomplished—for example, the numbers of classes taught, counseling sessions conducted, educational materials distributed, and participants served. Outputs have little inherent value in themselves. They are important because they are intended to lead to a desired benefit or change for participants or target populations.

  If given enough resources, managers can control output levels. In a parent education class, for example, the number of classes held and the number of parents served are outputs. With enough staff and supplies, the program could double its output of classes and participants.

FIGURE 12.3 *The Traditional Service Program Model*

Source: Reprinted from *Measuring Program Outcomes: A Practical Approach,* 1996, Alexandria, VA: United Way of America. Used by permission of United Way of America.

ceived; however, that does not indicate that their status or their overall functioning has changed significantly. The chapter that deals with satisfaction studies tends to support this idea. Even when participants complete forms that demonstrate their satisfaction—with a teacher, for example—that satisfaction is no guarantee that they have learned or changed.

The traditional service model in Figure 12.3 lacks one important focus: the benefits participants derive from the program. No amount of input, activity, and output analysis can answer the question, "Are participants or target groups better off after receiving the service than they were before?"

The questions of whether, and how much, a program's participants have changed, how their status has improved, and how they have benefitted are answered by measuring the program's *outcomes*. Outcomes are the arrow beyond the outputs, as shown here.

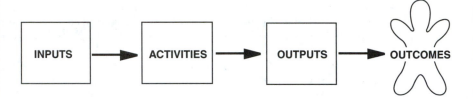

- **Outcomes** are benefits or changes for individuals or populations during or after participating in program activities. They are influenced by a program's outputs. Outcomes may relate to behavior, skills, knowledge, attitudes, values, condition, status, or other attributes. They are what participants know, think, or can do; or how they behave; or what their condition is, that is different following the program.

    For example, in a program to counsel families on financial management, outputs—what the service produces—include the number of financial planning sessions and the number of families seen. The desired outcomes—the changes sought in participants' behavior or status—can include their developing and living within a budget, making monthly additions to a savings account, and having increased financial stability.

    In another example, outputs of a neighborhood cleanup campaign can be the number of organizing meetings held and the number of weekends dedicated to the cleanup effort. Outcomes—benefits to the target population—might include reduced exposure to safety hazards and increased feelings of neighborhood pride.

FIGURE 12.4   *The Program Outcome Model*

Source: Reprinted from *Measuring Program Outcomes: A Practical Approach,* 1996, Alexandria, VA: United Way of America. Used by permission of United Way of America.

Here are some program components that agencies sometimes have trouble classifying as activities, outputs, or outcomes. These hints provide general guidelines and point out when exceptions may be appropriate.

- **Recruiting and training staff and volunteers, purchasing or upgrading equipment, and various support and maintenance activities.** These are internal program operations intended to improve the quality of program inputs. The number of staff recruited, number of volunteers trained, amount of equipment purchased, etc., indicate the volume of these internal operations. However, the operations do not represent benefits or changes in participants, and thus *are not outcomes.*

- **Number of participants served.** This information relates to the volume of work accomplished. In most cases, volume of service is an output. It tells nothing about whether participants benefited from the service and therefore *is not usually an outcome.*

  In public education programs where the program aims to encourage citizens to seek a service, such as cancer screening, the fact that citizens become aware of the importance of the service and seek it out reflects a change in knowledge or attitudes and behavior resulting from the program. Thus, the number of citizens who are motivated to seek a service by a public education program is an outcome of that program.

- **Participant satisfaction.** Most often, whether a participant is satisfied or not with various aspects of a program (e.g., courteousness of staff, timeliness of follow-up) does not indicate whether the participant's condition improved as a result of the service. Thus, participant satisfaction *generally is not an outcome.*

  In rare instances, participant satisfaction may be part of the series of changes a participant experiences in achieving a successful outcome. For example, if an individual's willingness to continue with long-term counseling is critical to the program's success and satisfaction is a key determinant of continuation, then satisfaction may be a necessary, although not sufficient, outcome. In programs whose purpose is to meet participants' basic needs, such as food kitchens and homeless shelters, it may be nearly impossible to track participants far enough beyond the immediate delivery of service to identify outcomes beyond being fed and sheltered. In these cases, the program may have to settle for participant satisfaction as the closest approximation of an outcome it can measure.

FIGURE 12.5 *Hints About What Are and Are Not Outcomes*

Source: Reprinted from *Measuring Program Outcomes: A Practical Approach,* 1996, Alexandria, VA: United Way of America. Used by permission of United Way of America.

FIGURE 12.6 *Examples of Diverse Programs and Possible Outcomes*[1]

Program	Possible Outcomes
Comprehensive child care	• Children exhibit age-appropriate physical, mental, and verbal skills. • Children are school-ready for kindergarten.
General Equivalency Diploma (GED) preparation	• Participants obtain their GED certificate. • Within 6 months after obtaining their GED, participants are employed full-time.
Outpatient treatment for adolescent substance abusers	• Adolescents increase knowledge about the effects of substance abuse and about substance abuse addiction. • Adolescents change attitude toward substance abuse. • Graduates remain free of substance abuse 6 months after program completion.
Emergency shelter beds on winter nights	• Homeless persons agree to come off the street and use the shelter. • Those sheltered do not suffer from frostbite or die from exposure to cold.
Homework guidance by volunteer tutors to children enrolled in after-school program	• Youths' attitude towards school work improves. • Youths complete homework assignments. • Youths perform at or above grade level.
Full-day therapeutic child care for homeless preschoolers	• Children get respite from family stress. • Children engage in age-appropriate play. • Children exhibit fewer symptoms of stress-related regression. • Parents receive respite from child care.
Overnight camping for 8- to 12-year-old inner-city boys	• Boys learn outdoor survival skills. • Boys develop enhanced sense of competence. • Boys develop and maintain positive peer relationships.
Congregate meals for senior citizens	• Participants have social interaction with peers. • Participants are not home-bound. • Participants eat nutritious and varied diet. • Seniors experience decrease in social and health problems.

[1]These are illustrative examples only. Programs should identify their own outcomes, matched to and based on their own experiences and missions and input of their staff, volunteers, participants, and others.

FIGURE 12.6 *Continued*

Program	Possible Outcomes
Interpreter services for non–English speaking patients at a health clinic	• Patients access needed health care. • Patients understand medical diagnosis and need for preventive measures or treatment. • Patients comply with medical recommendations. • Patients have decrease in health conditions that are preventable. • Patients recuperate from conditions that can be treated.
Personal safety training for residents of subsidized apartment building	• Residents initiate Neighborhood Watch Program. • Residents develop and implement action plan to make building more secure. • Residents feel safer. • Personal and property attacks decline.

Source: Reprinted from *Measuring Program Outcomes: A Practical Approach,* 1996, Alexandria, VA: United Way of America. Used by permission of United Way of America.

Virtually any program can and should have outcomes. Figure 12.6 shows a number of programs and the possible outcomes an agency may pursue within them. The examples should illustrate the distinctions made in the United Way system between outcomes and lesser achievements, such as activities and outputs.

Figure 12.7 gives the results of a community brainstorming session about the benefits of outcome measurement.

Planning and Implementing Outcome Measurement

Correctly planning and carrying out an outcome measurement program requires careful and strategic thought. Figures 12.8 and 12.9 present sample time lines for planning and implementing such a measurement. Figure 12.8 is completed and shows the various phases of the effort. The eight steps (the same as those in Figure 12.2) are carried out in order and by months. The chart also depicts the initial preparation, the trial run, and the implementation. Figure 12.9 is blank and available for planning one's own outcome exercise or for copying and using as a class exercise.

Of course, outcomes are not always perfect or final. At times they come in stages, such as in Figure 12.10. There can be three levels of outcomes, each a bit stronger and more lasting.

Focus groups, which are discussed in the chapter on needs assessment, are also used in other contexts—outcome planning, for example. The definition of and

Summary of Brainstorming by Agencies in Pierce County, Washington

- Provide a communication tool to let people know what's being done and the difference that it makes
- Reaffirm that we are on the right track
- Get information to use for program development
- Focus on programs that really make a difference for clients
- Make programs tangible by describing expected outcomes
- Benefit the agency and its long-range planning efforts
- Benefit families that use the services
- Let clients have a say in services
- Do a better job for our clients
- Have data to show quality
- Help focus on primary tasks
- Use for future planning
- A reality check
- Demonstrate "intangibles"
- Collect information as a routine part of what we are doing
- Get information that will be useful for decision-making
- Develop a model that will stop us from having to do ongoing testing
- Keep us from being penalized for things we cannot measure
- Communicate to funders a balance of outcomes and outputs
- Help justify existence
- Help the Board
- Be accountable and cost-effective
- Take pride in accomplishment and quality

FIGURE 12.7   *Examples of Potential Benefits of Outcome Measurement*

Source: Reprinted from *Measuring Program Outcomes: A Practical Approach,* 1996, Alexandria, VA: United Way of America. Used by permission of United Way of America.

suggestions for operations of focus groups shown in Figure 12.11 are helpful for any use of this methodology.

Figure 12.12 describes the ways in which indicators and outcomes connect with one another. It gives a variety of programs, their desired outcomes, and the indicators that are used to determine how close a program has come to reaching its outcomes. These concrete examples should clarify more specifically what the United Way of America means by outcomes and some of the indicators that show movement toward achievement of those outcomes.

Step	Initial Preparation Month 1	2	3	4	5	6	7	Trial Run Month 8-?	?+1	?+2	?+3	Implementation Month ?+4	?+5
1. Get Ready	X	X											
2. Choose the Outcomes You Want to Measure			X	X									
3. Specify Indicators for Your Outcomes					X								
4. Prepare to Collect Data on Your Indicators						X	X						
5. Try Out Your Outcome Measurement System								XXXXX					
6. Analyze and Report Your Findings									X	X	X		
7. Improve Your Outcome Measurement System												X	
Launch full-scale implementation													X →
8. Use Your Findings									X	X	X	X	X →

This sample allows 7 months for initial preparation. The amount of time for Step 5, which starts in Month 8, is left open because it can vary so widely. After Step 5, the sample shows 3 months for Step 6 and 1 month for Step 7. Full-scale implementation starts 5 months after the data collection trial ends.

FIGURE 12.8 *Form for Time Line to Plan and Implement Outcome Measurement*

Source: Reprinted from *Measuring Program Outcomes: A Practical Approach,* 1996, Alexandria, VA: United Way of America. Used by permission of United Way of America.

The United Way of America system requires the collection of data. Figure 12.13 describes the various data collection methods that may be used as well as their characteristics.

As one learns in basic research courses, the study of existing records is the simplest and least expensive data collection method. However, it may not yield the most comprehensive and useable results. The other three methods—self-administered questionnaires, interviews, and ratings by professionals—are each valuable but each more costly and complicated. The idea is that programs will

Program: _____

Step	Month																		
1. Get Ready																			
2. Choose the Outcomes We Want to Measure																			
3. Specify Indicators for Our Outcomes																			
4. Prepare to Collect Data on Our Indicators																			
5. Try Out Our Outcome Measurement System																			
6. Analyze and Report Our Findings																			
7. Improve Our Outcome Measurement System																			
Launch full-scale implementation																			
8. Use Our Findings																			

FIGURE 12.9   *Time Line Worksheet*

Source: Reprinted from *Measuring Program Outcomes: A Practical Approach,* 1996, Alexandria, VA: United Way of America. Used by permission of United Way of America.

choose the data collection method that best balances their need for information and their willingness to expend time, money, and other resources on collecting data. (Appendix 2 includes one United Way's program description form using the outcomes approach used in this chapter, as well as a statement of outcomes and indicators for senior adults in that community.)

Conclusion

Increasingly, social programs are required to evaluate themselves in concrete and specific ways. This chapter has covered some of the more common and effectively

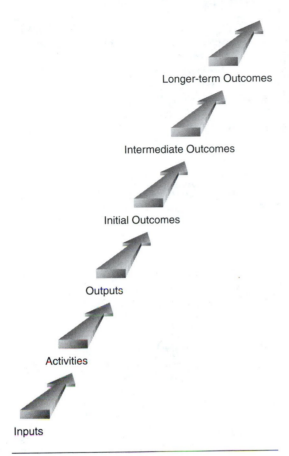

Longer-term Outcomes

Intermediate Outcomes

Initial Outcomes

Outputs

Activities

Inputs

FIGURE 12.10 *Inputs Through Outcomes: The Conceptual Chain*

Source: Reprinted from *Measuring Program Outcomes: A Practical Approach,* 1996, Alexandria, VA: United Way of America. Used by permission of United Way of America.

used evaluation and assessment tools and systems in the human services. Organizations are always subject to documenting the quality of their work and its effectiveness in the modern context. In many situations, financing depends on an organization's ability to demonstrate effectiveness through the documentation of the achievement of outcomes.

Several different systems are presented here, many from the mental health field. Indicators, score cards, and other devices are discussed. In addition, the United Way of America's *Measuring Program Objectives* approach is explicated in detail. It is a model that is increasingly used by private social welfare agencies and other human services programs that receive funds from United Way organizations in the United States. These measurement devices are likely to be increasingly

1. Invite approximately 8–12 participants to participate in each focus group. Consider offering an incentive for participation.

   Group members can be chosen from lists of current and former participants. The main criterion is that they have had experience with the program. If program participants are diverse in age, race/ethnicity, income, or other characteristics, the full range of your participants should be represented. Note, however, that conversations may be freer if each group is relatively homogeneous. If your program serves entire families, conduct separate focus groups with adults and young people.

2. Schedule the meeting for a maximum of two hours. Hold it in a comfortable, accessible location. Soft drinks and snacks might be provided.

3. Select an experienced focus group facilitator for the session.

   The purpose and conduct of focus groups are different from those of task-oriented meetings. Choose a facilitator who knows and is experienced with the differences. Do not select as facilitator a staff person who works with any of the focus group members. This could inhibit an open sharing of participants' views.

4. After introductions and an overview of the session's purpose, the facilitator asks the participants open-ended questions to elicit their views on the benefits the program provides—what changes participants want, expect, or have experienced. Pose the question in several ways, such as:

   - What did you expect to change for you as a result of being in the program?
   - If the program really helps you, how will you be better off?
   - Are there things you don't like about the program?

   The facilitator encourages each participant to express her or his views on these questions. The facilitator's job is to establish an open, non-threatening environment and obtain input from each participant. To do this, the facilitator accepts anything participants say and does not attempt to explain the program, correct misconceptions participants may have, or gain agreement or consensus among group members.

5. Someone, such as a member of the work group, serves as recorder. Soon after the session, the reporter and facilitator summarize what was said.

   Note that focus groups are purely qualitative in their method. The summary does not attempt to quantify how many persons expressed various views or seemed to share the same position.

FIGURE 12.11 *Conducting Focus Groups*

Source: Reprinted from *Measuring Program Outcomes: A Practical Approach,* 1996, Alexandria, VA: United Way of America. Used by permission of United Way of America.

FIGURE 12.12   *Example Outcomes and Outcome Indicators for Various Programs*[1]

Type of Program	*Outcome*	*Indicator(s)*
Smoking cessation class	Participants stop smoking.	• Number and percent of participants who report that they have quit smoking by the end of the course • Number and percent of participants who have not relapsed six months after program completion
Information and referral program	Callers access services to which they are referred or about which they are given information.	• Number and percent of community agencies that report an increase in new participants who came to their agency as a result of a call to the information and referral hotline • Number and percent of community agencies that indicate these referrals are appropriate
Tutorial program for 6th-grade students	Students' academic performance improves.	• Number and percent of participants who earn better grades in the grading period following completion of the program than in the grading period immediately preceding enrollment in the program
English-as-a-second-language instruction	Participants become proficient in English.	• Number and percent of participants who demonstrate increase in ability to read, write, and speak English by the end of the course
Counseling for parents identified as at risk for child abuse or neglect	Risk factors decrease. No confirmed incidents of child abuse or neglect.	• Number and percent of participating families for whom Child Protective Service records report no confirmed child abuse or neglect during 12 months following program completion
Employee assistance program	Employees with drug and/or alcohol problems are rehabilitated and do not lose their jobs.	• Number and percent of program participants who are gainfully employed at same company six months after intake

[1]These are illustrative examples only. Programs should identify their own outcomes and indicators, matched to and based on their own experiences and missions and input of their staff, volunteers, participants, and others.

(continued)

FIGURE 12.12 *Continued*

Type of Program	Outcome	Indicator(s)
Homemaking services	The home environment is healthy, clean, and safe. Participants stay in their own home and are not referred to a nursing home.	• Number and percent of participants whose home environment is rated clean and safe by a trained observer • Number of local nursing homes who report that applications from younger and healthier citizens are declining (indicating that persons who in the past would have been referred to a nursing home now stay at home longer)
Prenatal care program	Pregnant women follow the advice of the nutritionist.	• Number and percent of women who take recommended vitamin supplements and consume recommended amounts of calcium
Shelter and counseling for runaway youth	Family is reunified whenever possible; otherwise, youths are in stable alternative housing.	• Number and percent of youth who return home • Number and percent of youth placed in alternative living arrangements who are in that arrangement six months later unless they have been reunified or emancipated
Camping	Children expand skills in areas of interest to them.	• Number and percent of campers who identify two or more skills they have learned at camp
Family planning for teen mothers	Teen mothers have no second pregnancies until they have completed high school and have the personal, family, and financial resources to support a second child.	• Number and percent of teen mothers who comply with family planning visits • Number and percent of teen mothers using a recommended form of birth control • Number and percent of teen mothers who do not have repeat pregnancies prior to graduation • Number and percent of teen mothers who, at the time of next pregnancy, are high school graduates, are named, and do not need public assistance to provide for their children

Source: Reprinted from *Measuring Program Outcomes: A Practical Approach*, 1996, Alexandria, VA: United Way of America. Used by permission of United Way of America.

FIGURE 12.13   *Comparison of Major Data Collection Methods*

	Data Collection Method			
Characteristic	*Review of Program Records*	*Self-administered Questionnaire*	*Interview*	*Rating by Trained Observer*
Cost	Low	Moderate	Moderate to high, depending on how administered	Depends on availability of low-cost observers
Amount of training required for data collectors	Some	None to some, depending on how distributed	Moderate to high, depending on collectors' previous experience and survey complexity	Moderate to high, depending on complexity, subtlety of observations
Completion time	Short, depending on amount of data needed	Moderate to long, depending on how distributed	Long	Short to moderate
Response rate	High, if records contain needed data	Depends on how distributed	Generally moderate to good	High

Source: Reprinted from *Measuring Program Outcomes: A Practical Approach,* 1996, Alexandria, VA: United Way of America. Used by permission of United Way of America.

encountered by social workers in practice throughout the nation. They are a factor that influences the operation of many agencies—perhaps most—in the twenty-first century.

Questions for Further Study

1. Define the possible relationship between management information systems and the use of indicators and outcomes for evaluation of programs.

2. How does the United Way of America distinguish between outcomes and outputs? Give two examples of each that are *not* discussed in this chapter.

3. Note that funding agencies such as the U.S. government and the United Way of America often finance the plans for outcome measures and indicators. Speculate, in two or three paragraphs, about why financing sources have a special interest in these tools.

4. Assume you are director of a Big Brothers or Big Sisters "mentoring" program. Describe the ways in which you might define the four elements of the United Way system for such a program: inputs, activities, outputs, and outcomes.

References

Altshuler, K. Z., & Rush, A. J. (1999, March). Computerized Texas medication algorithm project undergoes testing. *Outcomes and Accountability Alert, 1*, 10–11.

Ginsberg, L. H. (1998, October). *Behavioral Health Outcomes,* Georgia Department of Human Resources, Division of Mental Health, Mental Retardation, and Substance Abuse. (2000). *1999–2000 Performance profile, MHMRSA statewide survey.* Atlanta, GA: Author.

Goldstein, M. G. (Ed.). (1998, October). Ohio task force readies an innovative mental health outcomes evaluation system. *Behavioral Health Outcomes, 3,* 10, 13.

Kamis-Gould, E., & Hadley, T. R. (n.d.). *Toolkit: A model of indicators and a report card for assessment of mental health plans' and systems' performance.* Philadelphia: University of Pennsylvania Department of Psychiatry.

Packard, T. (2000, Winter). The management audit as a teaching tool in social work administration. *Journal of Social Work Education,* 39–52.

Posavec, E. J., & Carey, R. G. (1997). *Program evaluation: Methods and case studies* (5th ed.). Upper Saddle River, NJ: Prentice-Hall.

United Way of America. (1996). *Measuring program outcomes: A practical approach.* Alexandria, VA: Author.

13

Evaluating Large Government Programs

Larry Nackerud
University of Georgia

The most prominent legacy of social workers in large government programs in the United States is one of direct service. This powerful direct service legacy helps fuel the profession's interest in the evaluation of large government programs. For decades, members of the social work profession have insisted that public policies and programs—particularly as a function of federal and state governments—demonstrate a meaningful impact on social problems. Direct social work practitioners have tended to ask of government policy makers and government programs: How much difference does this policy or program make to those persons who suffer from the effects of the social problem?

Social work practitioners are also generally able to recognize that judgments about the merits of a legislatively developed policy or a government-implemented program cannot be made without reference to the original understanding of the social problem. Policies should not be created and programs should not be implemented in the abstract or in relation to more or less random ideas about the nature of the social problem toward which they are directed as a solution (Chambers, 2000).

A discussion of evaluating large government programs inevitably leads to the debate about what has been the contribution of the social sciences to social problem resolution. Also, what impact has evaluation research conducted by social work practitioners had on social policy construction and social program implementation? Put simply, the central issue is: Have constructed and implemented social intervention strategies via large government programs been effective? In spite of the vast scholarship describing such problems as poverty, dependency, crime, health, and mental health, the value of the social sciences may reside merely in their fundamental ability to provide some semblance of reliable information for public discussion of social problems. Efforts to evaluate large government programs contribute directly to that public discussion of social problems (Epstein, 1997).

In hopes of making a positive contribution to that discussion, this author attempts to do three things in this chapter. First, two common pitfalls in the process of evaluating large government programs are identified. Second, as a means of illustrating the pitfalls, a brief review of three large government programs—Head Start, Model Cities, and Intensive Family Preservation Programs—is provided. Finally, the chapter highlights the evaluation methodology designed and implemented by a team of researchers affiliated with the School of Social Work at the University of Georgia as they fulfilled a contractual obligation to evaluate the impacts of welfare reform.

Evaluation Pitfalls

The evaluation of large government programs has two major pitfalls. First, evaluators tend to overly rely on the achievement of design rigor through the use of the classic experimental designs of the sort described in Chapter 10 (Epstein, 1997). The problem with the achievement of rigor in this fashion is that it is most often very expensive (Mowbray, Bybee, Collins, & Levine, 1998). The political, programmatic, and financial costs associated with the ability of evaluators to assign program participants in a large government program to treatment and control conditions are usually quite high. There is no question that this ability to assign to treatment and control is a design feature necessary for adherence to the demands of the classic experimental design. Adherence to the prescriptive norm of randomization in the scientific method is another example. However, although the use of the scientific method leads evaluators to always desire random selection in sampling and random assignment to conditions, the reality of evaluating a large government program is seldom so accommodating (Yegidis, Weinbach, & Morrison-Rodriquez, 1999).

The second pitfall is that evaluators of large government programs often focus only on the immediate question at hand and fail to see unusual opportunities to contribute to policy formulation and social science theory. For example, in any current evaluation of welfare reform there are a number of questions that come immediately to mind. In a most direct, simplistic, but yet important effort to evaluate program effectiveness, the only question that needs to be answered is: How effective has welfare reform been in driving down the numbers of persons in receipt of cash assistance? Sadly enough, a number of states, counties, and municipalities are limiting their welfare reform evaluative efforts to only that immediate question.

The questions and evaluation inferences in welfare reform, however, deserve to be more complex and become so as other questions are considered. Questions such as: How do those persons who remain on Temporary Assistance for Needy

Families (TANF) compare with those persons who have left TANF? How are persons who have left TANF faring?

An evaluation opportunity is missed in the evaluation of an innovative large government program, such as welfare reform, if only the immediate questions are addressed. It is necessary not only to attend to urgent issues of immediate relevance for the sake of the welfare reform impact debate, but also to include, as much as possible, in any evaluation effort a long-term analysis of the newly developed, power shifting, increasingly complex intergovernmental policies. The overarching policy of devolution contained in this iteration of welfare reform has tremendous implications for intergovernmental relations. Welfare reform evaluation efforts, at both the federal and state levels, can easily include the consideration of broader theoretical issues. Examples of these issues include federalism, categorical programs versus block grants, the issues of entitlements, the balance of dependency versus self-sufficiency, and the interplay between public policy and the underlying dynamics of human development, family functioning, and community well-being (McClintock & Colosi, 1998).

Head Start, Model Cities, and Intensive Family Preservation Programs

A brief review of three large government programs that have undergone extensive evaluative efforts—Head Start, Model Cities, and Intensive Family Preservation Programs—follows. Reader are reminded that a host of large government programs could have been selected for this review. Also, please keep in mind that the amount of information related to evaluations on any of these programs is exhaustive and only broached slightly here. These three programs, however, are highly amenable to the goal of illustrating the two common pitfalls. Evaluations of these programs illustrate the seemingly unending debate about reliance on the classic experimental design as a means to achieve rigor. They also illustrate the tension between the need to address immediate questions and the desire to include bigger issues.

It goes almost without challenge to say that no large social program in the United States has endured more rigorous and varied evaluation efforts than Head Start. Evaluations of this large government program have been conducted seemingly forever and by evaluators from a myriad of disciplines, including education, sociology, anthropology, social work, and economics. The nationwide and still most famous evaluation of Head Start programs was conducted by the Westinghouse Learning Corporation in the late 1960s. The design of the evaluation was a posttest-only quasi-experiment. Complex retrospective matching was completed on variables as varied as alumni status. An effort to control for a small number of variables, such as socioeconomic status, was also included in the Westinghouse evaluation. The analyses found full-year Head Start programs to be ineffective or only marginally effective for cognitive development. It would be an understatement to say that the Westinghouse findings were politically and socially controversial. Subsequently, there has been a three-decades long evaluative debate regarding the impact, or lack thereof, of Head Start. These evaluations have all been conducted within the context of Head Start being a highly popular government intervention program. This popularity extends to participating families, policy makers, and the general public. Even when the data revealed a lack of desired impact, Head Start was still seen as government doing the "right thing" (Currie & Thomas, 1995; Wu & Campbell, 1996).

The methodological rigor and wizardry of the follow-up evaluations of Head Start have been mind boggling. For example, Wu and Campbell (1996) were able to demonstrate how extending latent variable Lisrel analyses of the 1969 Westinghouse Head Start evaluation allowed for the discovery of a complex set of effectiveness results for black and white children and for full-year and summer attendees. Currie and Thomas (1995) emphasized in their recent evaluative effort, which focused on the development of economic models, the need to recognize the selection bias question (e.g., income eligibility requirements) and the difficulties regarding effect size estimates inherent in the early attempts to evaluate this large government program. Of course, those perceived weaknesses were most often attributed to a lack of strict adherence to the features of the classic experimental design, which includes a diminishing of any selection bias by the use of random selection and random assignment.

The Model Cities Program is another large government program that has undergone a multitude of evaluations. The Model Cities Program (which was created by the federal Demonstration Cities and Metropolitan Act of 1966) was a central component of the Lyndon B. Johnson administration's Great Society attempt to provide federal assistance to distressed urban communities. The evaluation attempts of this large government program were also varied and highly controversial. Again, a major point of contention was the failure of the original evaluators to adhere to the features in the classic experimental design—namely randomization in selection and assignment to condition and the inclusion of a basis of comparison after assignment to a treatment and control condition. Interestingly, lessons learned in evaluation efforts of the Model Cities Program reportedly were helpful in the creation of evaluation plans for the Empowerment Zone Program under the first Clinton administration. The need to ensure that coordination between the federal government and local communities actually occurs is the most often cited example of program learning. Major lessons learned and included in evaluation planning for the Empowerment Zone Program were not, however, related to the classic design features of randomization and assignment to treatment and control conditions. Instead, they involved: (1) measurement issues, such as the rectification of the Model Cities Program's vague designation criteria for communities as being in need, and (2) evaluation requirements of local constituencies, particularly with regard to the inclusion of contextual data (Rubin, 1994).

The creation of Intensive Family Preservation Programs followed on the heels of the Adoption Assistance and Child Welfare Act of 1980 [P.L. 96-272]. Bath and Haapala (1994) extensively critiqued the design of Intensive Family Preservation Programs evaluations. After a survey of recent evaluations with both positive and negative outcomes, Bath and Haapala focused on three widely reported experimental evaluations and concluded that the previously heralded equivocal findings must be treated with great caution. Their recommendations include consideration of alternative research strategies, such as those that include the use of mixed quantitative and qualitative methods. They support consideration of smaller scale, localized evaluations because they allow for greater control over experimental variables. Bath and Haapala report that they are led to this conclusion by the emergence of meaningful evidence from smaller, localized evaluations that appear to support the efficacy of Intensive Family Preservation Programs.

Smith (1995) also demonstrated empirically the efficacy of smaller scale, localized evaluations, which includes: (1) careful consideration of purposeful admission criteria in a locally based family preservation program and (2) more-definitive outcome measures used to judge program impact. Furthermore, Eamon's (1994) evaluative research denounces a lack of adequate consideration of preexisting poverty conditions during impact assessments of Intensive Family Preservation Programs. Her conclusion is that until family poverty is significantly reduced, or adequately controlled for during evaluation efforts, Intensive Family Preservation Programs evaluations adhering to classic experimental design expectations will continue to reveal disappointing results.

Addressing the Overreliance Pitfall

Why do endless numbers and variety of evaluators continue to attempt to explain, understand, and compensate for any lack of adherence to all standards of the classic experimental design in the Westinghouse or other early evaluation efforts of Head Start? The general public is not listening. Policy makers are hardly listening. With all due respect to Wu and Campbell, well-respected research design and evaluation experts in their own right, only a small percentage of evaluators understand and can apply to any reality-based policy question the nuances of data analysis based on analyses of the intensity of feelings about a program such as Head Start. That percentage becomes miniscule when such understanding is expected of the general public. One speculative answer is that some evaluators continue in their plight because of a fascination with, and clear overreliance on, the merits of the classic experimental design in the evaluation of large government programs.

Historically, and currently, evaluators face a multitude of design constraints in adapting research models to field conditions. If evaluation efforts and results are to be applicable to the realities of policy making and program implementation, evaluators may need to take a more realistic approach to resource needs and constraints. This point of view does not suggest weakening support for strong evaluation designs. For many large government interventions, definitive conclusions concerning the effectiveness of alternative service models cannot be obtained without rigorous designs. However, if the decision that the evaluation results feed into is availability of some services versus no services for a given risk population and the evaluation is based on an improvement-oriented, incremental process of feedback and change, then the need for rigorous designs is certainly less compelling. Evaluation practices recommended by several well-regarded evaluators emphasize that there should be less concern with whether an evaluation has produced the best knowledge possible and more concern on whether the knowledge produced will suffice, particularly given what policy makers need to know to achieve program successes (Mowbray et al., 1998).

Addressing the Immediate Concerns versus Bigger Issues Pitfall

Attending to the expressions of program theory in a large government program is one possible way for evaluators to strike a balance between attending to immediate, relevant impact questions and including a concern for broad theoretical issues (Nackerud, 1993).

With attention focused only on the immediate concern of whether welfare rolls have declined, it is easy for any evaluation to conclude that welfare reform has been a success. In July 1998, barely one year after all states had implemented TANF, the President and the secretary of Health and Human Services were hailing such facts as a 37 percent drop in welfare rolls nationwide. Although welfare rolls had been relatively flat from the mid-1970s through the end of the 1980s, they jumped by almost 30 percent between 1989 and 1993. This jump contributed directly to the political climate that resulted in the demise of AFDC. However, understanding the drop in welfare rolls after passage of the Personal Responsibility and Work Opportunity Reconciliation Act of 1996 is not so simple. The welfare rolls had actually begun to decline several years before the passage of TANF. The number of welfare recipients nationwide fell by 20 percent between January 1993 and January 1997. An additional variable that makes any evaluation effort of welfare reform more complex is the state of the economy. A report by the Council of Economic Advisers attributed 44 percent of the decline in welfare rolls to economic growth, 31 percent to welfare-to-work waiver demonstrations in various states, and 25 percent to other factors. There is no question, however, that the decline in welfare rolls accelerated after the passage and implementation of TANF. The number of welfare recipients dropped by 37 percent from August 1996 to December 1998. There were even more dramatic changes in many states: more than 75 percent in Idaho, Wyoming, and Wisconsin; more than 60 percent in West Virginia and Mississippi; and more than 50 percent in Florida, South Carolina, Colorado, Alabama, and Georgia. Simply using the decline in the TANF rolls as the prime indicator of success in welfare reform, however, is misleading (Joseph, 1999; Tweedie & Reichart, 1998).

Dye and Presser (1999) exemplified how evaluators who focused on welfare reform might include more broad-based, theoretical issues when they chose to review the "illegitimacy ratio" question. Even addressing a question such as whether welfare reform resulted in a diminished "illegitimacy ratio" requires the inclusion of some truly high inference variables (Yegidis et al., 1999). Variables such as marital status, abortion data, birth rates, infant mortality, and the ratio of abortions to live births are complex and hard to mesh together. Furthermore, data used to calculate the "illegitimacy ratio" and the ratio of abortions to live births are subject to random fluctuations.

Consideration of program theory can help broaden the focus during attempts to evaluate large government programs. Program theory is the source from which program activities are drawn. Program theory is essential to understanding program design, which, in turn, is essential to program management and essential for evaluations of large government programs that are not simply focused on an immediate concern (Chambers, 2000).

For example, simply because the number of persons in receipt of cash assistance has declined is no reason to automatically conclude that welfare reform was the sole cause. The situation is much more complex. A decline in the welfare rolls may also signal that serious consequences for more broad, theoretical issues have resulted. Welfare reform has undoubtedly impacted the relationship between the federal and state governments, redefined the concept of poverty in the United States, diminished the entitlement rights of all persons, and had serious consequences for the interplay between public policy and the underlying dynamics of human development, family functioning, and community well-being (McClintock & Colosi, 1998).

A thorough analysis of the program theory that undergirds a large government program can move an evaluation's focus from the immediate concern to an inclusion of more broad-based, theoretical concerns. For example, only a cursory examination of the language that leads into the TANF state plan for Georgia allows an evaluator to conclude much about its program theory. The plan clearly indicates: (a) adherence by the state to the parameters of the national legislation, (b) program design and implementation with local discretion, (c) a shift from a structural to an individual theory of poverty with an emphasis on personal responsibility, (d) an end of an entitlement for cash assistance, and (e) a nearly complete emphasis on work as the solution to poverty (Epstein, 1997).

Welfare Reform in Georgia

This chapter highlights the evaluation methodology designed and implemented by a team of researchers affiliated with the School of Social Work at the University of Georgia as they fulfilled a contractual obligation to evaluate the impacts of welfare reform. Rather than reporting on the findings of the evaluation, this presentation demonstrates how the two previously described pitfalls were addressed. Overreliance on the classic experimental design, and accompanying worries about rigor, were dealt with by building of a number of bases of comparison and by using a stratified random sampling technique. The use of an extensive in-home data collection process helped address the pitfall of immediate concern versus bigger issues.

Basis of Comparison and Sampling[1]

The welfare reform research project hosted by the School of Social Work at the University of Georgia, with its evaluative focus primarily on persons who continued to receive TANF, took seriously the opportunity to work collaboratively with other researchers. Included by the funder, Georgia's Division of Family and Children Services (DFCS), in a research team they developed were social scientists from Georgia State University, Clark-Atlanta University, and two additional entities at the University of Georgia: the Vinson Institute of Government and the Demographics Center. A number of bases for comparison were built between the data sets developed through the cooperative efforts of these varied researchers.

The most prominent basis of comparison used was the data set developed by the Georgia State researchers, which had an evaluative focus solely on persons who had left TANF, and the School of Social Work's data set, which focused solely on persons who continued to receive TANF. A priori efforts to design the interview guide together (see Appendix 2) and to select the same standardized measures that focused on the variables of happiness, self-esteem, perceived control, depression, optimism, life satisfaction, and self-efficacy proved extremely valuable as a basis of comparison post data collection.

A major challenge for the welfare reform evaluation was associated with the size of Georgia as a state. With 159 counties, Georgia is geographically the largest state east of the Mississippi River. Thus, Georgia reflects significant variations in population and economic factors associated with, among others, migration, employment, education, and overall quality of life.

Two factors were used to build further bases of comparison. First, a classification system of the 159 counties developed by Professor Doug Bachtel, a noted demographer at the University of Georgia and author of the *Georgia County Guide*, was used. Variations in factors that characterize the quality of life in a particular geographic region, such as income, employment, education, population migration, and housing, were used as a basis for the classification of the counties. According to the classification system, each county was classified into one of four categories: urban, suburban, rural growth, or rural decline. Of the 159 counties, 7 were identified as urban, 35 were considered suburban, 77 were viewed as experiencing rural growth, and 40 were characterized as in decline.

With populations of more than 50,000, the urban counties characteristically represented the heart of Georgia's metropolitan urban centers. Although a significant portion of the population has the general skills and resources to take advantage of the economic opportunities available in these areas, an equally large number of people are young and poorly educated and live at or below the federal poverty level. The suburban counties are, for the most part, metropolitan because

[1]The author would like to thank Dr. Lynne Billard of the Statistics Department at the University of Georgia, who developed the sampling procedure. The sampling methodology and its relation to evaluation findings can be found in additional publications. The author also would like to thank the Georgia Department of Human Resources and Division of Family and Children Services, which funded the welfare reform research projects.

a significant number of the residents living in them commute to the urban areas to work. These areas generally are predominantly white and affluent. Likewise, many residents in these areas possess a high degree of educational attainment and income level. Another group comprises those counties identified as "growing rural Georgia." Although scattered across the state, these rural counties tend to be concentrated in the north. These areas are usually associated with having either scenic beauty or some type of landscape that makes them attractive places for tourism. These areas also are located near some regional growth centers that contribute to the counties' economic development. Conversely, the counties identified as "declining rural Georgia," arguably are the areas considered to be in the greatest peril. These counties are characterized as experiencing long-term population loss, lack of employment opportunities, and low levels of supportive services. Historically, these areas have a legacy of low educational attainment and skill development. Thus, many of the residents in these counties are dependent on social welfare services. Figure 13.1 shows the county classifications.

Second, an administrative distinction in welfare cases was used to build another basis of comparison. The DFCS has designations for two types of recipient cases that receive cash assistance: child-only cases and family cases. In child-only cases, children in a particular family are the clients and the sole beneficiaries of cash assistance. Adult parents or guardians of the children are not included in the determination of the assistance award. In these instances, the adults associated with a child receiving benefits are not required to comply with federal or state work requirements for welfare. On the other hand, family cases are those cases in which an adult, along with a child or children, is included in the award for welfare assistance. In family cases, the adult who is the beneficiary must comply with the personal responsibility and work requirements associated with welfare reform. Figure 13.2 illustrates how this basis of comparison facilitated the presentation of findings.

To investigate accurately the impacts of welfare reform in Georgia, randomly selected recipients responded to an interview guide consisting of 185 quantitative and qualitative questions formatted in eight comprehensive sections. The items were developed after a thorough review of the scholarly and professional literature and notation of the program theory of Georgia's TANF plan. Extended conversations also were held with more than 200 county-based DFCS county directors, Family Connection directors, and members of the Georgia SAFETY-NET, an advocacy group concerned about the potential negative outcomes of welfare reform (Nackerud, Risler, & Brooks, 1998). Quantitative questions generated data on specific life issues and variables impacted by welfare reform, such as housing and family relationships, family income and resources, health care, job availability and employer behavior, education and work history, and child well-being. In addition, participants in the evaluation completed several standardized measures associated with psychological well-being. Finally, as a means to highlight current relevant issues from those directly affected by Georgia's TANF program, respondents were asked several open-ended questions.

After receiving approval from the Office of Human Subjects Review at the University of Georgia, use of the interview guide and standardized measures was

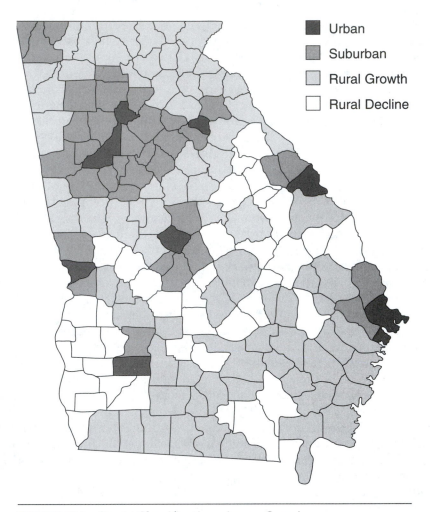

FIGURE 13.1   *Strata Classifications Across Georgia*

pilot tested on approximately 60 TANF recipients selected proportionately from Bibb, Dekalb, Habersham, and Seminole counties, which represented the four previously mentioned county classifications. Analysis of the pilot data allowed for necessary adjustments to particular items in the interview guide and determined the appropriate population parameters used in the selection of a representative sample of current welfare recipients from the strata, based on the degree of accuracy (92.5 percent) desired in the data. Essentially, the degree of data accuracy desired is associated with the concept of representativeness or how findings from the sample can be generalized to the total population of remaining TANF recipients. Thus, the cases selected in the research sample were considered

	Respondent	Family	Child-Only
Case Designation		55%	45%
Average Age	36	29	44
Female Gender	97%	98%	96%
Ethnicity (African American or White)	78% AA 22% W	83% AA 17% W	71% AA 29% W
No. of Children	2.3	2.4	2.3
Monthly Income	$1,052	$889	$1,257
Monthly Benefit	$201–$300	$201–$300	$101–$200
% With no High School Degree or GED	47	43	52
% With a Health Problem	49	35	67
% Who Are Working	34	39	28

FIGURE 13.2 *The Recipient Profile*

representative of the remaining TANF recipients. Accordingly, the evaluation utilized a well-developed stratified random sampling procedure (Yegidis et al., 1999).

The reported July 1999 caseload ($N = 56,260$) of all individuals in Georgia listed as receiving TANF was the population used in the sampling procedure. Based on each recipient's county of residence, the total July welfare population was initially stratified according to one of the four county designations. To achieve a confidence level of 92.5 percent in the data, a representative sample of 201 recipients was randomly selected to participate in the research evaluation. Although all the July recipients had a known chance of being included in the study, the recipients selected for the sample were in proportion to the total number of recipients in each of the four classified strata. The results were as follows: urban, 77; suburban, 45; rural growth, 53; and rural decline, 26.

All three bases of comparison—the data sets developed by the School of Social Work at the University of Georgia and researchers at Georgia State University, the county classification strata foundation for the stratified sampling technique, and the child-only and family case designation—assisted in building rigor in the research design. This rigor was achieved in the absence of the ability of evaluators to assign program participants to a treatment or a control condition.

In-Home Data Collection

The in-home data collection process was intensive, time-consuming, and costly, particularly from a person power standpoint. The data were collected between August and mid-November 1999. The interviews took place in the recipients' homes and took approximately one hour to complete. Following the interviews, recipients were compensated $25.00 each for their cooperation and time.

A research team comprised of social workers at all levels completed the interviews. These social work professionals—some faculty, some MSW and BSW-level graduates, and the rest MSW and PhD students—were selected based on their interest in poverty politics and social welfare policy. The positive impact of using social work professionals with the abilities to engage TANF recipients in their homes in an interview process, to build rapport quickly, and to probe for additional information cannot be underestimated. This skill of operationalization allowed the evaluation effort to go beyond the immediate concern of describing the remaining TANF population and the barriers to self-sufficiency.

The intense community-based and in-home nature of the data collection process helped bring to the surface questions and resulting data that addressed bigger issues. These issues included such things as: (1) the merits of a large government program founded on the concept that everyone could work, (2) whether poverty in a rural southern state was no longer a poverty borne of resource deprivation, (3) the relationship between federal disability programs, welfare reform, and persons with a health problem (physical or mental) that did not rise to the level of federal disability, and (4) speculations about family configuration.

Program theory depiction, evaluation design features that emphasized the development of multiple bases of comparison rather than merely a focus on the ability (or lack thereof) to assign program participants to treatment and control conditions, the building of rigor through attention to sampling issues, collaboration among researchers, and in-home data collection all helped to build an evaluative effort that was ultimately viewed with respect. The findings were accepted by all audiences (e.g., the funding agency, state legislators, research consortium members, and the general public) as rigorous and applicable to the demands currently being placed on policy makers. The findings were regarded as directly applicable to questions about the efficacy of continuing welfare reform as promulgated in the 1996 federal act or modified, particularly as the lifetime limits draw closer and closer for the first large cohort of remaining TANF recipients in Georgia. Initially 400 copies of the evaluation report were delivered to the funder, DFCS. An additional 300 copies were recently requested.

Conclusion

Although the goal of this evaluation was to ascertain the impacts of welfare reform on the families and children of Georgia, the chapter had a different goal. Hopefully, the material describing the welfare reform evaluation effort has depicted the realities of addressing the pitfalls of overreliance on the classical experimental design and immediate concern versus bigger issues in the evaluation of a large government program.

Questions for Further Study

1. What can be done in the evaluation of a large government program to ensure that the findings are perceived as meaningful in a local context?

2. What are the design features in the classic experimental design, and why are they desired in an evaluation of a large government program?

3. If a large government program like Head Start is so well regarded by the public, why do evaluators continue to use such complex methodology?

4. The Supplemental Security Income (SSI) program is a large government program that provides disability benefits to adults and children, as well as assistance for older adults. The Personal Responsibility and Work Opportunity Reconciliation Act of 1996 made it harder for children to be eligible for disability under SSI. If you were evaluating this change, what immediate concern would you focus on and what bigger issues might you tackle?

References

Bath, H. I., & Haapala, D. A. (1994). Family preservation services: What does the outcome research *really* tell us? *Social Service Review, 68,* 386–404.

Chambers, D. E. (2000). *Social policy and social programs: A method for the practical public policy analyst* (3rd ed.) Boston: Allyn & Bacon.

Currie, J., & Thomas, D. (1995). Does Head Start make a difference? *The American Economic Review, 85,* 341–364.

Dye, J. L., & Presser, H. B. (1999). The state bonus to reward a decrease in 'illegitimacy': Flawed methods and questionable effects. *Family Planning Perspectives, 31*(3), 142–147.

Eamon, M. K. (1994). Poverty and placement outcomes of intensive family preservation services. *Child and Adolescent Social Work Journal, 11,* 349–361.

Epstein, W. M. (1997). *Welfare in America: How social science fails the poor.* Madison: University of Wisconsin Press.

Georgia's State Plan. Temporary Assistance for Needy Families. (1999, November). Atlanta, GA: Georgia Department of Human Resources, Division of Family and Children Services.

Joseph, L. B. (1999). Families, poverty, and welfare reform: Confronting a new policy era. Champaign, IL: University of Illinois Press.

McClintock, C., & Colosi, C. (1998). Evaluation of welfare reform: A framework for addressing the urgent and the important. *Evaluation Review, 22*(5), 668–694.

Mowbray, C. T., Bybee, D., Collins, M. E., & Levine, P. (1998). Optimizing evaluation quality and utility under resource constraints. *Evaluation and Program Planning, 21*(1), 59–71.

Nackerud, L. (1993). The Central American refugee issue in Brownsville, Texas: Seeking understanding of public policy formulation from within a community setting. San Francisco: Mellen.

Nackerud, L., Risler, E., & Brooks, F. (1998). *The Georgia welfare reform research project: Emerging patterns and questions* (Report No. 1). Athens, GA: Division of Family and Children Services.

Rubin, M. M. (1994). Can reorchestration of historical themes reinvent government? A case study of the Empowerment Zones and Enterprise Communities Act of 1993. *Public Administration Review, 54*(2), 161–169.

Smith, M. K. (1995). Utilization-focused evaluation of a family preservation program. *Families in Society, 76,* 11–19.

Tweedie, J., & Reichart, D. (1998). *Tracking recipients after they leave welfare: Summaries of state follow-up studies* [Online]. Available: www.ncsl.org.

Wu, P., & Campbell, D. T. (1996). Extending latent variable LISREL analysis of the 1969 Westinghouse Head Start Evaluation to Blacks and full-year Whites. *Evaluation and Program Planning, 19*(3), 183–191.

Yegidis, B. L., Weinbach, R. W., & Morrison-Rodriquez, B. (1999). Research methods for social workers (3rd ed.). Boston: Allyn & Bacon.

14

Examples of Program Evaluations

This writer was once teaching an evening, adult education class on social group work in a town some distance from my home campus. For weeks I had talked about group dynamics, group behavior, and the stages of group development. About six sessions into the course, one fairly verbal student stood up somewhat angrily and asked, "What is all this about groups? Why do we spend so much time on groups? Why are they important?" Of course, that is what we had discussed, but he might have thought a course on social work was about all of social work—and he could not understand why groups were such a preoccupation.

It was easy to see that the objectives of the course were not clear to at least one student, whether or not they were clearly written and distributed to the class (I thought they were clear and I know they were distributed). However, since that time, I have tried to provide concrete examples of the main subject matter of each course. Although there may still be confusion, it is probably at least reduced.

This chapter is about sound examples of program evaluations. Of course, program evaluations are provided in the professional human services journals regularly. This is especially true of research journals because much of the research conducted in the United States, especially social work research, is about program evaluation. The degree to which social welfare programs achieve their objectives and avoid unintended consequences is a major concern of Congress, the federal executive branch, state governments, and the broader public. In many cases, no one really knows what the results will be for new approaches to social welfare. In such circumstances, evaluations become even more important than for other endeavors. Therefore, there is a priority placed on evaluative research. The examples provided here are primarily studies of large public programs; however, some of the same program evaluation techniques are useable in smaller and voluntary programs.

There is an effort throughout this book to include a variety of program evaluation examples—not solely experiments, case studies and descriptions, or accreditations, but a combination of the myriad evaluation techniques discussed. Some of the evaluation studies here simply document what a program did. This is helpful for those who might be interested in trying the same programs in their own communities. They also provide useful information on exactly what was done, how it was achieved, how much it cost, and difficulties that were encountered in implementing them.

Several of the studies follow experimental designs, with an experimental group compared with a control group to determine how much difference a program made in the lives of participants as opposed to nonparticipants.

Satisfaction is the subject of some of the studies, which surveyed participants to determine how well they accepted the programs. This, of course, is especially significant at a time when the new national welfare law, the Personal Responsibility and Work Opportunity Reconciliation Act of 1996, is being implemented around the country. That law is the most significantly different approach to welfare the nation has seen since the passage of the Social Security Act in 1935. As such, examples of its use in various states and localities are an important subject for evaluation. Because the new law gives greater flexibility to the states in deciding how they will carry out welfare programs, studying specific examples and their variations also provides important information for understanding and eventually revising welfare in the United States.

The success of an evaluation in being considered by programs and policy makers is due in part to the quality of the presentation. Royse and Thyer (1996) include suggestions for presenting evaluation results. Morris, Fitz-Gibbon, and Freeman (1987) authored a brief book on communicating evaluation findings. Many evaluators devote extensive time to planning the presentation of their results in addition to the evaluation activities themselves.

Among the organizations evaluating social welfare programs on a regular and intensive basis is the Urban Institute, a Washington, D.C.-based policy research organization that was founded in 1968. It has been especially active in studying the effects of the 1996 act. Its periodic publication, *New Federalism: Policy Research and Resources,* is something of a newsletter that summarizes current Urban Institute research and evaluation. It is available in libraries, on the Internet, and by mailed requests. The postal address is 2100 M Street, N.W., Washington, DC 20037. Its web site is http://www.urban.org/uipress. They also have a toll-free telephone number, 1-877-uipress.

Current welfare reform is the subject of many other, intense evaluation efforts. One example, which was reported at Evaluation '99 (the 1999 annual meeting of the American Evaluation Association in Orlando, Florida), looked at the ways in which the results of welfare reform could be studied in the Appalachian region of Ohio (Longo, 1999). It discusses an effort to create the Appalachian Partnership for Welfare Reform. That effort worked to ensure that the more rural, Appalachian area of the state was represented in decisions about welfare reform as well as the often more influential metropolitan areas. The partnership also helped local areas—which had greater flexibility to implement changed programs—develop the skills and leadership necessary to assume greater responsibility. The partnership assisted program implementation while developing performance measures to consistently evaluate movements toward reform objectives.

Manpower Demonstration Research Corporation

One of the premiere evaluation organizations in the United States is the Manpower Demonstration Research Corporation (MDRC), which has headquarters in New York City and San Francisco. It primarily studies government-sponsored work programs for public assistance clients. The corporation, which celebrated its twenty-fifth anniversary in 1999, focuses on work programs such as those that began in the 1970s called Work Incentive Programs. Most of the information produced is intended for policy makers and students of human services. However, one popular book, *The Underclass* (Auletta, 1999), was published out of MDRC research and serialized in the *New Yorker* magazine.

The organization has a distinguished board of directors from the social sciences, economics, and education. The chairman and treasurer, for example, is a former chairman and chief executive officer of Alcoa. I became involved with MDRC in the 1980s, when the agency I headed, the West Virginia Department of Human Services, agreed to have its Community Work Experience Program (CWEP) evaluated by the organization. CWEP grew out of President Ronald Reagan's welfare reforms in 1981 through the Omnibus Budget Reconciliation Act. One of its provisions was to allow states to establish community work programs for clients as a condition for receiving assistance. West Virginia had a long and successful history of operating such programs, and in this case the state decided to require male clients to perform community service work at the minimum wage, which was then paid through its assistance grants. MDRC, in cooperation with some foundations, evaluated the program for several years to determine the extent to which the West Virginia approach was successful in helping clients make the transition from welfare to employment.

The evaluation research conducted by MDRC is typically financed by a combination of funds from the U.S. government, the state government in which research is conducted, and one or more private foundations, especially the Ford Foundation, which has had a special interest in MDRC's work. The organization's mission is to design and rigorously field-test promising education and employment-related programs that are designed to improve the well-being of disadvantaged adults and youth. It also aims to give policy makers and human service practitioners evidence about the effectiveness of social programs. MDRC works to enhance the quality of public policies, and it also helps organizations implement the kinds of programs it is interested in studying. It has worked with 40 states, dozens of local communities, private philanthropies, and the federal government.

MDRC has many full reports available, which can be obtained from its offices at 16 East 34th Street, New York, New York 10016 or 88 Kearny Street, Suite 1800, San Francisco, California 94108, or through its web site, www.MDRC.org. Its catalog lists all of the studies that have been conducted that are available to the public. Some examples of MDRC reports give an indication of the range of studies that are conducted and the methodology used to evaluate components of welfare programs and the work programs associated with them.

Vermont Welfare Restructuring Project

This MDRC report (Bloom, Michalopoulos, Walter, & Auspos, 1998) is an evaluation of the Vermont Welfare Restructuring Project (WRP). Under the program, single-parent recipients of the system are required to work in jobs that pay wages after they have received benefits for thirty months. Adults in two-parent families must work, in most cases, after fifteen months. This program was established before the 1996 welfare law was implemented. The intention in Vermont is to provide assistance through wage-paying work rather than cash assistance. Those clients who cannot find work on their own are provided with subsidized, minimum-wage community service jobs when their time limits have run out.

To test the validity of the restructuring project, about 8,000 clients were randomly assigned to one of three groups from July 1994 to June 1995 in the six districts of Vermont that were scheduled for intensive study. The first group was the WRP group, for which the time limits described previously were imposed and financial work incentives were provided. Those who left welfare and entered employment that was not subsidized were able to receive financial incentives from the state agency in return for taking over their own support. The second group was an Aid to Needy Families With Children (ANFC) group, who had to follow the welfare rules that existed before WRP began. The third group was the Incentives Only group, who received financial incentives for becoming self-supporting but were not subject to time limits. The participants were assigned to groups by chance and, therefore, MDRC evaluators thought that any differences in rates of employment, receipt of welfare, or any other outcomes would be the results of different policies.

The study found that those who participated fully in WRP had modest increases in employment before they reached the time limits of 15 or 30 months. Sixty-eight percent of the participants in the full WRP approach worked at some time during the 21 months they were studied, compared with 63 percent of those who received ANFC. One of the major findings was that time limits made a major difference in the receipt of welfare. The researchers observed that the closer participants came to reaching their time limits, the proportion of those who were working while they received assistance increased substantially.

Two-parent families involved in the ANFC program were not as changed by WRP as single-parent families because two-parent families had other stringent work requirements through their involvement with the Vermont welfare system. The evaluation found that 79 percent of the families in the WRP group that were two-parent families worked, whereas 73 percent of the families in the ANFC group were employed. Therefore, parents who were involved in WRP were slightly more likely to work.

They also found that the time limit increased employment in two-parent families when one of the parents was incapacitated. Therefore, the group receiving assistance under the two-parent family program was more likely to have one of the parents employed. Fifty percent of the families in the WRP group had at least one working parent, compared with 40 percent of the WRP's Incentives Only group.

Of course this is an experimental study because it compares three different groups. (One of the attractive facts about reports from MDRC is that they are generally modest and do not take credit for having accomplished more than they can prove they accomplished. The term "modest increases" seems to appear quite frequently in their literature.) The study results showed that the time limits appeared to work. Until the deadlines, most of those who were receiving ANFC benefits, regardless of the group to which they were assigned, seemed to have about the same work participation. However, when those who had deadlines came close to them, they began more seriously looking for and obtaining employment.

Los Angeles Jobs-First GAIN Evaluation

MDRC evaluated the Los Angeles County Department of Social Services's Welfare to Work Program, which they called Jobs-First GAIN (Freedman, Mitchell, & Navarro, 1999). GAIN is an acronym for greater avenues for independence. Initially, the program focused on basic education, but that later transformed into getting people into jobs quickly. The research was especially significant because Los Angeles County has the largest welfare population of any county in the United States.

The redesign of the Los Angeles program came in 1993 when, instead of placing most clients who were eligible for assistance in basic education programs, the Department of Social Services instead focused on helping people find jobs and on encouraging recipients to start working as quickly as possible in order to become self-sufficient. The new approach, which was implemented in 1995, developed client job skills, helped clients search for jobs, suggested that time limits would be imposed on clients who did not engage in work, and showed clients that the combination of work and welfare would benefit them financially. The redesigned program was implemented before the new federal welfare law but it is continuing under the 1996 act. MDRC was asked to evaluate the Jobs-First GAIN program, and it embarked on the evaluation with funds from Los Angeles County, the U.S. Department of Health and Human Services, and the Ford Foundation.

In the evaluation research, MDRC randomly assigned 21,000 single parents and members of two-parent households who first attended a Jobs-First GAIN orientation to one of two groups: experimental and control. Those in the experimental group were given messages about the importance of finding work and the positive consequences of doing so. They were given mandatory participation requirements and were told that if they did not prepare for work, search for work, and ultimately find work, they could have a reduction in their assistance. The members of the control group were not given the same orientation, and they continued to be eligible for financial assistance and food stamps. They also used other services in the community. Both groups were provided with a combination of welfare and wages under formulas that made the combination of these attractive.

The evaluation research showed that those who participated in the experimental group increased their earnings by $750 for the first year, or 31 percent, compared with the control group. Two-parent families in the experimental group increased their family earnings by $1,082, or 44 percent, relative to the control group. Increases by men in the experimental group averaged $1,449, although the experimental group women's extra earnings were not as large. The experimental group members were less likely to continue receiving assistance than control group members. Participants in the experimental group had a total, however, of about the same money from a combination of welfare and work earnings as they had with welfare, alone. They replaced welfare dollars with their own earnings.

Most significantly, the Jobs-First GAIN approach seemed to be much more successful than the education approach that had been used in the past. The increases seemed to prove positive effects for all sorts of clients—those in the central city, those in the outer areas of the county, various ethnic groups, those with little education, and those with significantly more education.

Clients who volunteered for early entry into the program seemed to do rather well. This suggested that volunteer participants in welfare-to-work programs who are eager to participate seem to have significant advantages over those who are not early participants.

Influences that MDRC found made a difference were: the strong message about the importance of work, the warning of time limits, an intensive orientation to the program, help in finding jobs, assistance with developing job-search skills, and strongly enforcing the program.

Washington Works

In 1992, the state of Washington established a program called Washington Works. The evaluation was conducted by MDRC (Gooden, 1998) with funds from the Charles Stewart Mott Foundation and the Rockefeller Foundation. The program, which began in 1992 and was located in downtown Seattle, Washington, was designed to provide connections between assistance recipients and employers. The project focused on signing contracts with organizations that would be expected to place low-income individuals in jobs. The basis for paying a contract was an organization's performance in effectively locating jobs for participants.

In this evaluation, MDRC principally documented the program and the contracts, which were based on performance. This evaluation functioned more as a case study than as an experiment. The report shows how the program was planned, designed, and implemented, and it also discusses results, such as that many welfare recipients were placed in jobs and earned above-entry-level salaries.

Big Cities and Welfare Reform

Another major study by MDRC (different than ones already mentioned) was *Big Cities and Welfare Reform* (Quint et al., 1999). After the passage of the 1996 federal act, MDRC initiated a study of the ways in which the new law was being implemented and the reactions of clients in four urban counties spread throughout the United States. The counties were Cuyahoga County, Ohio, which incorporates Cleveland; Los Angeles County, California; Miami-Dade County, Florida; and Philadelphia County, Pennsylvania.

Eleven private foundations located throughout the United States funded the study. In some ways, this study is a combination of two kinds of evaluations: first, the documentation and description of what actually happened and, second, a survey of client reactions (which is similar to a study of satisfaction) in the counties that were studied.

The researchers found that three of the counties—all but Philadelphia—had passed on some of their decision making power to local governments. None had used draconian measures on their poor citizens. They also noted that several organizations that had not been involved in welfare in the past were now participating in the reform efforts in the four counties because there had been substantial privatization of welfare programs in some of the sites. Several had used private corporations to implement new elements of public assistance in line with the new legislation.

Again, the programs focused on time limits and the work-first emphasis that was found in other areas. Putting clients to work, except those exempt by law, was a major challenge in all locations. Of the four counties studied, only Miami-Dade sanctioned or reduced benefits at a significantly higher rate than in the past.

The clients, based on the surveys of them, understood that they had to deal with time limits and the like. Some were concerned about the reduction in opportunities to participate in longer-term education—as opposed to training—under the new federal law. The 1996 act focuses on short-term training for immediate job placement, whereas earlier laws made provisions for basic education and, in some cases, higher education.

Many clients approved of job-search and mandatory work requirements. They believed (as many nonclients did) that job searches would eliminate people who were capable but unwilling to work from assistance rolls. However, there was a high degree of concern about supervision of children and how their children would fare in care and supervision under the new law. This study was of great value to policy makers and the larger public because it provided early information on the ways in which the 1996 act affected clients and on client reactions.

New Hope for People with Low Incomes

MDRC worked with a program called New Hope Project, Inc., which was a demonstration in two low-income areas that began in 1994 and ended in 1995 in Milwaukee, Wisconsin. The demonstration enrolled 1,360 people (Bos et al., 1999).

The project was designed to serve working poor people, not recipients of assistance. The 1,360 subjects were randomly assigned to one of two groups: an experimental group, who would receive benefits from New Hope for three years, and a control group, who would not receive New Hope benefits. MDRC evaluation began with the program. The operators of New Hope were strongly committed to evaluation research. The evaluation was sponsored by the state of Wisconsin, the U.S. government, and several private foundations.

Of the participants, 37.5 percent were employed at the time they enrolled in the program, and 84.9 percent had been employed full-time during some part of their adult lives. A majority (59.8 percent) had never married; 18.3 percent were separated, divorced, or widowed; and 21.8 percent were married. Over a fourth of the sample were men, and 37.1 percent were not receiving any welfare assistance programs. The average age of the participants was 32 years old.

The program components were an earnings supplement to raise the household income of the experimental group participants to the poverty level, health insurance that they could afford, financial assistance for child care, and a full-time job opportunity for the people who could not find jobs on their own.

The program appeared to have significant benefits for those who received the services. The study found that the community service jobs that were made available for those who did not find jobs were important.

In terms of comparison between the experimental and the control groups, those who were not employed full-time when they were selected for the experimental or control group had significant increases in their employment patterns and their earnings. That is, those who were participants in and received the benefits of New Hope were significantly better off than those who were assigned to the control group.

Of course, the New Hope project demonstrated that providing people with work, helping them develop better incomes, and making health insurance available at affordable prices, made a major difference in the lives of people who participated in New Hope compared with those who did not receive the benefits from the program.

The overall costs of the project were not large. The participating families cost about $7,200 each during two years of involvement with New Hope. The full cost was $9,000, but when the cost of welfare assistance to the families and the value of the work that participants produced in community service jobs were subtracted, the overall total was $7,200. The significant results, such as moving people from welfare to work, improving family relations, and otherwise improving the families, suggested that the costs were reasonable or even low compared with the benefits of the project.

Parents' Fair Share Project

An interesting study of helping families leave welfare for other means of support is found in the Parents' Fair Share Project (Doolittle, Knox, Miller, & Rowser, 1998), in which noncustodial parents of children who were receiving welfare (primarily fathers) were offered the opportunity to obtain help in finding more-stable and better-paying jobs, to pay child support payments for which they were responsible, and to play a larger role as parents to their children. Those who work in the U.S. public welfare system realize that a large portion of welfare dependency results from fathers being unable to pay child support. Many public efforts are used to locate and enforce child support orders throughout the United States. If those who are required by courts to pay child support (most of whom are absent fathers) actually paid, many children would not need public support to meet their basic needs.

The federal government, state and local governments, and private foundations came together to demonstrate ways to improve this situation. The noncustodial parents were referred to a program that would provide employment and other services on a mandatory basis. Participants were not living with their children and were not receiving welfare assistance themselves. If they had jobs, they were low-paying and temporary. Participants' work and payment of child support was carefully monitored by each agency and by a child-support enforcement unit that administered the overall collection of child-support payments and the allocation of the money to the families. About 5,500 parents in seven sites (Dayton, Ohio; Grand Rapids, Michigan; Jacksonville, Florida; Los Angeles, California; Memphis, Tennessee; Springfield, Massachusetts; and Trenton, New Jersey) were involved. A control group and an experimental (or assistance-receiving group) were created.

The study identified the kinds of job-improvement activities that were most effective in helping people enhance their employment and in retaining the interest of the noncustodial parents.

Child support payments actually increased before job-improvement activities began. A higher percentage of those who were involved in the work improvement program paid child support than the control group. However, there was not any statistically significant difference between the two groups in the amount of support that was provided. Some of the sites—Dayton, Grand Rapids, and Los Angeles—had a greater impact on the payment of child support than the others. When all the sites were considered, there was no statistically significant impact on either employment or earnings. There appeared to be great variation among the sites. Some were highly successful and others less successful. Overall, it appeared that local efforts, local conditions, and local administration made major differences in the effectiveness of the program.

In any case, the research and demonstration were important because child support payments are a critical factor in deciding whether and to what extent a family might need assistance.

New Chance for Young Mothers in Poverty and Their Children

One of the persistent concerns about welfare has been the young, unmarried woman with children. New Chance was an experiment designed to test methods of helping that population at 16 sites throughout the United States, from the East to the Far West and including the Upper Midwest and the South (Quint, Bos, & Polit, 1997). The program began in the mid-1980s, and it was designed to help young mothers complete educational qualifications, such as the GED, using better-quality day care and taking other steps that would help them leave the welfare system. Both experimental and control groups were used.

The experimental group received more services and had greater successes, however, the differences between the experimental and control groups were not great. In general, although the experimental groups had certain successes, they were left far from self-sufficiency (in keeping, perhaps, with this being one of the most stubbornly difficult groups to help with alternatives to the welfare system). As Dr. Judith Gueron, MDRC's president, said (Quint et al., 1997) "the outcomes for the mothers have improved since they enrolled in New Chance. The sobering news is that the absolute levels of progress leave these young families far from self-sufficiency, and for most outcomes the New Chance program did not improve progress over and above that shown by an equivalent group of young women who did not attend New Chance" (p. vi). She adds that there were some unintended consequences for those receiving help. "For example, mothers at high risk for depression reported higher levels of parental stress than their counterparts in the control group. They also believed that their children were doing less well on measures of social behavior" (p. vi).

The conclusion after several years of study was that it was important to prevent the problems, which are associated with school failures, dropouts, and teenage births. Overcoming them, despite strong efforts to do so by the mothers, seems much more difficult than preventing them.

Ron Stodghill, II (2000) reported on another recent evaluation conducted by the Manpower Demonstration Research Corporation, which he calls a nonpartisan research center. MDRC evaluated a program in Minnesota that provided day care payments in 1994 for a mother who had a low paying job, which she might have left had she not been provided with child care. By 2000, she was earning $45,000 per year as manager of a regional telephone company while she raised her two children.

MDRC conducted the study of the Minneapolis, Minnesota, welfare reform project, which has been in operation for six years. They found that the level of welfare client employment was 35 percent and that marriage rates and school success among families receiving assistance also had increased. MDRC found that the assistance with making the transition from receiving public help to work made a big difference in the Minnesota successes.

Work Incentives and Welfare Transitions

The Social Research and Demonstration Corporation of Canada, which is a partner of MDRC, conducted a study in two Canadian provinces (Berlin, Bancroft, Card, Lin, & Robins, 1998) of the effects of an earnings-supplement program, The Self-Sufficiency Project. The effort was designed to determine whether an earnings supplement for people who left welfare for full-time employment would have the unintended consequence of enticing working poor people to resign from their jobs and join the welfare rolls as a means of increasing their overall earnings. A careful study of the earnings supplement recipients through the use of focus groups and other means found that for a variety of reasons, the unintended consequence did not occur.

Somewhat comparable to the MDRC studies is the work of Morris and Orthner (1998), who examined, with the help of grants from the U.S. Department of Health and Human Services and the North Carolina Department of Health and Human Services, the transition of people from welfare to local jobs. The support of this research demonstrates, as do the MDRC studies, the high degree of interest that governments, both federal and state, have in better understanding the transition from welfare to employment.

The researchers found that the availability and quality of the jobs in local labor markets had more influence on exiting welfare than personal characteristics. Factors such as local wage rates are examples of significant characteristics that encourage people to leave welfare and enter the labor market. One of their findings was that employment decisions were made in a family context. That is, opportunities for other family or household members were significant considerations for them, as well as for the targeted welfare client. Having a preschool-aged child seemed to suppress departures from welfare, along with the receipt of welfare for a long period of time. Researchers also found that returns to welfare by families who had left to take jobs in the local labor market were fairly common.

Two Florida Evaluations. The Anti-Drug Abuse Act of 1988 (ADAA-88, PL 100-690) established the Edward Byrne Memorial State and Local Law Enforcement Assistance Formula Grant Program (Byrne Program) whose purpose is to assist states in carrying out specific programs aimed at improving the functioning of the criminal justice system and advancing national drug control priorities.

State governments are given authority to fund state and local programs for enforcing state and local laws that establish offenses similar to those identified in the Controlled Substances Act—emphasizing prevention and control of violent crime and serious offenders, and improving the functioning of the criminal justice system. The federal funds pay for 75 percent of the activities and the state and local recipients contribute 25 percent of the total cost. Three states—Ohio, Louisiana, and Florida—share the administrative funds of the program with local entities.

Florida chose to provide 10 percent of the administrative monies to local governments and commissioned an evaluation of those local expenditures with the Florida State University Institute for Health and Human Services Research (McNeece, Crook, O'Quinn, Rasmussen, & Jones, 1999). The evaluation demonstrated that the funds were properly spent and that they helped achieve some of the objectives of the Byrne program.

One influential evaluation was one that was conducted of Florida's Medicaid waiver for frail elderly people (Vinton, Crook, & LaMaster, 1997). This program, which began in 1995 and was evaluated in 1997, allows Medicaid funds to be used for care of older people in assisted living facilities. The purpose of using the waiver is to delay nursing home admission, which is more expensive than care in assisted living facilities.

A careful research project was done to compare those who lived in assisted living facilities as part of the program and those who did not. The evaluators studied four different samples—Medicaid waiver recipients who began receiving services between February 1995 and June 1996, another group that received services between July 1996 and December 1996, people who resided in the assisted living facilities and who were on a waiting list for funds from the waiver before January 1997, and another sample of everyone who had received long-term care between July 1996 and October 1996.

The evaluation concluded that the waiver and the use of Medicaid funds in assisted living facilities was cost effective. The waiver has continued. This evaluation is a good example of the use of evaluations in policy-making.

Temporary Assistance for Needy Families

Some of the most important evaluations are those conducted by government agencies to satisfy the demands of legislative bodies such as the U.S. Congress. When the Personal Responsibility and Work Opportunity Reconciliation Act was passed in 1996, the law required annual reports from the Department of Health and Human Services on the effects of the program and its impact on clients. The second annual report to Congress (U.S. Department of Health and Human Services, 1999) provided detailed information on the program as it had been carried out after its implementation in July 1997.

The department reported that the new law was paying off. Between 63 percent and 87 percent of adults who left the welfare rolls had worked since leaving. About three fifths of single mothers (57 percent) were employed. The figure for the same group in 1992 was 44 percent. The agency also reported that welfare rolls were at their lowest levels in 30 years—a decline of almost half from the beginning of the Bill Clinton presidency through the next-to-last year of that administration.

Continuing employment for those who leave assistance and obtain work is defined as the next challenge by the federal welfare administration. They point out that those who have child care are much more likely to continue working than those who do not receive such help. Included in the 250-page report are examples of welfare reform projects around the nation, including some of those described previously by the Manpower Demonstration Research Corporation.

These carefully designed and implemented evaluations are sound examples of many of the ways in which program evaluations are carried out. The results are used to help determine changes in programs and to document the effectiveness of the efforts. Both formative and summative evaluations are included in the several projects mentioned here. Methods such as cost-benefit analysis, examination of unintended consequences, case studies, and experimental studies are used.

American Evaluation Association

The American Evaluation Association (AEA) meeting in 1999 produced several papers with special significance for social work. Myers and Rittner (1999) presented a pilot study on the adult functioning of children raised in an orphanage. Much social work literature has suggested that group-care experiences, such as living in children's homes, has less favorable outcomes than other arrangements. However, these authors suggest residential care may be more positive in the long term than the common belief. The 94 former residents of the United Methodist Children's Home in Florida who were studied had average or above-average economic and social success in their later years, based on their completion of two standardized instruments and a questionnaire. The authors developed the questionnaire themselves. The two standardized instruments were the Index of Peer Relations (one of the Hudson scales discussed in Chapter 8) and the *Quality of Life Inventory* (Frisch, 1997). Their evaluation and analysis could have significance for future programs of care for children unable to live with their biological families.

Another report from the 1999 meeting suggested that school-based case management services for Hispanic students and their families who were migrants, rural, and at-risk could contribute to their well-being (Armijo, Stowitschek, Smith, & Valdez, 1999). The lead author is an evaluation specialist with a program designed to work with the study and teaching of at-risk students. The paper's contribution to effective work with the growing U.S. Hispanic population may have long-term significance.

Still another report from the conference dealt with night incarceration from 6 P.M. to 6 A.M. in Oklahoma County (Masmes et al., 1999). The researchers found they could save the government more than $25 million by using night incarceration and providing treatment services to the inmates. Conferences such as AEA's provide a significant quantity of information about many social welfare programs.

Personal Encounters with Program Evaluation

My interest in program evaluation is longstanding. My professional career began long before I began teaching graduate social work students at the University of South Carolina. For almost 10 years in the late 1960s and the 1970s, I served as dean of the West Virginia University School of Social Work. During that time, I was also an evaluator for Head Start programs in several states. From 1977 until 1986, I was a West Virginia state government official in the fields of human services, social welfare, and higher education, before coming to South Carolina.

Federal Programs and Program Evaluation

As a social work dean during the U.S. presidential administration of Richard M. Nixon, I learned, as did my colleagues around the country, of the major emphasis that administration placed on the results of the social programs it helped finance. Social work educators were highly interested in the federal government's posture on supporting education. In fact, social work students and faculty were heavily financed throughout the United States by grants in fields such as mental health and child welfare. Several deans, including myself, met with the late Elliot Richardson, then secretary of Health, Education, and Welfare. He emphasized the importance of developing data to justify funded programs and to demonstrate the results of the financing. As suggested in Chapter 1, the importance of evaluation and some of the methods for conducting reliable evaluations began emerging during these times, when the national administration was not especially enamored of or closely tied to social work.

What specific benefits accrued to human services programs, Richardson wondered, by having professionally educated social workers staffing them? It was a question that was new for social work deans. Under Nixon's most recent predecessors, John F. Kennedy and Lyndon B. Johnson, relations between social work and the U.S. government were relatively warm. Many of the priorities of those presidents were to be carried out by the social work profession, so there had been no question about the value of augmenting the complement of professional social workers available in the United States. Social work relations with the federal government had been close—a different state of affairs than under Nixon. Under Kennedy and Johnson, social workers had served on advisory groups, met frequently with federal human services officials, and had been viewed as meeting federal priorities, without detailed evaluation reports to document their successes. That was not typically the case with Richard Nixon's people. After his presidency—and that of President Gerald Ford, who moved from Vice-President to President after Nixon's resignation—Jimmy Carter, a Democrat, was elected. Again, relations between social workers and their organizations and the federal government were warmer and friendlier.

However, when Carter was defeated for reelection by Ronald Reagan in 1980, while I was still a state official, some of the tensions between social workers and the federal establishment resurfaced. One of the initiatives of the Reagan administration was to eliminate categorical social welfare programs and turn decision making power over to the states, which would receive block grants. Before the Reagan administration, federally funded state programs were carefully monitored by federal officials. However, the new president wanted to reduce the size of the federal government, largely by eliminating federal jobs, which was one of his campaign pledges. President Reagan and his supporters wanted to transfer the authority to design and operate programs to the states. Therefore, states were placed in the posture of not only operating programs but of also evaluating them and justifying them to federal funders. Instead of federal monitors inspecting programs, the states would inspect their own programs by conducting evaluations and by contracting with accountants to monitor expenditures. It was a decidedly different kind of environment for educators and state government officials. That environment has persisted through the George Bush and Bill Clinton presidencies, as well. Clearly, these approaches to federally supported social work education and social services are a major factor in enhancing the significance of program evaluation.

State Government Examples

During my first months as commissioner of Welfare in West Virginia, a position that was later renamed commissioner of Human Services, I recall some shortcomings in carrying out required program evaluations. The governor, John D. Rockefeller, IV—who was as new to running a state as I was to running a welfare department—said that the welfare program should be evaluated, a request that came to me from a top member of his staff. Of course, there were then, as there are now, extensive criticisms of the departments of welfare—some, no doubt, legitimate, but others simply part of the mythology and folklore that consistently surround public welfare departments. Citizens as well as elected officials thought there were too many recipients, that irresponsible recipients were being supported by government when they should be supporting themselves, that staff costs were very high, and that the staff seemed awfully large.

There actually were some serious problems in the department about which I initially knew nothing. I was told about them by friendly federal officials who monitored such matters. There were members of the staff who were nervous about what they had heard and seen or who had been, in their opinions, mistreated by powerful people in the agency. For example, a person with strong financial management skills and with a powerful and high position in the department had used a state purchase order to buy electronic entertainment equipment for, it appeared, his personal use. The store that sold him the equipment brought it to the attention of department investigators—several months before I was appointed. The department leadership in place before my administration decided to require the man to repay the department for his purchases but took no further action against him.

In another case, the state was in the process of seeking a computer software program for one of its more complicated programs. The company that won the contract also employed some key department staff—who had made the decision to purchase the software from that company—as consultants to spread the word about the virtues of the company. There was a congressional committee investigation of the firm, and some department personnel testified about what appeared to be a conflict of interest. Ultimately, the software company failed to provide the program that it was supposed to provide, and it was no longer successful in securing contracts from states for such software programs.

With regard to an overall evaluation of the agency, I was not quite certain what was desired or how to achieve it. I did not then know (as I now do) that evaluations are often initiated as a means of responding to critics, whether or not they are fully informed about programs. Such efforts often satisfy or divert the critics. Welfare was simply unpopular with some people—a fact of which I was quite aware. It is possible that the attacks on the agency had less to do with the quality of its operations than with its mission. Some welfare critics do not want welfare services provided to anyone under any circumstances. My impression was that the department was a relatively efficient organization, although it might have spent funds a bit lavishly. It was far from a generous organization. Assistance grants for low-income people were modest. Eligibility was difficult to achieve. Staff salaries were relatively low.

To comply with the request for an evaluation, I ultimately contracted with a small firm that had intelligently, I thought, conducted a careful study of the costs and benefits of social work education on behalf of the federal government (which financed and continues to pay for much of social work education). My school was a subject of their evaluation. I contracted with them for what was a substantial amount of money at the time—$40,000, as I recall—to design and conduct the evaluation. However, my instructions to them were not sufficiently specific. The criteria that I wanted them to use in evaluating the program were not very clear, either. Of course, the instructions under which I was operating also were not especially clear.

One of my concerns was to examine the cost and value of what seemed to me to be a lavish public information program, which had been instituted by the previous state administration. The public information program produced a great deal of material and seemed effective in producing information about the welfare programs. But staff salaries were low and public assistance grants to low income families were far below the poverty line. An expensive public relations program seemed inappropriate. I thought it was a problem and shared my concern with the evaluators.

The evaluators, however, saw no problems with the public relations program. It was small and cost very little in relation to its productivity. Why worry about it?

Overall, the evaluators thought the department was fine—that it spent no more than comparable departments around the country that provided the same level of services. The evaluators, who were not social workers but who were fiscal and systems experts, generally believed that the department needed only minor administrative modifications to improve. After fairly intensive study, the evaluators rendered a report with some modest recommendations. I have often thought that if the task had been more sharply defined, I might have obtained better guidance and results from the evaluation.

I later brought in a former colleague who was then involved in public information activities in the federal government to make another judgment about the public information program. He and a coworker in the federal system came to West Virginia for several days to evaluate the program. They also thought that it was fine and needed no modifications. At least there was no expenditure for their services other than expenses.

Of course, I now know that the program evaluation activities and criteria that I used were inappropriate. The decisions I was charged with making had to do with available resources and politics, not with the efficiency or the performance of the programs. I, along with those to whom I reported and key staff in the department, needed to make decisions about the issues that were of concern without necessarily using program evaluation results at all.

I have since seen other organizations grapple with similar contradictions—displeasure with staff directors or programs, for example—by commissioning program evaluations. Some evaluators are willing to make recommendations that satisfy those who have employed them, regardless of the data they gather. Such results are unethical for both the evaluators and those who may have employed them with pre-ordained results. Agency boards and mangers have the right and the power to act on their judgments. Using formal program evaluations to justify their actions may, at best, seem manipulative and, at worst, backfire.

Overstaffing

As for the efficiency of the staff, the former administration had added department employees to a level that could only be sustained for six months of the fiscal year. Without extensive additional money from the state legislature, which was unlikely to be forthcoming, the department had to eliminate hundreds of positions and terminate the employees who filled them. The reductions had to be made—and they were. Some were achieved by eliminating jobs, but many were the product of attrition. When people left, as many did each month, they were simply not replaced. (It was interesting that, despite the significant reductions in staff, the external evaluations of the department, such as quality control measures carried out by the federal government, stayed the same or actually improved with fewer staff. Precisely how that happened is difficult to determine.) Program evaluations did not help the department make decisions—decisions that had to be made because of political realities and financial difficulties.

I also remember a program evaluation process that probably caused me to lose what appeared to be the best job I ever had. I was chancellor of higher education in West Virginia, after my almost eight years as the commissioner of Welfare and Human Services. The chancellor was responsible for all the colleges and universities in the state and reported to a board of regents, who were appointed by the governor and who represented a balance of political parties and regions of the state. One of the processes that had been developed at the board's direction was a periodic evaluation of every president of the thirteen colleges and universities in the state. The evaluations were conducted by staff and teams of members of the board of regents, who followed a specific outline to evaluate each of the presidents.

When I became chancellor—a job I did not hold very long—I discovered that some of the presidents had serious deficits that the staff and board had simply tolerated or ignored for years. There were cases of strange financial dealings, expenditures for renovations of the official residences of the presidents that seemed out of line, charges of sexual harassment, and charges that presidents had denied faculty, staff, and students their rights under the rules and statutes governing higher education in the state.

I immediately began working with the board to do something about the serious deficits. There were some time pressures. The board was under the threat of termination as the governing body for higher education in the state, and the threats were often the product of the presidents who were the subjects of those periodic evaluations. We reassigned some presidents and took a variety of other actions to try to deal with the most obvious and difficult of the problems. I also reassigned the staff member who had run the evaluations for a long time and who had been heavily involved in the selection process for new presidents. He was proud of the position he held and the credibility he communicated by being the top staff member on presidential appointments and evaluations.

I assigned another staff member to coordinate the team and dictated detailed instructions to that person about what to look for in the evaluation of one particular president, who was well-regarded and who had a long tenure in his position. I gave the staff member questions to ask and weaknesses that I thought I perceived in the president's performance. I gave the dictation tapes to my secretary to transcribe on her computer. The evaluation was conducted, the president seemed to answer all the questions correctly, and he was recommended for continuation in his position.

At roughly the same time, a major foundation contracted with an educational evaluation organization to evaluate and recommend the future for the board of regents. I was naïve about the ways in which such an evaluation might evolve. The presidents of several institutions that functioned under the board wanted the organization eliminated. So did several major supporters of the state's largest university. I cooperated with the foundation and the evaluation organization, but, in retrospect, I should have avoided the evaluation or replaced it with a much more carefully defined and designed process. (But that is hindsight.)

A year later, after Governor Rockefeller had moved on to the U.S. Senate and his often foe, Arch A. Moore, Jr., was governor, there were changes in the board composition. It was interesting that the new governor suggested in his annual message to the legislature that the board of regents be abolished. He also withheld budgeted funds appropriated to higher education from the board of regents. In consultation with the board president, I initiated legal action to restore the funds to education—and won in the state Supreme Court. I also lobbied in the legislature for the continuation of the board, which I also won. However, Governor Moore now had authority over the appointments of several of the regents—enough, really to constitute a majority. Suddenly I was confronted with evaluations of my own work, including that earlier presidential evaluation and (although I am not sure of it) perhaps my reaction to the external evaluation, as well. The board was supplied with verbatim copies of the notes I had given the staff member raising questions about the performance of the president. Someone had pilfered my notes from the secretary's computer, I concluded—a relatively easy achievement for someone who understands computer methods, partly because none of the office doors in our building were ever locked.

The president whose performance I had questioned was outraged, and he, who had something of a strong relationship with Governor Moore, managed to outrage other board members, several of whom had been my supporters in the past. Before long, I was asked to resign, which I did. Ironically, some dozen years later, the president whose performance had aroused my suspicions was pressured to resign after long tenure in the same presidency, based in large measure on the kinds of concerns I had expressed somewhat naively, or at least without adequate self-protection, much earlier. Lawsuits and grievances from faculty and students were used to raise questions about his leadership.

Conclusion

The examples of program evaluations that begin this chapter, as well as the personal evaluation experiences that conclude it, demonstrate the broad range and complexity of evaluation in human services work.

It is noteworthy that some of the personal examples of evaluations while the author was a government official either backfired or were of little practical use to the supposed user of the evaluation results. Thomas J. Stanley (2000), who is an expert on millionaires and multimillionaires, mentions several times that the most financially successful people he studies usually recite their lifelong problems rather than their successes as the bases for their financial triumphs. This author's notions are somewhat similar. Perhaps I learned enough about evaluations to write about them because of some of the results of evaluations in which I have been involved. Fortunately, though, those are not the whole story.

Also, of course, over the years I have worked as an evaluator or as the recipient of evaluations in many other ways. At one point, I led an evaluation of a program that was to be conducted by a group of graduate students. We thought the evaluation was fair and helpful. Much of the work was associated with documenting what was taking place. The evaluation was a condition of an agency, a mental health program, receiving its operational grant. The evaluation was funded with federal government resources. Nevertheless, the program was displeased with—or hostile to—the evaluation, and our team was cancelled. There was even an evaluation of the evaluation, which lent credence to the agency's resistance to the work our team performed. The balance of the evaluation was to be conducted in-house by staff of the agency.

For many of the years I have spent in social work, I have been involved in evaluations—sometimes as their subject and sometimes as an evaluator. Those evaluations have included accreditations, needs assessments, and the use of formal research designs. Evaluations are a crucial element in securing and maintaining quality in the human services. Without evaluations, many clients and communities would suffer and many of the resources for human services would be wasted. However, evaluations are not always pleasant experiences, a fact that is well-known to many social workers but not widely reported in the professional literature.

It is clear that program evaluations are often controversial, resisted by those who are evaluated, and the source of conflict. From personal experience, I know that too often they are typically much more than objective, scientific exercises in searching for the truth. The methods and approaches discussed in this text are far from dry examples of business as usual. Program evaluations are often fraught with anxiety, sometimes-hidden agendas, and results that may be unpredictable.

Questions for Further Study

1. The chapter describes evaluations in several states. How are the Vermont and Wisconsin programs different and how are they similar?

2. In your opinion, what impact could the "New Chance" program have on American social welfare?

3. In what ways did evaluations negatively affect the work of the author of this text?

4. List three considerations that should be involved in contracting for evaluations that are suggested in this chapter.

5. Discuss two types of evaluations that are described in this chapter's examples.

References _____

Armijo, E. J., Stowitschek, J. J., Smith, A. J., Jr., & Valdez, O. G. (1999). *School-based case management for migrant and at-risk rural Hispanic students and their families.* Unpublished manuscript, University of Washington at Seattle, Center for the Study and Teaching of At-Risk Students.

Auletta, K. (1999). *The underclass.* Woodstock, NY: Overlook Press.

Berlin, G., Bancroft, W., Card, D., Lin, W., & Robins, P. K. (1998, March). *Do work incentives have unintended consequences?: Measuring "entry effects" in the Self-Sufficiency Project.* Ottawa, Ontario: Social Research and Demonstration Corporation.

Bloom, D., Michalopoulos, C., Walter, J., & Auspos, P. (1998, October). *WRP: Implementation and early impacts of Vermont's restructuring project* [Executive summary]. New York: Manpower Demonstration Research Corporation.

Bos, J. M., Huston, A. C., Granger, R. C., Duncan, G. J., Brock, T. W., & McLoyd, V. C. (1999, August). *New hope for people with low incomes: Two-year results of a program to reduce poverty and reform welfare* [Executive summary]. New York: Manpower Demonstration Research Corporation.

Doolittle, F., Knox, V., Miller, C., & Rowser, S. (1988, December). *Building opportunities, enforcing obligations: Implementation and interim impacts of parents' fair share* [Executive summary]. New York: Manpower Demonstration Research Corporation.

Freedman, S., Mitchell, M., & Navarro, D. (1999, June). *The Los Angeles Jobs-First GAIN evaluation: First-year findings on participation patterns and impacts* [Executive summary]. New York: Manpower Demonstration Research Corporation.

Frisch, M. B. (1997). *Quality of life inventory.* Minneapolis, MN: NCS Assessments.

Gooden, S. (1998, March). *Washington works: Sustaining a vision of welfare reform based on personal change, work preparation, and employer involvement.* New York: Manpower Demonstration Research Corporation.

Longo, P. J. (1999). *Anticipating outcomes in welfare reform: Blending federal, state, and local expectations in Ohio Appalachia.* Unpublished manuscript, Ohio University at Athens.

Masmes, T., Martin, M., Marcus-Mendoza, S., & Hall, K. (1999). *An evaluation of the Oklahoma County nighttime incarceration program.* Unpublished manuscript, University of Oklahoma at Norman, Institute for Public Affairs.

McNeece, C. A., Crook, W. P., O'Quinn, N. K., Rasmussen, D., & Jones, J. M. (1999). *Evaluation of the administrative component of Florida's Byrne Fund program* [Research report]. Tallahassee, FL: Florida State University, Institute for Health and Human Services Research.

Morris, L. L., Fitz-Gibbon, C. T., & Freeman, M. E. (1987). *How to communicate evaluation findings.* Thousand Oaks, CA: Sage.

Morris, L. A., & Orthner, D. K. (1998). *Exit from welfare and local entry-level labor markets.* Unpublished manuscript, University of North Carolina at Chapel Hill, School of Social Work.

Myers, L. L., & Rittner, B. (1999). *Adult functioning of children raised in an orphanage: A pilot study.* Unpublished manuscript, University of Georgia at Athens, School of Social Work.

Quint, J. C., Bos, J. M., & Polit, D. F. (1997, October). *New chance: Final report on a comprehensive program for young mothers in poverty and their children* [Executive summary]. New York: Manpower Demonstration Research Corporation.

Quint, J. C., Edin, K., Buck, M. L., Fink, B., Padilla, Y. C., Simmons-Hewitt, O., & Valmont, M. E. (1999, April). *Big cities and welfare reform: Early implementation and ethnographic findings from the project on devolution and urban change* [Executive summary]. New York: Manpower Demonstration Research Corporation.

Royse, D., & Thyer, B. A. (1996). *Program evaluation: An introduction* (2nd ed.). Chicago, IL: Nelson-Hall.

Stanley, T. J. (2000). *The Millionaire Mind.* Kansas City, MO: Andrews McMeel.

Stodghill, R., II. (2000, June). Off the dole: Minnesota's welfare reform proves a winner. *Time,* 65.

U.S. Department of Health and Human Services, Administration for Children and Families, Office of Planning, Research, and Evaluation. (1999, August). *Temporary Assistance for Needy Families: Second annual report to Congress.* Washington, DC: Author.

Vinton, L., Crook, W., & LaMaster, K. (1997). *Final report on the evaluation of Florida's Medicaid 1915C home and community based assisted living waiver for the frail elderly program* [Research report]. Tallahassee, FL: Florida State University, Institute for Health and Human Services Research.

Appendix 1

United Way of Rochester

The following are materials from the United Way of Rochester, New York. First is a form for agencies to use when preparing their program descriptions. It is followed by a table identifying outcomes and indicators for senior programs in that community. These outcomes and indicators have been adopted by the United Way, the city and county governments, and other organizations as a common set of outcomes that the community is working to achieve.

United Way of Greater Rochester
1999–2000 Program Description

Date: _____

Program Name: _____   Program #: _____

Provider Name: _____   Provider #: _____

Program Site(s): _____

_____

Contact Person: _____

Telephone: _____

# of Beneficiaries (2/98 report) _____   98/99 UW Investment _____

# of Beneficiaries (2/99 report) _____   Total Program Budget _____
(Direct Service beneficiaries = group + individual)

Program Year _____

Impact Area: *Please check only one.*   ____ Success By 6
                                                    ____ Kids On Track
                                                    ____ Strengthening Families
                                                    ____ Helping Seniors
                                                    ____ Overcoming Disabilities

Community Wide Outcome: (Primary): _____

(Secondary): _____

Indicators:

1) _____

2) _____

3) _____

Service Continuum: Using a line or brackets, identify where on the service continuum your program fits.

1 _____   2 _____   3 _____   4 _____   5 _____   6 _____   7 _____   8 _____

| Community Development/
Community Education | Primary
Prevention | Early
Intervention | Treatment |

(see definitions in Program Description Instructional Guide, page xx)

Chief Volunteer Officer

Name _____   Signature _____   Date _____

Chief Professional Officer

Name _____   Signature _____   Date _____

Program: _____   **Provider:** _____

Program Goal:

Methodology

Target Population

a. Describe the population served by this program.

b. How/why is this population in need of this service?

c. What is the total level of community need for this type of service (Citywide or Countywide)?

Service Integration

Program: _____   **Provider:** _____

Performance Projections and Previous Outcomes: (You may include up to 5 Outcomes)

1.a) Outcome Objective

b) Performance Section

Indicator of success:				
	Previous Year Projection (a)	Previous Year Actual (b)	% (b/a × 100)	Next Year Projection
Time frame				
Total # of Participants				
# Successful				
% Successful				
Basis for Next Year Projection: (source & relevant statistic)				

c) Performance Measure
1. Measurement instrument: name, if applicable, and brief description (include copy)

2. Measurement timetable

d) Analysis and Plans for Continuous Program Improvement

REPEAT THIS SEQUENCE AS NEEDED FOR EACH OUTCOME OBJECTIVE

Program Description Addendum

Use this format for reporting on previous year's outcomes for objectives that will no longer be part of the Program's plan.

a) Previous Objective:

b) Performance Section

Indicator of success:			
	Previous Year Projection (a)	Previous Year Actual (b)	% (b/a × 100)
Time frame			
Total # of Participants			
# Successful			
% Successful			
Basis for Next Year Projection: (source & relevant statistic)			

(or use Alternative Performance Section for measuring whole group changes)

c) Explain why this Outcome Objective is being dropped.

REPEAT THIS SEQUENCE AS NEEDED FOR EACH DISCONTINUED OBJECTIVE

Alternative Performance Section
Measuring Changes for a Whole Group

b) Performance Section

Indicator of success:				
	Previous Year Projection (a)	Previous Year Actual (b)	% (b/a × 100)	Next Year Projection
Time frame				
Total # of Participants				
Group – Baseline (1)				
Group – Final (2)				
Group – Change (2 – 1)				
Basis for Next Year Projection: (source & relevant statistic)				

Source: 1999–2000 Program Description form developed by United Way of Greater Rochester. Used by permission of United Way of Greater Rochester.

Rochester Area Logic Model   Program/Project Time frame: _____

Program/Project: _____   Agency: _____   Date: _____

Program/Project Goal: _____

Inputs (*$s, staff, volunteers, materials & other resources required*) Quantify inputs wherever possible (e.g., "2.5 FTE social workers" "270 volunteer hours")	Activities (*What the program does with the inputs to achieve its outcomes*) Activities should be quantified (e.g., 2 support groups/10 moms ea./2 hrs/wk for 4 mos.)	Projected Outcomes (*Effects on knowledge, attitudes, skills, behavior, condition or status during or after the program/project*)	
		Shorter-term Outcomes put an "*" next to those you will measure	**Longer-term Outcomes** put an "*" next to those you will measure

Source: Rochester Area Logic Model developed by a consortium of funders and providers under the auspices of the Rochester Effectiveness Partnership. Used by permission of United Way of Greater Rochester.

United Way of Greater Rochester Communitywide Outcomes and Indicators

HELPING SENIORS

Communitywide Outcomes	Indicator
Seniors enjoying mental and physical well-being	• Improved or maintained health status • Lower rates of preventable and untreated physical and mental health problems • Increased or maintained levels of mental and emotional wellness for seniors and their nonprofessional caregivers
Seniors exercising independence	• Increased frequency of seniors living in appropriate, affordable, and desirable housing • Increased ease of mobility outside the home • Increased independence in daily living
Productive seniors	• Increased rates of paid and volunteer employment • Decreased social isolation
Financially secure seniors	• Decreased frequency of seniors in poverty • Increased ability to afford desired health care • Increased ability to protect and manage assets
Personally safe seniors	• Decreased frequency of preventable household accidents • Decreased physical, emotional, and financial elder abuse and neglect • Decreased crimes affecting seniors • Increased sense of safety in neighborhoods

Source: Sample Communitywide Outcomes and Indicators used by permission of United Way of Greater Rochester.

Appendix 2

Interview Guide

Georgia Welfare Reform Research Project
TANF Recipient Survey

Code # _____ Gender _____ Race/Ethnicity _____

County # _____ Age _____ Child Only _____

Address _____

City _____ County _____ Zip Code _____

We are very interested in how individuals and families who are currently on TANF are getting along. The State of Georgia knows that welfare reform has cut the number of folks on welfare, but no one is really sure how the folks still on TANF are doing. Because of this, we'd like to ask you a few questions about the ways in which your life has gotten better or worse as a result of the changes in the welfare laws. We would also like some basic information about your income and financial resources as well as your employment and education. Since we will be comparing folks on TANF around the state, your individual responses are very important in developing a clear picture of the impact of welfare reform. Please know that your privacy is important to us and that your responses will be confidential.

Section 1   Personal History and Family Relationships

1.1   Are you currently residing in the county where you were born?
  1. Yes
  2. No

1.2   What year were you born? _____

1.3   What is your current marital status; are you married, widowed, divorced, separated, or never been married?
  1. Married
  2. Widowed (go to 1.3.1)

3. Divorced (go to 1.3.1)
4. Separated (go to 1.3.1)
5. Never been married (go to 1.3.1)

1.3.1   Are you living as a couple with a boyfriend/girlfriend or partner?
   1. Yes, living as a couple
   2. No

1.4   Do any of your children under the age of 18 currently live somewhere other than your household? (CHECK ALL THAT APPLY)
1. Yes (go to 1.4.1)
2. No (go to 1.5)

1.4.1   Where are they living?
   1. Foster care (go to 1.4.2)
   2. Living with other parent
   3. Living with other relative
   4. Living with a friend
   5. Living in a group home or behavioral correction facility
   6. Has independent child under 18

1.4.2   How many months has your child been in that location?
   _____ (insert #)

1.4.3   Is that child receiving TANF benefits?
   1. Yes
   2. No

1.5   How many adults over 18 are now living in your household?
   _____ (insert #)

1.6   How many children, UNDER 18 are now living in your household. Please include the child's age, gender, and your relationship with them **(circle focal child).**
   _____ (number of children)

	Name	Age	Gender	Relationship
Child # 1	_____	_____	_____	_____
Child # 2	_____	_____	_____	_____
Child # 3	_____	_____	_____	_____
Child # 4	_____	_____	_____	_____

1.7   How old were you when your first child was born?
   _____ (insert age)

END SECTION 1

Section 2   Living Arrangements

2.1   As a place to raise your children, how would you rate your neighborhood?
1. Excellent
2. Very good
3. Good
4. Not too good
5. Awful

2.2   Do you currently own your own home, rent, live with family, live in a group shelter, are homeless, or have some other housing arrangement?
1. Own your home
2. Rent your home/apartment/room
3. Live with family
4. Live in a group shelter
5. Homeless
6. Live in some other housing arrangement
7. Other _____

2.2.1   How much do you pay each month for rent/mortgage?
_____ (insert amount)

2.3   Approximately how many times have you moved in the last year?
_____ (insert #)

2.4   Thinking of your last move, what was the main reason you moved?
1. Took another job
2. Got married
3. To live closer to work
4. Could afford a better place/better neighborhood
5. Bought a home
6. Could not afford the rent or house payment
7. Conflict with spouse or partner
8. Was homeless
9. Other _____

END SECTION 2

Section 3   Health Care

3.1   Do you currently have health insurance for yourself, including Medicaid?
1. Yes (go to 3.1.1)
2. No, uninsured (go to 3.2)

3.1.1   What type of health insurance do you have for yourself?
1. Medicaid
2. Medicare

3. Employer provided insurance
4. Insurance you have purchased on your own

3.2 Does your child have health insurance?
1. Yes (go to 3.2.1)
2. No, uninsured (go to 3.3)

  3.2.1 What type of health insurance do they have?
  1. Medicaid
  2. Employer provided insurance
  3. Insurance you have purchased on your own
  4. PeachCare for Kids
  5. Different plans for different children

3.3 How often is your child sick?
1. All the time
2. 4 times a month
3. 2–3 times a month
4. Once a month
5. Less than once a month

  3.3.1 Does your child have a health problem?
  1. Yes
  2. No

  3.3.2 What kind of health problem is it?
  _____

3.4 Where do you go when your child is sick?
1. Nowhere, care for child at home
2. Family member/friend
3. County Health Dept.
4. Hospital emergency room
5. Private doctor

3.5 How much time does it usually take for you to travel to get help for your sick child?
Amount of time in minutes _____

3.6 Is your child currently on medication prescribed by a doctor?
1. Yes
2. No

  3.6.1 Name of medication _____ What for _____

3.7 Have you ever lost a job because you had to care for a sick child of your own?
1. Yes
2. No

3.8   Please rate your child's health.
1. Excellent
2. Good
3. Fair
4. Poor

3.9   Please rate your own health.
1. Excellent
2. Good
3. Fair
4. Poor

3.10   Do you have any health problems?
1. Yes (go to 3.10.1)
2. No (go to 3.11)

3.10.1   What kind of health problem do you have?

_____ (open-ended)

3.10.2   How much does this problem limit your ability to work?
1. Cannot work at all
2. Can do some light work
3. Does not interfere with my ability to work
4. N/A, Retired/Grandparent

3.11   When was the last time you saw a doctor?
1. Less than 1 month ago
2. 1 month to 6 months ago
3. More than 6 months to 12 months ago
4. More than a year ago

3.12   Do you or your child have a disability?
1. Yes (go to 3.12.1)
2. No (go to Section 4)

3.12.1   What is the type of disability?

_____ (Circle Child/Adult)

3.12.2   What type of benefits or payments does the person with the disability receive?
1. Federal Disability Insurance (OASDI) (circle C/A)
2. Federal Disability (Workmans comp., Veterans disability, Black Lung) (circle C/A)
3. Permanently Disabled Aid (SS, APDT, Title XIV) (circle C/A)
4. Aged, Blind & Disabled Aid (SS, AABD, Title XIV) (circle C/A)
5. Supplemental Security Income (SSI, Title XIV) (circle C/A)
6. None

3.13 Have you ever been in counseling for an emotional or mental illness?
    1. Yes
    2. No

3.14 Have you ever been hospitalized for an emotional or mental illness?
    1. Yes
    2. No

3.15 Have any of your children ever been in counseling for an emotional or mental illness?
    1. Yes
    2. No

3.16 Have any of your children ever been hospitalized for an emotional or mental illness?
    1. Yes
    2. No

    3.16.1 Do any of your children use alcohol or drugs?
        1. Yes
        2. No

3.17 Have you ever been in treatment (inpatient/outpatient) for a substance abuse problem?
    1. Yes, inpatient only
    2. Yes, outpatient only
    3. Yes, both inpatient and outpatient
    4. No

    3.17.1 Have any of your children been in treatment (inpatient/outpatient) for a substance abuse problem?
        1. Yes, inpatient only
        2. Yes, outpatient only
        3. Yes, both inpatient and outpatient
        4. No

3.18 Do you drink alcohol?
    1. Yes (go to 3.18.1)
    2. No (go to 3.18.3)

    3.18.1 Do you feel like you are a normal drinker?
        1. Yes
        2. No

    3.18.2 How much do you typically drink in a week?
        _____ (include volume and type)

    3.18.3 Have you ever gotten into trouble at work because of your drinking?
        1. Yes
        2. No

3.18.4 Have you ever lost your job because of your drinking?
    1. Yes
    2. No

3.18.5 Have you ever experienced a blackout from drinking?
    1. Yes
    2. No

3.18.6 Do members of your family or your friends think you have a drinking problem?
    1. Yes
    2. No

3.18.7 Have you ever been in trouble with the law for using drugs or alcohol?
    1. Yes, drugs only
    2. Yes, alcohol only
    3. Yes, both drugs and alcohol
    4. No

END SECTION 3

Section 4 Education

4.1 Are you currently attending school?
    1. Yes (go to 4.1.1)
    2. No (go to 4.2)

    4.1.1 What type of school are you attending?
        1. Tech school
        2. Adult Ed./GED
        3. College/University

4.2 Did you graduate from high school or get a GED?
    1. Yes (go to 4.2.1)
    2. No (go to 4.2.2)

    4.2.1 Which did you earn?
        1. HS degree
        2. GED

    4.2.2 What was the highest grade you completed in school?
        _____ (insert grade)

    4.2.3 What was the main reason you dropped out of school?

        _____

4.2.4   Were you ever placed in special ed. classes when you were in school?
    1. Yes
    2. No

4.3   Did you attend college?
  1. Yes (go to 4.3.1)
  2. No (go to 4.4)

4.3.1. Did you receive a college degree?
    1. Yes
    2. No

4.4   Did you receive any other degree or certificate through a vocational school, a training school, or an apprenticeship program?
  1. Yes (go to 4.4.1)
  2. No (go to Section 5)

4.4.1   What type of educational program did you attend?
    1. Nursing
    2. Vocational
    3. Office administration
    4. Adult Ed./GED
    5. Other _____

END SECTION 4

Section 5   Employment and Work History

5.1   We would like to know what you do—are you working now, looking for work, retired, keeping house, or a student?
  1. Working now
  2. DFCS work program
  3. Temporarily laid off (sick leave, maternity leave, etc.)
  4. Looking for work/unemployed
  5. Retired
  6. Disabled permanently/temporarily
  7. Keeping house/caring for child
  8. Student
  9. Other _____

5.1.1   What kind of job do you have?
    1. Food service
    2. Office services (secretarial/clerical)
    3. Housekeeping/janitorial
    4. Manufacturing/production
    5. Retail

6. Technical/vocational
7. Child care
8. Medical
9. Military/government
10. Professional/management
11. Other _____

5.2   How many jobs do you have where you earn money?
_____ (insert #)

5.3   How many hours a week do you now work?
_____ (insert #)

    5.3.1   Which shifts do you normally work?
       1. Days (9–5)
       2. Evenings (3 to midnight)
       3. Third shift (Midnight–morning)
       4. Weekends
       5. Rotating (Cycle days)

    5.3.2   How easy has it been for you to find child care for the hours that you work?
       1. No problem
       2. Somewhat a problem
       3. A major problem

5.4   How much is the take home pay from your job?
_____ (insert amount)

5.5   Is this hourly, weekly, biweekly, monthly, or annually?
1. Hourly
2. Weekly
3. Biweekly
4. Monthly
5. Annually

5.6   How long have you had this job?
1. 1 month or less
2. 2 to 6 months
3. 7 to 11 months
4. 1 to 2 years
5. More than 2 years

    5.6.1   How satisfied are you with the job you have?
       1. Very satisfied
       2. Somewhat satisfied
       3. Neither satisfied nor dissatisfied
       4. Somewhat dissatisfied
       5. Very dissatisfied

5.6.2   How long do you think you will keep this job?
1. 1 month
2. 2 to 6 months
3. 7 to 11 months
4. More than 1 year

5.6.3   Overall, how interesting or boring do you find your job?
1. Very interesting
2. Somewhat interesting
3. Neither interesting nor boring
4. Somewhat boring
5. Very boring

5.6.4   What do you dislike most about your job?
1. Work responsibilities
2. Difficulties with coworkers or managers
3. Low pay/not enough hours
4. Physical discomfort
5. Lack of transportation/location

5.6.5   Would it be enough reason to quit?
1. Yes
2. No

5.7   What do you like most about your job?
1. Relationships with coworkers and managers
2. Positive work environment
3. Good pay/hours
4. Location

5.8   If you are not working now, when did you last work?
1. 1 month ago
2. 2 to 6 months ago
3. 7 to 11 months ago
4. More than 1 year ago

5.9   How long have you been looking for work?
1. Not looking for work
2. Less than 1 month
3. 1 month to 6 months
4. More than 6 months to 12 months
5. More than a year

5.10   What have you been doing to find a job?
1. Filling out applications
2. Visiting employment/labor office
3. Interviewing
4. Talking with friends/contacts
5. N/A (I am retired, a grandparent, or a student)
6. Other _____

5.10.1 How many hours a week are you actively looking for a job?
1. 1 to 5 hours
2. 6 to 10 hours
3. 11 to 20 hours
4. More than 20 hours

5.11 Why are you no longer at your last job?
1. Personal health problem
2. Family health problem
3. Pregnant/newborn child
4. Laid off/fired
5. Business closed
6. Retired
7. Moved
8. Other _____

5.12 What did you like the most about your last job?
1. Relationships with coworkers and managers
2. Positive work environment
3. Good pay/hours
4. Location

5.13 Thinking of your last job, what kind of job was it?
1. Food service
2. Office services (secretarial/clerical)
3. Housekeeping/janitorial
4. Manufacturing/production
5. Retail
6. Technical/vocational
7. Child care
8. Medical
9. Military/government
10. Professional/management
11. Other _____

5.13.1 How many hours a week did you work on your last job?
1. Less than 10 hours
2. 10 to 20 hours
3. 21 to 30 hours
4. 31 to 40 hours
5. 41 to 50 hours
6. More than 50 hours

5.13.2 How much did you earn each week on your last job?
1. Less than $100
2. $100 to $200
3. $201 to $300
4. $301 to $400

     5. $401 to $500
     6. More than $500

5.14 How old were you when you had your first job?
     1. 12 and under
     2. 13 to 16
     3. 17 to 20
     4. 21 to 30
     5. Over 30
     6. Never had a job

END SECTION 5

Section 6   Welfare Experience

6.1 Who in your family is currently receiving TANF?
     1. Parent and child
     2. Only child/Parent custody
     3. Only child/Grandparent or relative custody

    6.1.1 Have you received AFDC/TANF in the past?
        1. Yes, for myself and my child
        2. Yes, but only for my children
        3. No

    6.1.2 Of the following options, which BEST describes why you stopped receiving benefits?
        1. Got a job
        2. Got married
        3. Moved
        4. Had to do too much, too many rules
        5. No child in household
        6. Denied benefits (sanctioned)
        7. Exceeded asset limit
        8. Graduated
        9. Approved for SSI disability
        10. Other _____

6.2 How much money from benefits do you receive each month?
     1. Less than $50
     2. $50 to $100
     3. $101 to $200
     4. $201 to $300
     5. $301 to $400
     6. $401 and over

6.3   While on TANF, has your benefit payment ever been reduced because of a DFCS requirement?
1. Yes (go to 6.3.1)
2. No (go to 6.4)

6.3.1   What was the main reason your benefit payment was reduced? (Check the main reason) (INTERVIEWER: PLEASE READ LIST)
1. Work requirement
2. Personal responsibility plan
3. Establishment of paternity of child
4. Child did not attend school
5. Children were not immunized
6. Other _____

6.4   When you were a child, did your family receive welfare?
1. Yes (go to 6.4.1)
2. No (go to 6.5)

6.4.1   Who else in your family received welfare benefits?
1. Grandparents
2. Grandparents and parents
3. Parents
4. Parents and siblings
5. Siblings

6.5   How old were you when you first had your own case number?
1. 10 to 15
2. 16 to 19
3. 20 to 24
4. 25 to 30
5. 31 to 40
6. 41 and older

6.6   How many months have you received welfare benefits?
1. Less than 6 months
2. 6 months to less than 12 months
3. 12 months to less than 2 years
4. 2 years to 4 years
5. More than 4 years

6.6.1   How long have you been receiving benefits under the new law? (Since January 1997)
1. Less than 6 months
2. 6 months to 12 months
3. 13 months to 24 months
4. More than 24 months

6.7   How many times have you gone off welfare and had to return?
1. Once
2. Twice
3. Three times
4. Four times
5. More than five times
6. Never have gone off welfare

6.8   How confident are you that you will get off of welfare in the next two years?
1. Extremely
2. Somewhat
3. Not so confident
4. Not at all
5. N/A, child-only case

6.9   What do you need most to increase your chances of getting and staying off welfare?
1. Education & training
2. Job opportunities
3. Child care
4. Transportation
5. Good wages and salary
6. SSI Approval
7. Extra time/extension
8. Other _____

6.10   How satisfied are you with the help your caseworker has given you in preparing you to leave welfare?
1. Very satisfied
2. Satisfied
3. Neither satisfied nor dissatisfied
4. Dissatisfied
5. Very dissatisfied
6. N/A, child-only case

6.11   How satisfied are you with the amount of help your case worker has given you with job training information, helping you to find child care, and/or helping you with transportation obstacles?
1. Very satisfied
2. Satisfied
3. Neither satisfied nor dissatisfied
4. Dissatisfied
5. Very dissatisfied
6. N/A, child-only case

6.12   How many hours of job training/experience have been provided for you while on TANF?
1. 0–5 hrs/week
2. 6–10 hrs/week

3. 11–15 hrs/week
4. 16–20 hrs/week
5. N/A, child-only case

6.13 What type of job training have you received while on TANF?

_____

6.14 What is the lifetime limit that you can receive TANF benefits in Georgia?
1. 2 years
2. 4 years
3. 6 years
4. 8 years
5. Don't know

6.15 If a woman who has been on TANF for a year in Georgia has a baby, her welfare payments will increase.
1. True
2. False

6.16 If a person leaves TANF, his/her Medicaid benefits will end.
1. True
2. False

6.17 Teenagers who are mothers are not required to stay in school to receive TANF benefits.
1. True
2. False

6.18 If you are currently involved with a husband/boyfriend/partner, how supportive is he/she toward you returning to work or finding a job?
1. Very supportive
2. Somewhat supportive
3. Indifferent
4. Somewhat unsupportive
5. Very unsupportive
6. Currently not in a relationship

6.19 If you are currently involved with a husband/ boyfriend/partner, how supportive is he/she toward you returning to school?
1. Very supportive
2. Somewhat supportive
3. Indifferent
4. Somewhat unsupportive
5. Very unsupportive
6. Currently not in a relationship

6.20 Have you been a victim of domestic violence since January 1997?
1. Yes
2. No

6.21 Have you been a victim of domestic violence prior to January 1997?
    1. Yes
    2. No

END SECTION 6

Section 7   Child Issues

Section A: (A7.1–A7.18) Complete section if **focal child** currently in day care.
Section B: (B7.1–B7.9) Complete section if **focal child** currently attending school.
General section (G7.17–G7.28) Complete all items about child well-being.

Subsection A: Focal Child in Day Care

A7.1 What type of day care is your child attending?
    1. Child care center, nursery school, preschool
    2. Head Start
    3. Family day care (in the home of a nonrelative)
    4. Relative care (in your home)
    5. Relative care (in a relative's home)

A7.2 How many days a week is your child in this child care arrangement?
    1. 1 to 2 days a week
    2. 3 to 4 days a week
    3. 5 days a week
    4. More than 5 days a week

A7.3 How many hours a day is your child in this child care arrangement?
    1. 1 to 3 hours
    2. 4 to 6 hours
    3. 7 to 9 hours
    4. More than 9 hours

A7.4 How long has your child been in this child care arrangement?
    1. 1 month
    2. 2 to 6 months
    3. 7 to 11 months
    4. More than 1 year

A7.5 How much do you pay for this child's care each week?
    _____ (insert amount)

A7.6 Do you receive money from anyone to help you pay your day care costs?
    1. Yes (go to 7.6.1)
    2. No (go to 7.7)

A7.6.1 Who helps you with your child care costs?
1. The government (subsidy program through DFCS)
2. Child's father
3. Other relative
4. Friend or someone else

A7.7   How have your child care costs effected your overall financial situation? (Check all that apply)
1. No impact on financial situation
2. Used up savings
3. Gone into debt
4. Sold assets (car, home)
5. Dropped health insurance
6. Lost or quit job
7. Went on TANF
8. Borrowed money from family and friends
9. Had to move because could not afford rent
10. Other _____

A7.8   How many children are in your child's group (room) at day care?
_____ (insert number)

A7.9   How many child care workers are there for this group/room?
_____ (insert number)

A7.10 (for coding purposes only, child/worker ratio) _____

A7.11 Is this child care facility licensed by the state of Georgia?
1. Yes
2. No

A7.12 In your opinion, how well trained are the worker(s) who care for your child?
1. Very well trained
2. Adequately trained
3. Not well trained
4. Very poorly trained

A7.13 How many different child care placements has your child been in over the past year?
_____ (insert number)

A7.14 Would you like to change your child's care facility?
1. Yes
2. No

Thinking again about (**focal child's**) current primary care arrangement, I am going to ask you some questions about (**focal child's**) and your experience with the care she/he is receiving. Please look at **card B.** For each of the following statements, please let me know which answer best describes your child care experience.

		Never	Some-times	Often	Always
A7.15	(**focal child**) feels safe and secure in (primary child care)	1	2	3	4
A7.16	(**focal child**) gets lots of individual attention in (primary child care)	1	2	3	4
A7.17	(**focal child's**) child care provider is open to new information and learning	1	2	3	4
A7.18	(**focal child's**) child care provider plans activities for the children	1	2	3	4

<u>Subsection B:</u>   Focal Child Attending School

B7.1   What is your child's current school grade?
_____ Grade

B7.2   Has your child ever been assigned to special ed. classes?
1. Yes
2. No

B7.3   For this school year, how many days has your child missed more than half of the day from school because of illness?
_____ (insert number of days)

B7.4   Does your child eat breakfast at school under the Federal School Free Breakfast Program?
1. Yes
2. No

B7.5   Does your child eat free or reduced-price lunches at school under the Federal School Lunch Program?
1. Yes
2. No

B7.6   Do you attend PTA/PTO meetings at your child's school?
1. Yes
2. No

B7.7   For this school year, how many times have you visited your child's classroom?
_____ (insert # of times)

B7.8   For this school year, how often have you spoken with your child's teacher?

_____ (insert # of times)

B7.9   What does your child do on a regular basis after school?
1. After school program
2. Stays with parents/relatives
3. Stays with neighbors or friends
4. Stays by him or herself

B7.9.1 If anything, how much does this cost you?
_____ (insert amount)

Subsection G: General Issues About Child Well Being

G7.17   How often do you or someone else in your home read to your child?
1. Never
2. Rarely
3. Occasionally
4. Often
5. Very often

G7.18   Approximately how many hours a week do you take your child with you on activities outside of the home?
1. 1 to 2 hours
2. 3 to 5 hours
3. 6 to 10 hours
4. More than 10 hours a week

G7.19   How many books does your child have?
_____ (insert #)

G7.20   How often do you talk to your child while you are working around the house?
1. Always
2. Often
3. Occasionally
4. Rarely
5. Never

G7.21   Have you ever been called to go to the school or day care center to discuss your child's behavior?
1. Yes
2. No

G7.22   Is the child's noncustodial biological parent still living?
1. Yes
2. No

G7.23 Does the child's noncustodial biological parent live in the household?
1. Yes
2. No

G7.24 In the past 12 months how often has your child seen his/her non-custodial biological parent?
1. Every day
2. Around three times a week
3. About once a week
4. 1–3 times a month
5. 2–11 times in the past 12 months
6. Once in the past 12 months
7. Child has not seen his/her noncustodial biological parent in more than a year
8. Child has never seen his/her noncustodial biological parent

G7.25 How satisfied are you with the amount of love and caring the child's noncustodial biological parent has shown for him/her?
1. Very satisfied
2. Somewhat satisfied
3. Neither satisfied or dissatisfied
4. Somewhat dissatisfied
5. Very dissatisfied

G7.26 How satisfied are you with the amount of money and help the child's noncustodial biological parent has shown in the past?
1. Very satisfied
2. Somewhat satisfied
3. Neither satisfied or dissatisfied
4. Somewhat dissatisfied
5. Very dissatisfied

G7.27 Has your child ever been in trouble with the police and had to go to court?
1. Yes (go to G7.27.1)
2. No (go to Section 8)

G7.27.1 What did your child go to court for?
_____ (name offense)

G7.27.2 What happened when your child went to court?
1. Case dismissed
2. Informal probation
3. Probation
4. Committed to the state

G7.28 Do you have a working computer in your home?
      1. Yes
      2. No

END SECTION 7

Section 8   <u>**Family Income and Resources**</u>

8.1   COUNTING ALL SOURCES, how much money was brought into the home in the past month?
    _____ Respondent income from work
    _____ TANF Benefit
    _____ Food stamps
    _____ Child support
    _____ SSI
    _____ Other income or support
    _____ **Total**

8.2   Does anyone else in your household have a job?
      1. Yes (go to 8.2.1)
      2. No (go to 8.3)

    8.2.1   How much did s/he contribute to the household expenses last month?
        _____ (insert amount)

8.3   Has your application for SSI ever been denied?
      1. Yes
      2. No

8.4   Besides a job, what else do you do to earn money?
    _____ (Open-ended, e.g., do hair, yard work, etc.)

    8.4.1   From this, how much extra income is brought in monthly?
        _____ (insert amount)

8.5   What was your total income for the 1998 tax year?
    _____ (insert amount)

8.6   Did you file an income tax return last year?
      1. Yes
      2. No

    8.6.1   Did you receive an earned income tax credit when you completed your tax return?
        1. Yes
        2. No

8.7   All things considered, your financial security today compared to 3 years
      ago is:
      1. Greatly improved (go to 8.7.1)
      2. Slightly improved (go to 8.7.1)
      3. Not changed
      4. Slightly worse (go to 8.7.2)
      5. Much worse (go to 8.7.2)

      8.7.1.   The primary reason for the improvement is:
               1. TANF benefit
               2. Increased income/more hours
               3. Relocation
               4. SSI approval
               5. Better money management
               6. Personal issue resolved
               7. Additional relative help
               8. Other _____

      8.7.2   The primary reason my finances are worse is:
               1. Reduction in TANF benefits
               2. Loss/reduction of income
               3. Family crisis
               4. New addition to family (e.g., new baby, stepchild, etc.)
               5. Increased expenses

8.8   How do you *usually* get to work (if unemployed ask about most recent
      job)? Do you drive, walk, get a ride with someone, use public trans., or
      some other way?
      1. Drive (go to 8.8.1)
      2. Walk
      3. Ride with someone
      4. Public transportation
      5. Some other way
      6. N/A, Work at home

      8.8.1   Do you own a car or truck that is operational?
               1. Yes
               2. No

      8.8.2   What is the make and year of your vehicle?
               Year _____

8.9   How many minutes does it take you to travel, one way, from your home to
      your place of work? (if unemployed, ask about most recent job). Please
      include the additional time it may take to drop your children off at school
      or child care.
      _____ (insert how many minutes)

8.10 Over the past 12 months, have you and your children had enough food to eat?
1. We have had enough to eat and the kinds of food we wanted.
2. We have had enough to eat, but not always the kinds of foods we wanted.
3. Sometimes we don't have enough food to eat.
4. Often we don't have enough food to eat.

8.11 If you did not have food to eat, what would you and your family do?
1. Would go hungry
2. Got meals or food at shelter/food kitchen
3. Got meals/food/money from church
4. Were given food or money for food by friends/relatives
5. Other _____

8.12 Do you believe the lifetime limit is fair?
1. Yes
2. No

8.13 Do you believe the lifetime limit should apply to you?
1. Yes
2. No

8.14 Should anyone be exempt from the lifetime limit? If so, who?
_____

8.15 If your TANF benefits ran out tomorrow, what would you do?
_____
_____

8.16 What are your plans for the future with regard to child care, employment, and/or education and training?
_____
_____

8.17 Is there anything else that you would like to share about how the new welfare laws have impacted your quality of life?
_____
_____
_____

END SECTION 8

END OF INTERVIEW GUIDE

Source: TANF Recipient Survey used by permission of Larry Nackerud.

Index